Buyers' Guide
to
Outboard Boats

by

David H. Pascoe, Marine Surveyor

D. H. Pascoe & Company, Inc.

Buyers' Guide to Outboard Boats

Published by D. H. Pascoe & Company, Inc.
www.yachtsurvey.com

First Printing 2002

Printed in the United States of America by Rose Printing, Tallahassee, Florida

ISBN 0-9656496-2-8

To order copies, visit our web site
www.yachtsurvey.com

Introduction

This book kicks off with a question that one is unlikely to find in the literature on any manufactured product. Are you a good candidate for being a happy boat owner? I ask it for one very simple reason: Far too may people spend huge sums of money on a boat, only to discover the hard way that they didn't have time for it, couldn't really afford it, or just plain don't like boats as much as they thought they might. Tens of thousands of dollars is a lot to spend on an experiment. For that reason we start by taking a hard look at what boat ownership is all about in the first chapter.

During my three decades of work consulting with boat buyers, it has become abundantly clear to me that the boat buying public needs more information than they are getting. The idea of writing a boat buyers' guide came to me about 10 years ago, but it has taken me all these years to figure out how to execute it. In large part, the reason for this is because of the huge variety of boats out there. My idea of what would constitute a good buyer's guide is more than just brief descriptions of the available products; that's been done. Yet our email box receives thousands of letters from our web site **www.yachtsurvey.com** every year with prospective buyers asking where they can obtain definitive information on a particular type of boat they are contemplating buying.

Most people are amazed when I tell them that there are no such reliable sources available. Most folks don't fully grasp the fact that the boat building industry, despite the fact that it produces very large and expensive products, is a marginal industry. As industries go, it is small and highly vulnerable to economic downturns. What that means is that there is not a huge amount of money to be made on producing information, much as one finds with the auto industry.

Name any particular style boat and one can come up with literally hundreds of different builders over the years. There are simply too many small companies building small numbers of boats for anyone to be able to examine, test and provide reliable information about what amounts to hundreds of thousands, if not millions of boats. Ultimately, this means that all anyone has to rely upon when considering a purchase is his own knowledge and ability to evaluate the caliber of a boat. Unless, of course, one chooses to hire a professional to do that.

The idea of writing such a book seemed easy in theory but in reality runs smack into a problem similar to people attempting to perform a medical self-diagnosis. It takes a physician over a decade of training to become a good doctor. Developing a truly useful buyers' guide is not too far off attempting to teach boat buyers to perform marine surveys.

Indeed, within limits, the purpose of this book is to teach you how to evaluate boats for yourself. While some surveyors might complain that I am attempting to put them out of business, that is far from the truth. When it comes to small boats, I would estimate that at least 95% of used outboard boats are purchased without a survey. Buying a used boat without a survey is not a smart thing to do. Unfortunately, most marine surveyors are not much interested in the small boat market because most surveyors feel that the fee a small boat buyer is willing to pay is too low.

With these realities in mind, the ideas for this book began to blossom. Ultimately, I realized that there are two main difficulties: (1) I can't make surveyors out of boat buyers, and (2) any book that deals with the subject of how to check out a boat thoroughly before purchase would necessarily cover an awful lot of technical detail and therefore runs the risk of overwhelming the first-time buyer with technicalities. Too much detail without experience leads only to confusion.

For those who are seeking quick and easy solutions to the problem of too many choices, rest assured that there aren't any. The most frequently asked question is, "Who builds the best boats?" This is a question for which no one has the answer, for one has to ask, "In what year"? The simple fact is that consistency of quality is one of the industry's greatest problem. As this is being written, the national economy is in recession. Hundreds of boat builders will be going broke, while many others are struggling to survive. Will that have an effect on quality? You can bet it will.

Then there are issues that revolve around the maxim that one man's trash is another man's treasure. What is acceptable quality to one, is not to another. Indeed, it's an open question as to how long a boat should be made to last. Should they be like cars and end up going to the grinder within ten years? Traditionally, we expect boats to last longer than that, if not because they are so expensive, then it's because we don't have the habit of changing them like dirty socks.

Today there are a fairly large number of builders turning out high end, very high quality center console boats. These are boats that typically sell for close to $100,000 and more. They are boats that are built to last, as boats should be built. However, one should understand that these boats will outlast wooden boats by a long shot. Thus, their value is far greater than what the industry standard was fifty years ago. Indeed, there are many good quality boats built back in the 1970's that people find worthwhile refurbishing, so that the life expectancy of well designed, good quality boats can be measured in decades.

The reader will find that throughout this book I frequently make reference to the standards that high end builders employ. When it comes to a boat, if one wants it to last, and not be faced with high maintenance costs, things must be done right, and with top quality materials. The plain fact of boating life is that second rate materials don't last the way we'd like. It is therefore by necessity that boats are judged by the standards of the best, not the least.

Virtually all of us who are not rich, and cannot afford the absolute best, are faced with the difficulty of compromising with the devil, e.g. the second and third best. Whether one is contemplating a new or used boat, the purpose of this book educate the reader sufficiently to be able to make his own intelligent decisions. Along the way, I will occasionally offer my own opinions on various issues.

The bottom line on boating is that it is an expensive hobby, sport, recreation or what-ever you want to call it. It used to be called "yachting" and was once considered the exclusive sport of the very rich. Then an industry developed that did its best to turn it into a mass recreation, attempting to put a boat in every garage or slip. Judging from some of the emails I get, there are those who believe that they have a God-given right to a good quality boat at a price they can afford. They are entitled to their beliefs, but there is no agency yet established that forces boat builders to do so.

With the Internet Bubble and the Enron debacle, and the stock market in general, we've seen what can happen when people buy things without knowledge. The word to the wise when buying a boat is caveat emptor. After reading this book, I am confident that you will be.

Don't get disillusioned; get educated. After all, boating can be a lot of fun, particularly when you can afford to own what you own.

David H. Pascoe
Destin, Florida
February, 2002

Contents

Chapter 1

Basic Considerations for First-time Buyers

Unlike most marketing media that hype boating with visions of paradise, eternal fun-in-the-sun pictures of bright, sunny days, calm waters and coconut palm studded white sand beaches with the ubiquitous scantily-clad mermaids somewhere nearby, this book is going to present you with a more realistic view of boat buying and ownership.

We start with the fact that it involves considerable responsibility and financial resources, plus elements of risk in the activity itself. If you are adverse to risk taking, perhaps you might want to rethink your desire to become a boat owner.

One of the things that has long attracted so many people to boating in the past is the sense of adventure and the presence of danger. Without the element of risk, many would find boating as boring as driving a car on a crowded road. After all, that's one of the things we seek to get away from.

What Are the Risks?

The dangers of operating a boat are often not obvious. Unlike driving a car, a boat floats on a fluid, water, which can be shallow or deep, clear or murky, moving or not moving. Dangers include running aground, getting caught in storms, becoming lost, and becoming stranded due to engine failure or running out of fuel. There is also the risk of sinking resulting from striking a submerged or floating object, as well as the failure of some internal plumbing component.

With a car, you can park it in a driveway or garage and more or less forget about it. Not so with a boat, for a boat left unattended for long periods of time while afloat may sink, or at the least will deteriorate at a rate that is disconcerting, for boats require a substantial amount of care.

The newcomer to boating should be aware that despite all our high technology and the fairly good safety record of boat builders, to go boating safely one still needs certain knowledge and skills. The need to learn something about seamanship has not disappeared. Seamanship is not just a term that applies to ships on the high seas; it also refers to the skill needed to operate vessels safely on rivers, lakes and bays where storms, wind and waves may not be the only danger.

Another important factor goes beyond yourself. As boat owner and operator, you are responsible for the safety of your passengers. That means that if you don't know what you're doing, you can be held liable for your mistakes that end up in injury to others. There is a very good reason why, in days of old, the captain of a ship possessed the powers of a sovereign: Ultimately he is responsible for the ship and its passengers since, while in the midst of the ocean he cannot call upon the services of a policeman. In the immediacy of a crisis, all decisions are his to make, including the taking of all actions to ensure safety. Thus, the responsibilities of boat ownership are greater than for any other type of vehicle you could own.

Many boat owners attempt to forgo the effort it takes to learn how to read and use charts, and navigation aids which are the mariners "road maps". This lack of knowledge is most often the cause of running boats aground, which can damage the hull and engines. In addition to nautical charts, the intelligent boater also learns to read the weather. He knows by experience the very serious dangers of getting caught in severe weather.

Seaworthiness

Ranking very high among the most common causes of boating accidents is the failure to maintain a boat in seaworthy condition, so let's be sure we understand what the term seaworthy means. Seaworthiness does not have an absolute definition, but is actually a legal term that is relative to how a vessel is to be operated. Here is the dictionary definition:

> *The fitness of a vessel for a particular voyage with reference the condition of its hull and machinery, the extent of its fuel and provisions, the quality of crew and officers and adaptability to the type of voyage proposed.*

In other words, the boat is made reasonably safe to do what the operator intends to do with it for the proposed outing only. And by "reasonably safe" we mean as judged by a knowledgeable seafarer. Moreover, in the event of a mishap that led to litigation of any type, it would be the opinions of other experts as to what constitutes seaworthiness that would apply, and not merely the judgement of the vessel owner or operator.

The point here is that whereas with road vehicles we have a precise set of rules and laws that define a motorists behavior, in the realm of maritime law, the rules are less well defined owing to the broader range of circumstances and risks to which a vessel is subjected. A car that is not road worthy may simply end up not drivable, and so the driver just gets out and walks or calls a taxi. When the engines of a boat quit running, the boat and passengers are likely to be subject to great danger, such as being washed up on the rocks, sinking, or being swept under a low bridge.

So it is that the primary risks involved in owning and operating a boat involve the maintenance condition of the boat, weather and navigation skills. Most boating accidents occur as a direct result of the boat owner having insufficient knowledge and experience. That is because seaworthiness is directly related to a boat's maintenance condition.

The most difficult part of boat ownership is the work of learning how to keep a boat in seaworthy condition so that it remains afloat, and the engines in good condition so that they don't break down and leave you stranded at the worst possible time. A boat owner who knows little or nothing about his boat and its systems is a boat owner who has no capacity for knowing when something may be about to go wrong. That is why preventive maintenance needs to be of paramount importance to boat owners. Boats are similar to airplanes in that when something goes really wrong, you can't just get out and walk away from the problem. Poorly maintained boats are much more prone to suffering crippling breakdowns.

A boat owner should be a mechanically inclined person who has some interest in things mechanical and electrical and is not afraid or disinclined to learn more. Far too many boat owners today are the sort who have no interest in things mechanical, and who attempt to rely upon others to see to it that their boats are kept in good condition. And more often than not, such people will attempt to pay maintenance people as little as possible since maintaining a boat is costly. The faulty logic in this should be painfully obvious. In all things in this world, we basically get what we pay for, so that if we pay for cheap help and service, that is what we get.

The bottom line is that people who get the most out of their boats and boating are the sort who love boats for all that they involve, including the work, the adventure and the dangers. They see a challenge in every aspect, from fixing a bilge pump, to painting the bottom, to learning the art of navigation. If this describes you, then the odds are high that you'll love boat ownership and boating.

"There is nothing so fine as just messing around with boats." - Anonymous

"Ya gotta be nuts to own a boat" - An opinion expressed by thousands.

"A boat is a man's first love and first wife. Second loves and wives are optional and ill-advised."
- Barnacle Bill

Definition of BOAT: *Break Out Another Thousand*

No one thinking about buying his first boat should approach it with the idea of going boating without any training and education. There are simply too many risks to do that, and not expect to be courting disaster. One does not necessarily have to attend a boating course, though that is surely a good idea.

Self education is usually good enough, *so long as you are serious about it*. Perhaps most people learn about boating through friends with boats. After all, experience is the best teacher. One thing that you'll learn about boat owners is that they love to spout off about their hobby, so that all one needs to do is just ask in order to get an earful.

Going out on other people's boats is a great way to get hands-on experience. But what if you don't know anyone who owns a boat? Then it's either one of the many boating courses available, or buy the boat and see how many new friends you suddenly develop! With your own boat, it should not be difficult to find an experienced boater who's willing to spend a bit of time to help you.

Let me tell you about how I ended up becoming a crewman on a world-famous ocean racing sail boat. I simply started hanging out with small sail boat owners. These were people I did not know, but I hung around them and expressed my interest in learning. It wasn't long before one day a boat owner said that one of his crewman had failed to show up for a race, and he needed an extra hand. And so it was that I was off to the races. From there I worked my way up, just by being available when needed.

Here's another true story. This fellow bought a 26' boat when his neighbor died and his widow offered him the boat for half of what it was worth. He hadn't planned on buying a boat at this time, nor one this big, but he found the deal just too good to pass up. Never having operated a boat before, he and his brother would trail the boat down to the ramp on Saturday mornings, launch it, drive it around in a short circle and then load it back on the trailer and go home. He did this three times before one of the locals at the ramp noticed what he was doing and asked him about it.

Our new boat owner explained how he came by the boat, that he didn't know anything about it, and was reading a couple of books trying to learn. In the meantime, he was testing out some of the things he had learned.

The other guy rolled his eyes toward the heavens and said, "Geeze, buddy, you need help that bad why didn't you just ask someone? Put 'er back in the water and me and my buddy Calvin will help you get started." By mid afternoon, they had covered a few miles of the waterway, and our new boat owner had not only learned a bit of boat handling but navigation aids as well. From there he met other experienced boat owners that he invited to go out with him, and from whom he learned much. Four years later he was making fishing trips to the Bahamas on his own.

Are You a Candidate for a Being Happy Boat Owner?

A lot of people go out and buy a boat on what amounts to a whim, only to discover the hard way that there's a lot more to it than they anticipated. Chances are, if you've gone to the trouble to buy this book, that does not describe you. My purpose here is to help you try to anticipate whether you're really up for it.

Here are some of the reasons why people get into trouble with boats: Ownership usually proves more costly than they expected, it involved more work than anticipated, or it turned out that they didn't have as much time as they thought they'd have to use the boat.

It is very easy to get in over one's head financially through not taking the time to add up all the costs, and including a cushion for unanticipated expenses. Many people make the mistake of buying a new boat with the idea that the warranty and insurance are going to eliminate all maintenance and repair costs. Rest assured, these won't. I explain why further on in this chapter.

Maintaining a boat properly is a lot of work. Always has been, always will be; that's just the nature of boats, and unless you're willing to do the work yourself, or can afford to pay someone else (few can), then be prepared to see the resale value of your boat decline very rapidly. If the best you can do is just to tolerate the effort of taking care of it, if you don't really enjoy this sort of thing, perhaps you should reconsider.

Remember, as a boat owner, everybody loves you when you take them out for a day of fun, but the usual scenario is that when the fun is over and it's time to do the clean up, repairs and maintenance, those folks tend to disappear or have something better to do. When it comes time to paint the bottom, compound and wax the boat, clean the bilges, change the oil or lay it up for winter and whatnot, chances are you'll be doing it all alone. Those members of the family who so enthusiastically cheered your decision to buy a boat are nowhere to be found when work time rolls around.

It's like the perennial story of the child who wants a puppy. He begs, pleads and swears that he'll take care of it. A week later it's the parents who are cleaning up the endless little "accidents" and feeding it. Ah, the wonderful world of good intentions.

The amount of pleasure that you derive from a boat will be a function of whether you enjoy doing some maintenance, and how often you get to use it. If you get to use it seldom, chances are it will become a burden.

Why Are Boats So Damned Expensive?

Boats are expensive for two reasons, and one of them is not because people who buy boats have a lot of money, and that marine manufacturers therefore try to gouge them. No, that won't work in a free market economy.

The first reason is that boats exist in a very hostile environment. Salt water is extremely corrosive, and that requires the use of expensive, high quality materials to withstand this environment. Fresh water is a little better, but not much. The same engines that are used in road vehicles have to be "marinized," meaning adapted to the marine environment. Similar parts in cars that can be made of inexpensive iron and steel, in boats they have to be made of costly brass, bronze and stainless steel. Even electrical wire for boats is higher quality and more costly. Even the interiors of boats have to use higher quality materials than are normally found in high quality homes or automobiles because sooner or later parts of the interior get wet.

The second reason is "low production numbers." Undoubtedly you've heard the term "economy of scale." Well, when it comes to boats and marine equipment, there is very little in the way of economy of scale. Boaters do not benefit from products made by the millions or even hundreds of thousands, as with most other consumer products. Quantities of parts made and sold are usually no more than tens of thousands, as compared with millions for other consumer products. The numbers of boats built by any one builder are even less. And when we break it down by different models per builder, the numbers are fewer still. To give you an general idea, production runs typically number from 200 to several thousand, depending on boat size and price.

Boats are basically hand made items, which involve enormous amounts of labor, and so they are not cranked out of production lines like cars with cookie-cutter sameness. Both boats and houses are similar in that they are not amenable to being produced by machines.

Some Interesting Numbers

Consider the cost of basic materials. Fiberglass laminate costs roughly $7/lb. That doesn't include cost of labor, overhead or tooling. A typical twenty four foot outboard center console boat has an average laminate thickness (we include frames and stringers, etc. to arrive at this thickness) of approximately 1/2" . The square footage of a hull is approximately 250 square feet, and since one square foot of 1/2" of fiberglass weighs roughly 4 lbs, a typical 24' solid glass boat hull weighs roughly 1,000 lbs.

At a base materials cost of $7/lb., our fiberglass hull costs approximately $7,000 excluding labor and we haven't even added the deck yet. A board foot of mahogany, which is also one square foot, now costs upwards of $15/sq.ft. so if we still made boats out of wood, our boat would use up about $6,000 worth of mahogany and many more weeks of labor. Our glass boat hull takes two men two days. Plus, there is a lot of wastage when using wood and almost none with fiberglass.

While the wooden boat is theoretically cheaper, the labor costs will more than make up the difference over materials with fiberglass. Thus, fiberglass ends up as a cheaper material that lasts longer. So while fiberglass boats may seem to be outrageously expensive, they're really a pretty good deal when you consider how long they last.

The Nature of the Industry

The boat building industry is unique and unlike most other major industries that produce large, expensive products. As industries go, it is smallish and remarkably undercapitalized, unlike the auto industry which is very consolidated and limited to little more than a dozen giant international corporations with revenues in the tens of billions. The gross revenues of a General Motors or Toyota are greater than that of many nations. As for boat builders, their revenues may number from a few million to a few tens of millions; virtually *none* are in the billion dollar category.

At any given time there are around 1200 boat builders offering products in the US. Imagine if you had 1200 automakers to choose from! That the boat building industry has not consolidated and generated a "big three" (though it is not that some have not tried) is due to the fact that it is highly vulnerable to recessions and economic downturns. When the economy slows down, boat sales come to a near complete stop because pleasure craft are not a necessity like cars and appliances or homes. Every time we have a serious recession, about half of all builders go bust. Hence, few who understand this industry are willing to invest in it, for it is far too risky and so it is extremely difficult to raise capital by means of selling stock. The recent demise of OMC during boom times is a good case in point.

Yet another problem affects the small boat industry: per unit profits are so low due to strong competition that it becomes almost impossible for these companies to survive economic downturns. This is a case where competition tends to lower prices to the point of extinction. While it appears to buyers that boat builders are getting filthy rich, through what appears to them to be outrageous prices, the truth is that most won't make enough to survive the business cycle. I have personally witnessed this cycle seven times in my own lifetime, and there is no reason to believe that these cycles will not continue, or that the industry will fundamentally change in any way. The fact of life is that it is a marginal industry.

If you're wondering why, in spite of all this, there are still so many venerable old name boat builders still around, it's because old names are valuable for marketing. Most companies bearing names like Chris-Craft are companies that have gone bankrupt numerous times. It's just the trade name that keeps being reincarnated. There are very, very few builders that have been operating continuously for several decades.

This situation causes problems that seriously affect product quality and reliability. First, boat builders either can't afford, or won't hire, the kind of high priced engineering talent that is needed to assure high quality and reliability. The truth is that boat building pretty much fits that old saying about watching sausage being made. If you could see it, you probably wouldn't want to eat it.

Boat building now, as in the past, suffers from a serious lack of R&D, product testing and engineering skill. And now that it has entered the realm of high tech plastics chemistry and composites, the engineering skills required have become even more complex. Yet the industry continues to make-do as it always has on the basis of trial and error. Unfortunately, much of this kind of product testing is done at the consumer's expense, with the boat buyer as beta tester, which helps explain why the industry as a whole has had such a poor record of customer satisfaction.

The truth of this could not be more forcefully demonstrated than by a large number of boat builders returning to an idea that failed in the 1960's when it was first tried. This involved the use of cores in boat bottoms. A core is a method of attempting to increase strength while at the same time reducing the amount of costly materials by substituting cheaper materials. A core basically makes a sandwich of a cheaper material such as balsa wood or foam between two thin layers of fiberglass. What this does is essentially to create a truss that is stronger in certain situations, but not all.

The great risk of this method is the risk of water getting into the core since the materials used are porous and contain large amounts of air space. And when water gets into the core, boat bottoms begin to come apart. It was a bad idea 40 years ago, and is a bad idea now as cored bottom boats are now meeting the same fate as they did back in the 1960's and 70's.

With these things in mind, it only makes good sense to be careful about what you buy. Just because a company has been successful in promoting and selling its products is no guarantee of quality and good service. Just because a company offers what appears to be a good warranty is no guarantee that the warranty will be honored, especially if a recession hits and the company goes out of business. To show you that this is no idle threat, consider that in the recession of 1989-92, over 50% of all boat builders went bankrupt, including many of the industry's best known names like Bertram and Viking. When bankrupt companies get sold, typically only the assets are sold, without the liabilities, which means warranty liabilities. So, even though the brand name continues to exist, *the legal obligation to honor warranties given by prior ownership usually doesn't.*

Consider another point: Automobile models typically sell in units of hundreds of thousands and up into the millions. Boats don't come anywhere close to that. A boat model that sells a total of 500 units is a lot in this industry. The larger and higher priced the boat, of course, the lower total unit sales will be. What this means for the consumer is that very few boat models are in production long enough that whatever shortcomings they may have never gets time to be perfected. Obviously, the longer a model is in production, the more likely it is that it will become perfected as problems and weaknesses are discovered over time, and then get the opportunity to be corrected.

From year to year, in the auto industry, chassis and engines tend to remain the same, while it is only the shape of the outer wrapper and interior that is changed annually. In large part this is why the automakers have become so large and prosperous. Thus the fundamental and most important part of the car has the opportunity to become highly perfected. Boat builders do not have this advantage. The boat hull and deck is its chassis, and thus major model changes forces major changes in tooling. Hence, model changes are very costly and builder's profits suffer, as does product reliability.

Finally, for the most part, boats are hand made items. There is very little in the way of robotics in boat building. Some have criticized the industry for being primitive and backward in this respect. However, they fail to realize that the market simply will not support this kind of huge capital investment. And besides, no one has yet figured out how to design a robot that can lay up fiberglass at lesser cost.

We also have the same identical problems caused by low production numbers with engines. It was fortunate in the past that basic outboard engine designs tended to remain the same over periods of many years, so that basic designs, though perhaps faulty at the outset, eventually got perfected over the years. In large measure, the acute problems that have been encountered in recent years, were mainly caused by government mandates forcing major engine changes in a too short period of time. As manufacturers rushed to meet these mandates, there wasn't sufficient time to perfect the designs so that far less than perfect products ended up on the market.

Dealerships

If the boat building industry suffers from serious problems, it naturally follows that their dealerships end up suffering the same slings and arrows of misfortune. Owning an auto dealership can be like owning the keys to a gold mine. That is decidedly not true for boat dealerships since the nature of the product is so different. Boat builders and their markets are simply not large enough to support the kind of dealership networks and profitability that would result in dealership stability. Plus, as you already know, auto sales are the largest and longest running major league scam in the world. With their power, they can manipulate prices in ways that other industries only dream of. If anyone else engaged in these practices, they'd go to prison for fraud, collusion and antitrust violations. The boat building industry has no such political/economic power, and therefore cannot manipulate prices and sales practices to ensure their survival.

The history of boat dealerships is that they come and go rather like the seasons. Very few have shown any staying power, and those that do seem to change their product lines like they change their socks. That's because manufacturers (both boat and motor) are not very kind to their dealers; they do not instill dealer loyalty, and lacking that loyalty (or other economic motivation) dealers feel free to change whenever a better deal comes along.

Dealerships suffer from the same economic vulnerabilities as builders do, plus one more; in most parts of the nation it is a seasonal business. This factor alone results in a large reason for customer dissatisfaction. With a large part of the business rush coming in just a few months, it is impossible to meet demand and keep all customers happy. It's also hard to attract and keep skilled personnel, from salesmen to engine mechanics. Highly trained people are rarely available for part-time or seasonal jobs.

When you look around at dealerships, you'll probably find that the ones that have been around longest are those that operate marinas where their revenues are not completely dependent on sales and service. To be successful, and survive economic slow downs, a dealer has to have a revenue source other than sales and service. Dockage, storage and other services usually help them turn the trick, particularly when the water is frozen a good part of the year.

National vs. Regional Builders

It takes a lot of resources and a company has to be of a certain size before it can aspire to achieve a national sales network. There are, however, numerous builders who neither have the size nor the aspiration to become national. That is why there are a fairly large number of builders who have only a regional market.

These are often builders that do not have dealerships, and who sell direct. As a general rule, their products and services tend to be a cut above the rest. But, like all general rules, they are made to be broken. The downside to builder direct sales comes from logistics problems that arise in the event that warranty work becomes necessary. The boat has to go back to the builder to get fixed.

Buying Philosophy

The philosophy of always shopping for the lowest price may be without risks for many other kinds of products, but it is very risky when applied to boats. In fact, it is downright imprudent. When it comes to boats, lowest price means *de facto* lowest quality. If you would buy the lowest quality boat, you might as well buy the lowest price air plane and seek out the lowest priced doctors and surgeons. There are some things for which it is not wise to make selections based on lowest price, and boats are surely one of them.

As we discussed earlier, boats are so expensive because they require high quality materials to be durable. To reduce price, a builder has to reduce the cost of materials. The end result is usually a product that looks good in the showroom, but begins deteriorating rapidly once it is in the water.

On Quality and Reliability

There came a time when the boat building industry stopped building just "boats" and began creating "consumer products." There was also a time, not too long ago, when most boat builders were in the business for the love of boats. A time when making money did not reign supreme. Those days are largely gone, and most of boat building is corporate business, though there exists a fringe market of custom boats and high quality boat builders. Though the prices on their products are often stunning, they provide a good price contrast between high quality boats and the consumer market quality boats.

The term "consumer products" translates to mean boats were no longer designed and built to serve the functions that boats heretofore normally served. Instead, marketing designers and strategists were hired to help increase sales, the kind of people who perform psychological studies to learn what will most attract people to a product. Along with a chicken in every pot and two cars in every garage, their goal was to put a boat in every garage and dock. It didn't matter whether it was a fat chicken or an emaciated, starving bag-of-bones chicken, so long as it was a chicken. If the chicken was emaciated, never mind, the nice coat of feathers would hide the fact that there was no meat on those bones.

The new design philosophy was sex appeal and status symbols. Not to worry whether a boat is a practical vessel designed to navigate the waters with; what the consumer wants is a status symbol and fashion statement; the practicality of a boat is deemed irrelevant to getting them sold in large numbers. The marketing types know that if you can create a style trend, the style will perpetuate itself because people are like sheep in that they want what everybody else has as long as it is the latest fashion. So if stylish, sexy looking boats that are utterly impractical become the norm, then that is what people will buy. Vanity became the name of the game.

This could never happen unless boating could be turned into a mass recreation, and so the industry set about doing just that. Somewhere in the mid 1980's they succeeded and the number of boats in existence reached 22 million by 1990, a high water mark that has since receded to around 19 million and continues to drop.

Part of the problem can be laid at the feet of boat buyers themselves. Far too may people have been willing to spend very large amounts of money without an adequate understanding of what they're buying. No doubt they do so, in part, due to high levels of consumer trust in most other products, which can be badly misplaced when buying a boat.

Today, the industry and its leading association, the National Association of Marine Manufacturers, is deeply worried that too many first-time boat buyers are last-time boat buyers. Boat owner surveys show that customer satisfaction rates are poor and going lower. Dealer service satisfaction rates are even worse.

Yet another part of the problem with high cost stems from increased complexity and sophistication of the product, combined with increased luxury and equipment that is no longer optional but standard. When the buying public demands all the bells and whistles, all the luxury and pizzazz combined with a myriad of electronics, and all at an affordable price too, the net effect is to drive quality and reliability down as the builders struggle to keep prices down.

So why can't we have our cake and eat it too? Let me lay it out in fast format here.

- Boaters want "reasonable cost," luxury and every amenity imaginable. There's no way you can have a reasonably priced boat plus good quality plus all the bells and whistles unless you are well-heeled. Something has to give, and that something will always be quality.
- Largest Interior Spaces. The shape that would provide the maximum interior space that so many people demand would be a square or rectangle, though I trust you understand why square boats might be a problem. To yield best performance, a boat hull has to have a certain shape. That shape is not conducive to achieving floating patios and parlors. Hence, the majority of boats perform poorly even under moderate conditions.
- Boaters want fuel economy. The type of hull design that is most fuel efficient is also the one that is least sea worthy. Flat bottom boats will go fastest with the least horsepower and lowest fuel consumption. This also yields a ride that's like driving a car on a rail road track.
- Boaters want low maintenance. Low maintenance is achieved by using highest quality materials with a minimum of complexity. That flies in the face of low cost fanciness and luxury.

In other words, what most boat buyers really want is a contradiction in terms, but that doesn't have any bearing on wanting it. However, if you understand this, you're now better equipped to make some intelligent choices. Invariably, this will mean giving up some luxury and extras in favor of quality.

What Does Quality Mean?

Quality is not always immediately self evident on a boat. Much of it is invisible, or hidden, especially when a boat is new and sitting on a showroom floor. Even I can't tell whether a new boat has good or poor quality get coat, a finish that is going to turn to chalk within a year and become unrestorable. In most cases there's no way to determine if the wood used in the stringers is rot-prone pine or costly fir. And nowadays it's hard to determine even if a hull is cored or not. When a boat is new, everything looks good, but what will it look like a year later? For used boats, answering these questions is a lot easier, for we *are* looking at it years later. These questions can be answered by doing some serious checking, which is what the remainder of this book is all about.

It takes a lot of effort to go through a boat and size up all the materials, hardware and systems used in its construction. Is the electrical system well engineered, or was it put in as cheaply as possible to keep the price down? And how about the loads of upholstery in that eye-catcher, is it good quality stuff? Or is it vinyl and foam rubber stapled onto cheap plywood?

These are but a few of the questions you can begin to ask and perhaps they will begin to convince you of the reasons why good quality drives cost up by leaps and bounds.

Good quality first means that more thought went into the design of something to ensure that it works properly and gives long service. Second, that it is made with better, more durable materials, and with a process and skill that is superior to others. That, too, drives cost up costs.

If you are completely unfamiliar with boat quality, I would suggest a short field trip to go look over one or more of the many high end center console boats such as Jupiter, Regulator, Triton, Contender or Intrepid, as these are some of the highest quality production boats available. What you'll see is a certain plainness about them, marked by the highest quality materials and components with superior design and engineering, plus attention to detail. Instead of putting money into low cost eye candy designed to lure the uninitiated, the builder has put it into quality materials.

After you have looked over one of these beauties, you'll now be in a better position to judge quality. I'm not suggesting that you should be looking for this level of quality in an entry-level boat, for you surely won't find it. But if you think you might step up to a mid level quality boat, you'll be better prepared to make judgements as to whether it lives up to its billing.

In recent years many of my consulting clients have expressed concern over low resale values upon resale after a few years. They point out the huge depreciation losses usually involved with a buying a new boat. They are correct, in far too many cases, the first three years depreciation can run up to 50%. Even at a very, very low initial price, that is more than many people can bear. You can check this out for yourself by first doing an Internet search on asking prices of boats for sale and comparing them to the original, new cost.

It is said that one man's trash is another man's treasure, or, quality is in the eye of the beholder. This is true, up to a point. That point is surpassed when the durability of the product results in poor performance or rapid deterioration of the product to the point where his investment in the product depreciates far beyond what he had expected.

Most newcomers to boating look upon the purchase of a boat as all fun. They are soon to be profoundly disabused of that notion. Boat ownership is a lot of work, and anyone who approaches it with a "park-it-and-forget-it" attitude will soon find the value of his boat evaporating like summer showers on hot tarmac. The rule is: the more one puts into maintenance, the greater resale value will be, up to a point.

No matter how good they are, boats require both management and maintenance. In part that's because boats operate in a hostile environment, and in part because they receive rough treatment. To give you a general idea, a typical fifty foot sport fisherman usually requires the new owner to hire a full time professional just to manage the outfitting of the new boat, at least for the first several months. So if it takes a few weeks to straighten out the problems of a twenty or thirty footer, no one should be surprised. The large boat owner, if he's smart, doesn't trust the dealer to get everything right; instead he hires someone to oversee it on his behalf. This process is called "fitting out" and involves a "shakedown" cruise. That means shaking out all the problems that inevitably arise with a new boat, or even a used one.

The small boat buyer will usually want to do this himself, for his boat isn't so big and complex that it's all going to take that long. In the chapter on rigging I'll discuss how to do that and what to look for.

Small Boat Management

Even small boats are sufficiently complex that they demand of the owner considerable time toward managing them. This involves everything from the financial end, to insurance, dockage, and, of course, maintenance and repairs. Most boat owners end up with sizable boat files containing all their records. Yes, your new boat will leave a substantial paper trail which will testify to the amount of time you spend managing your new acquisition.

The amount of time this will demand of you will depend much on the proximity of where you live to where you keep the boat. If that is a considerable distance, it obviously will demand more time of you. For example, if you keep the boat at a rack-and-stack located twenty five miles from home, this will be a chore just to run over and check on something. If you keep it on a trailer in your yard or garage, the time demands will be minimal. In the former case, you're almost forced to pay others to do your maintenance unless you have a lot of time on your hands.

The key to keeping a boat well maintained starts with frequent inspections. It is always better to catch problems early-on before small problems become big ones. The more you learn about boats, the better you will get at this. Otherwise, you will have to pay others to do this for you. The alternative of waiting until things break down is vastly more expensive.

I would suggest that anyone purchasing their first boat, and who intends to keep it at a location a considerable distance from home, give careful thought to the high demands on your time this will create. It's likely to be a lot more than you anticipate.

When purchasing a new boat, you should be prepared to experience some problems at the outset. While that may not happen, if it does, at least you'll be less likely to be disappointed. The biggest problem is usually a matter of the amount of your time it takes to get problems resolved, combined with your proximity to the dealer from which you bought it.

As I said, buying a boat is not like buying a car wherein you expect to drive it off the dealers lot with no problems thereafter. There is no such thing as a perfect boat.

Finding a boat that meets all your requirements as well as fitting your budget is not an easy thing. My job is to try to help you do that, and to shorten the amount of time you have to spend searching as well as educating yourself.

If you are a newcomer to boating, and you plan to buy a fairly sizeable boat, you'll probably reach a point where you think to yourself that the more you educate yourself, the more confused you get. Relax, that's normal when there are so many decisions to be made. You already know the way out, which is to sit down with pad and pen, and make a list of your requirements. Once the list is roughed out, then prioritize it, starting with the must-haves and ending with the wishful thinking.

New -vs- Used Boats

First time boat buyers are prone toward purchasing new boats. Their reasoning is usually that they don't want to "buy into other people's problems." Their thinking is that if they buy a new boat, they won't have any problems. I've already explained why this rationale is likely to be erroneous.

Experienced boat buyers have a different philosophy. Theirs is that the first couple years loss in value isn't worth the price; that if they can buy a late model boat for half or two thirds of the new boat price, they are thousands of dollars ahead, even when the used boat may have problems to be fixed. For example, consider a boat that sells for $60,000 new and $40,000 two years later. That $20,000 saving could cover a lot of repairs with many thousands left over.

Everybody loves a new product be it a car, house or boat. But you pay dearly for that gleaming new shine that's going to fade away in a very short time. The fact is that used boats are tremendously good values. Another important point is that used boats have been tried and tested; new boats haven't. The significance of this is that if a boat is going to develop problems, those problems will have become manifest by now and with a survey, you can expect to discover them, if they haven't been successfully corrected. And if the problems are serious, you don't buy the boat.

True, with a new boat you have a warranty but the question becomes one of how much is that worth? If the product doesn't have a certain degree of quality, a warranty becomes like a Band-Aid over a wound: it covers the wound but doesn't kill the pain. It's trouble enough taking a car back to the dealer for warranty work, but with a boat, this can be a lot more troublesome when the dealer is not located nearby.

With some of the more unpleasant realities of boat ownership out of the way, we'll now move onto the nuts and bolts of how to evaluate what will be the best boat to fit your needs.

Should You Get a Professional Survey?

This book intended to help you make a reasonably informed inspection of any boat you propose to buy, new or used. It cannot, however, provide you with the years of training and experience that a marine surveyor has. This book was written because the cost of professional surveys for smaller boats is sufficiently high that most outboard boat buyers will not pay the price of a professional. Moreover, highly qualified surveyors exist, for the most part, only in the largest boating centers where it is possible for them to earn a living. Surveyors are not to be found in most inland regions, excepting the Great Lakes.

Even so, when spending a sizable portion of your income on a boat, and when in doubt about your own abilities to size up a boat, I'd certainly recommend that you hire a surveyor if one is available.

So there you have it: some tough talk about the realities of boat ownership. In this chapter I've discussed mostly the negatives and bad things that can happen without mentioning the potential good times. However, I will trust that the various advertising agencies and marketing departments have already done a commendable and better job of that than I could. Now, if you still think you really want to buy a boat, we'll get on with the nuts and bolts of how to go about sizing up those thousands of boats to choose from.

Chapter 2

Boat Types & Hull Design Basics

In order to get the maximum enjoyment and usage from a boat, it is very important to match boat types with the kind of weather and water conditions that prevail in the area you intend to do your boating. It doesn't make much sense to choose a relatively flat bottomed bow rider for use on the Great Lakes or an ocean. For large bodies of water without protected bays, the ability to handle rougher water with safety and greater comfort is all-important.

Naturally, the size of a boat also plays an important role in how well a boat can handle sea conditions. The rule of thumb that bigger is better is no myth. Not only size, but weight, as we will discuss in a later chapter, has a lot to do with who wins the battle of the waves. The boat or the waves? Bigger and heavier almost always wins that battle.

The great increase in inland boating has resulted in the creation of an entirely differ-ent class of boat which is rarely faced with big seas but, unfortunately, many of these boats are marketed in places they probably shouldn't be. Therefore, the first time boat buyer needs to be aware of what boat styles are best suited for varying areas of opera-tion.

Saltwater Boats

While attending the Fort Lauderdale Boat Show someone asked me what is the differ-ence between a "saltwater" boat and one that wasn't so designated. Indeed, there are some builders who make this reference but, for the most part it usually means lake type boats as opposed to ocean type boats. In other words, boats that are specifically de-signed for shallow, calm waters as opposed to those that aren't.

Many years ago there were inland based companies that built boats that were used predominately only in fresh water, and that lacked the high quality materials needed to endure saltwater use. These days the majority of builders build for saltwater use, al-though I have seen some obvious exceptions in the bass and pontoon boat categories. But, when it comes to distinctions in rough water performance, the products of some

Fig.2-1. The typical center console boat, the most widely sold boat style. Its strong point is lots of open deck space and typically deeper vee hulls for open water navigation.

builders are clearly more suited for protected waters over open water, i.e., large lakes or oceans.

Center Consoles

Whatever other design features it may or may not have, a center console boat is distinguishable by its stand-alone or free-standing center console. It may have a cabin up under the fore deck or not, it may have a cabin space within the console or not, but it's still a center console.

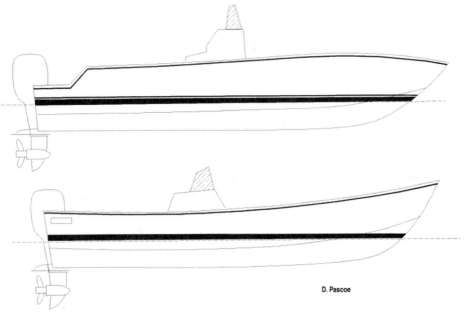

D. Pascoe

Fig 2-2. The two basic types of center console boat: above, the more modern integral platform design with reverse sheer, and the more traditional skiff type hull often preferred by fishermen. Note the prominent difference in sheer lines.

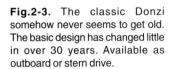

Fig.2-3. The classic Donzi somehow never seems to get old. The basic design has changed little in over 30 years. Available as outboard or stern drive.

When it comes to outboard boats, far and away the most popular type is the center console, distinguishable by — what else? — its center console. Many people call these fishing boats but really what they are is utility or multipurpose boats. They are most popular, not as a result of their great styling - I doubt anyone would call them sexy - but because they are so versatile. Water skiing, fishing, swimming and diving are but a few of the common but dedicated uses their owners put them to.

While they are great for water sports, they are less good for touring, partying or cocktail cruising due to the lack of convenient seating. The most used seats in these boats are usually the unupholstered gunwales, and more than a few people complain about getting bruised butts. Yet they put up with the lack of seating precisely because the lack of seats yields a lot of unrestricted deck space to move around in without risking falling over something. Their owners like the ability to move freely all around the boat which, of course, is what makes it so great for water sports.

Fig.2-4. Some boats defy pigeonholing. At first glance it looks like a walkaround, but isn't. With a small, raised cabin, it is basically a pocket cruiser or cuddy cabin runabout.

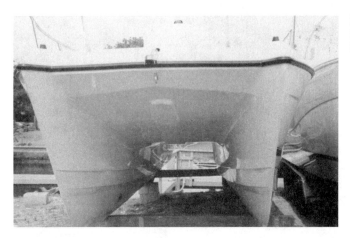

Fig. 2-5. The catamaran hull: what you gain in speed and economy you loose in interior hull space.

Its other drawback is the complete lack of protection from the elements. On a CC boat there is no escape from wind and rain and spray. While T-tops can offer a bit of shade when the sun is straight up, rainfall slants under the top whenever the boat is moving. And so does the sun when it is not straight over the yard arm. This is definitely an outdoorsy type boat.

Center consoles are most popular from the mid-Atlantic and South Atlantic to Gulf Coasts where the seasons are longer. In Florida and much of the south, the CC boat predominates by huge margins over any other style. Unless one is particularly sports minded, this may not be the best choice of boat for those places where the weather is more often inclement than not. However, with a little creativity, CC boats with T-tops are amenable to at least minimal enclosure with curtains.

Fig. 2-6. Two models of the Glacier Bay cats, center console and cruiser. Note the nifty boarding ladder and rails between the engines. Deck area is comparable to mono hull boats.

CC boats tend to have deeper rather than shallower hulls, owing to the predominate ocean usage. A CC boat without a deep hull is a tough sell in most places as CC boat buyers are amongst the most experienced and knowledgeable of boat owners. Be wary, however, that in recent years many smaller CC boats have been built that have very flat bottoms for use in shallow waters.

These boats can range from completely plain-Jane, very utilitarian boats with no frills, to heavily upholstered plushies, to the completely decked out sport fisherman. Sizes range from around 14 feet to 35 feet and even larger with triple engines and prices topping a quarter million dollars. Presently, there is an expanding market in very high end production and semi-custom boats, the prices of which can take the average boat owner's breath away. The high quality of some of these boats is truly remarkable.

Many center console boat designs have gone way beyond the utility fishing or day boat, incorporating large cabins up under foredecks, complete with berths, heads and small galleys.

Walkarounds

The walkaround style is another very popular type, primarily for fishermen who engage in bottom fishing or casting. It is distinguished by the ability to move from the cockpit to the fore deck area without having to climb over or through a windshield. As distinct from an express style, it usually has a recessed side deck that is lower than the gunwale. Indeed, even the fore decks are often "sunken" or recessed at a lower level than the gunwale.

This design has distinct pros and cons. While it provides the advantage of being able to move to the fore deck with relative ease, there is always a stiff price to pay for this convenience. Side decks take up space and necessarily squeeze the forward cockpit area, making it much narrower than any other style. This results in a very tight helm area that, in the case of most twenty four footers, will barely accommodate two persons. In some of these boats the helm area is so narrow as to be downright aggravating: be wary of this drawback.

The walkaround is most always a cabin boat An important consideration is how the side decks are designed. Deeply recessed side and fore decks seriously cut into cabin space, so that if cabin space is one of your main criteria, you need to consider this aspect carefully. Many walkaround designs have side decks that are extremely narrow, about six inches or so. That is so narrow as to make walking quite difficult. There's really no need for side decks to be recessed: those that are flush with the gunwale will provide more space and make walking easier. It's a peculiarity of the boating business that the same identical style boat that does not have recessed decks is usually not referred to as "walkaround".

The advantage of flush side and fore decks is that this does not reduce head room in the cabin, though it continues to squeeze the cockpit area. The bottom line for the walkaround style is to consider whether you're going to make use of those side decks enough to render the sacrifice of a more spacious helm area worthwhile.

My own view is that while the walkaround may be a great style for the dedicated bottom fisherman, it is far from ideal for a multi-purpose boat. The restricted forward cockpit area is an unacceptable sacrifice for a rather limited benefit. As boats get larger, say 28 feet and over, these effects of these limitations begin to disappear as wider beams allow for sufficiently wide cockpits.

Runabouts

The runabout, a boat that really has no other purpose than running around in a boat, has largely died out. The 20 foot Donzi is the quintessential runabout that has no other purpose than zooming around fast. It's not even very good for water skiing since there is so little cockpit space. Boats have become too expensive to be so frivolous and non utilitarian. Some small market remains for these boats in inland regions, boats that are being increasingly produced by the Japanese companies that produce jet skis, and which are often found with jet drives.

The outboard runabout has been largely displaced by the stern drive runabout because of inherent noise problems with sitting in close proximity to a roaring outboard motor, plus the problems that small outboards have always had with sinking.

Restoration of old runabouts like the Donzis and Bertrams has become very popular in recent years as there are a lot of them out there. Restored classics can offer good value at reasonable prices. However, you do have to be careful to ensure that the basic hull structure is sound as age and high speed can have serious effects. Anyone contemplating one of these should get a professional survey done.

Fig. 2-7. Left, an outboard pocket cruiser. At right, yet another of the seeming infinite varieties of center consoles, this one an inboard powered Shamrock keel hull. The engine is under the console with no loss of cockpit space.

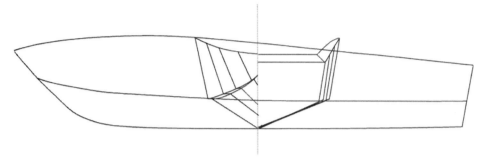

Fig. 2-8. The classic offshore hull design that incorporates a constant deadrise deep vee consisting of almost completely flat panels and very narrow beam. The style doesn't offer much in the way of interior space but is unquestionably the finest rough water hull form.

Offshore Types

Often referred to as a "Cigarette boat," offshore hull is the proper name for what is fundamentally a race or go-fast boat. Adapted from oceanic offshore racers these boats typically have constant deadrise deep vee hulls. Which means that the hulls are very deep, very inefficient and require huge amounts of horsepower (and fuel) to drive them.

Offshore hulls are also exceeding narrow, making them suitable for little more than merely going fast. Beginning in the 1980's, numerous pleasure boats were adapted from the offshore design. Later they became popularized as drug boats. The basic type never really caught on as a popular pleasure craft type due to the exceedingly narrow beams that created nearly useless interior spaces. Then someone had the bright idea of turning the style into a center console and a whole new style was born. One of the first success stories was the Wellcraft Scarab, a thirty foot center console with an 8'6" beam. Today, the vast majority of CC boats are variations of the offshore hull style, though almost none have the original constant deadrise hull shapes owing to the fact that it takes too much power to drive them.

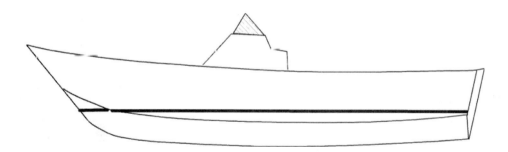

Fig. 2-9. An older skiff style reminiscent of the Chris Craft skiffs of the 1960's, 70's & 80s. Very sea kindly little boats, the design was adapted from wood to fiberglass. This boat has a conventional sheer line as compared with the reverse sheer line of the offshore type above and is usually mock lapstrake.

Bow Riders

These are popular choices for inland lakes, rivers and well-protected bays. Bow riders are basically runabouts with no fore deck, usually having a seating arrangement in that area, which makes up somewhat for the loss of space caused by outboard motor mounting. They are essentially touring boats that can double for a bit of fishing or water skiing.

Bow riders have several inherent weaknesses. The first is that due to the completely open bow, *they are not suitable for use on rough waters*, and can be particularly dangerous in places where strong currents and waves are present, such as inlets to oceans.

Then there is the effect that putting a number of passengers all the way up in the bow has on hull trim. Deep vee hulls necessarily create very pointy hulls that have very little flotation in the bow area. In order to support passengers in the bow, the hull has to have more flotation, meaning that the bow is wider and flatter, a fact that translates to a generally poor ride on rough water. Hence, the reason that these boats are mainly found in protected bodies of water.

Bow riders are to be found in both outboard and stern drive power options.

Catamarans

This basic type has been with us for hundreds of years, albeit as sail boats and not as powerboats, and we're most familiar with the Polynesian catamarans or "outriggers" of the Pacific. In recent years there has been a revival of this type. Along with it there has been an awful lot of advertising hype.

As with every type, the catamaran has its advantages and disadvantages. The basic advantage stems from having two very narrow hulls with minimal wetted surface area. This results in less drag or less resistance that translates into requiring less power to achieve the same speeds as a comparable mono hull. It can also provide for more deck space since the bows are not pointed and the sides are not tapered.

Fig. 2-10. At left, the deck boat type; at right the bow rider which is a form of runabout. Neither of these types are well suited to open water use.

The disadvantages are also significant. Although you get more deck space, the deck by necessity is much higher up, so for fishermen you're not going to be as close to the water as in a mono hull. You also tend to loose a lot of below decks storage space, and instead of having to attend to one hull, you've got two.

As far as performance goes, I don't suppose the endless arguments about which kind of hull produces a better ride will ever be settled. As with all other boat types some designs are better than others, so unless one evaluates a large number of them, it's hard to tell. Almost everyone who has one raves about how much better it is than a mono hull, but I am not convinced. Cats can produce a better ride under some conditions but not others. They're less prone to slamming in 2-3' seas but head-on into larger seas, and especially in taking head seas on the forward quarter, I'd award the trophy to the well-designed monohull. My personal opinion is that cats are best suited for large bays and lakes where nasty chops predominate, for that is where they truly excel.

The fact is that cat hulls behave differently than mono hulls, and whether that is for better or worse tends to be a matter of personal opinion. As a matter of fuel economy, the cat wins over a deep vee hull hands-down. All I can say is that if you're interested, get a demo ride in one and see for yourself.

Catamaran hull designs vary widely, and my experience has been that even minor differences in hull design can produce major changes in performance. The truth is that because of their relative newness on the market and the small numbers of them, not a lot is known about these variations. Surveyors like myself don't work with them on a daily basis as we do with monohulls. There are some boats that do not turn very well; they are hard to steer and turn. Some have their hulls so close together that they might more appropriately be called slotted hulls rather than cats. They turn more easily but it gets hard to see the advantage of such a boat.

Fig. 2-11. Deep vee outboard with heavy bow flare.

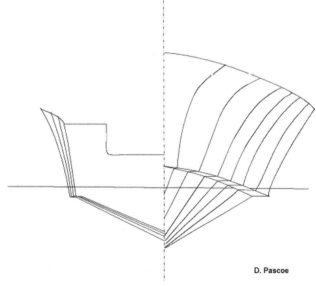

D. Pascoe

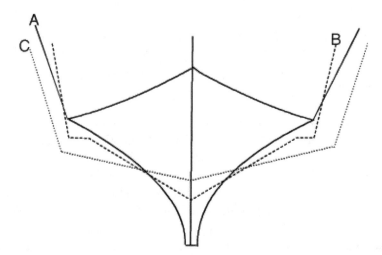

Fig. 2-12. Hull sections of the three major classes of hull shapes overlaid gives a general idea of how each type will perform in head seas. (A), the warped plane hull; (B), deep vee hull; (C), shallow vee hull.

The thing to be aware of with cats is the spacing of the two hulls. The closer they are together, the more it will behave like a mono hull. Some are so close that technically they are slotted hulls, not catamarans. Equally important is the beam of each of the hulls. The narrower the hulls, the softer the ride but less fuel efficient and possibly more difficult handling.

Turning ability can also be a sore spot. Some boats that I have tested tend to lean toward the outside of a turn, which is uncomfortable. Others, like the Glacier Bays turn quite nicely with a list toward the inside of the turn.

Pocket Cruisers

The so called pocket cruiser is a very old type that long ago went out of fashion but now seems to be making a comeback. It is distinguishable by a large part of its interior volume being given over to sheltered cabin space. These days, most pocket cruisers are stern drive powered though some few are made for outboards. How large can a pocket cruiser be? My answer to that is up to 25 feet, beyond which a boat becomes a normal sized cruiser. The 28 foot Bertram, for example, is clearly not a pocket cruiser.

These are essentially niche market boats because their very small size makes them unattractive to many boaters. With too much crammed into a too-small space, these can be ergonomic nightmares for all but the smallest people. On the other hand, there are some people who don't mind being cramped.

One big drawback for many of these boats is performance. The beam-to-length ratio is often very high, so that with considerably higher weights than other outboard boats, performance is often on the poor side both in terms of speed and fuel efficiency. And with a lot of weight up forward, they can be a lot tougher to get on and off trailers.

If you are seriously considering a boat of this type, the basic performance is one of the first things that need be researched to ensure that you don't end up disappointed with your purchase. Consider the taking of a test ride as mandatory.

Cruisers

These consist of any boat in which the major part of the interior is given over to cabin space. Usually, a cruiser is a boat 26 feet and larger. Whether it's called an express, convertible or whatnot, it's still a cruiser. Its primary features are facility for overnighting, as opposed to a day boat.

The main drawback of outboard cruisers is always weight. As discussed in the power options section, outboard motors are not the best choice for driving heavy boats. By the time a boat reaches around 8,000 lbs., it is reaching the limit for outboard motors to power them efficiently. Typically, cruisers get loaded down with more equipment and loose gear than any other kind of boat, so that the dry weight direct from the builder is only a starting weight. By the time it's loaded down with everything, it's going to weigh a whole lot more.

When considering buying a cruiser, give consideration to other power options as the outboard may not be the best power choice.

If you run across an outboard cruiser with a flying bridge, I would counsel you to be very cautious about that boat's stability. Outboard boats are not amenable to having flying bridges due to engine(s) being on the stern may not provide adequate ballast for the boat.

Pontoon and Deck Boats

These are specialty boats that are mainly designed for use in small lakes, bays and rivers. Beware of dealers who tout them as go anywhere, do anything boats. These are not open water boats and should not be used as such. If it's not designed like a deep water boat, don't take it in deep water. Deck boats are typically very rough riding when the water gets choppy.

There is, and has been, a substantial amount of litigation over accidents involving the use of these boats in open water. This includes a case in which I was involved where a woman had her back broken while sitting in a seat when the boat went off a wave, and was disabled for life. This occurred when the owner thought the boat could handle three foot seas. It couldn't, and that mistake about ruined his life, too.

You should approach the purchase of any specialty boat such as this with caution, making sure that the boat is designed properly for the conditions in which you intend to use it.

Fig.2-13. The center console, cuddy cabin strives to give the best of both worlds, a cabin and a console in a small open boat. The desirability of such designs depends on your demand for unfettered cockpit space. As can be seen here, this one is rather cramped.

The Importance of Hull Form

One of the difficulties that we have with communicating the importance of hull form is the tendency for people to think most often in terms of idyllic conditions — those bright, sunny warm days when the water is flat calm and there is little to interfere with your enjoyment of a beautiful day. Unfortunately, as every experienced boater knows, not only can weather conditions change fast but, more often than not, those idyllic conditions are all too rare, especially on weekends, the time when most boaters get the most use of their boats.

It's one thing if you are buying a boat to use only on small lakes or rivers, where wave height isn't much of a consideration. It's something else again if you're boating on the oceanfront or the Great Lakes where weather conditions are often highly uncooperative. Clearly, if you want to get the most use from your expensive boat, you need to take into consideration how well a boat is going to handle the most prevalent conditions. If a one to two foot chop is going to stop you cold, more often than not you'll remain tied to the dock.

This is where consideration of hull form comes in. Fishermen, of course, tend to understand this a lot better because they're a lot less inclined to allow weather to keep them in port. You got to go when the fish are running, and if you don't . . . well, no fish. Yet it's not only the avid fisherman that should pay attention to hull design and performance. With a properly designed hull, you run the prospect of easily doubling the amount of use you can get from your boat over one that has a rather flat bottom.

Offshore Mono Hull Shapes

We start talking about specific features of hull design when we are interested in more than just buying a boat because we like the way it looks, and when we are most concerned about its offshore performance, a term meaning how the boat handles when waves start getting uncomfortable.

The hulls that get the most attention are the center console boats because these are most often used offshore. By offshore, I mean in large bodies of water where how well a boat handles the seas becomes of critical importance. Not only are we interested in the depth of the hull, but other issues such as beam and bow flare and directional stability.

The standard 8'6" beam is standard because this is the maximum towable width allowed on the roads. The maximum beam always occurs at the deck since most hulls taper down to the water line. This, of course, reduces cockpit deck space considerably. So does bow flare. Bow flare exists to help keep spray and water out of the boat. A boat with perfectly straight up and down hulls sides would take a lot of water over the bow, and not just from spray.

Bow Flare and Sheer Lines

Thirty years ago, when the Cigarette offshore racing boats were first designed, these boats stood out because their sheer lines (the line defined by the point where the hull meets the deck) were a convex curve. The bow sloped downward so that the hulls had higher freeboard in the mid section than at either bow or stern. This isn't very practical as far as good seakeeping ability is concerned, but the reason for this design had nothing to do with sea keeping. After all, these are race boats. The reason for the lower bow is that with all the engine weight in the stern, the bow tends to rise up very high. The pilot needs to see over the bow, so the designer simply made it lower. Besides, raw speed was at issue here, not seaworthiness.

Unfortunately, people are trendy and fad conscious, and so offshore racing spawned thirty years worth of copycat design for no good reason. Thirty years later many builders are still designing them the same way, though the trend is slowly fading.

Ever wonder why ships have very high bows? The reason is pretty obvious, isn't it? With a very pointy, low bow, when seas get large, there is the risk of burying the bow into a wave. That is true for both head seas and following seas. So it just makes good sense for good offshore boat design to have higher rather than lower bows. Fortunately, that is exactly the current trend in serious offshore CC boats. Besides, you can't get any serious bow flare with a Cigarette type hull with a pointy snoot.

Bow flare is the amount of arc a hull side has as it runs up and outward. A boat can have a cockpit deck in the bow area that is two feet wide near the water line and be eight feet wide at deck level. That is extreme bow flare. But bow flare is not the only determining factor for how dry a boat is. The shape of the forefoot and the chine angle also plays a role. Some boats even have a double, or false chine, to further hold down the water that tends to run up the side of the hull. Bow flare helps prevent the wind from catching the water and blowing it back into the boat, something that is common to virtually all boats.

Bottom Shape

The amount of vee in a hull is called **deadrise**, and is measured in degrees from the horizontal plane as shown in Fig. 2-11 (page 25). Deadrise is always measured at the transom because of the fact that it is possible to greatly modify a vee hull into something else called a **modified vee**. A modified vee can be very deep up forward — the area called the forefoot — and taper off to almost nothing at the stern. This is also called a **warped plane** design. A good example of modified vee hulls are those designed by Jack Hargrave for Hatteras, bottoms that are highly irregular in shape, yet can be equally effective as the rather flat surfaces of a plain deep vee hull. A full vee hull has bottom panels that carry the same deadrise angle from end to end. The bottom panels are flat, but the two sides form a vee. This is called a constant deadrise hull.

If you take a piece of cardboard and, holding one end in each hand and twist in opposite directions, you have the essence of the warped plane hull in which the deadrise varies at different points on the hull. With this hull type, the bottom angle increases toward the bow. In extreme cases the stern section could be completely flat while the bow section is like a knife's edge.

So what's the point of this? Well, a knife slicing through water is not going to suffer from any slamming and neither will a knife edged bow. It all depends, of course, on what part of the bottom the boat is riding. We now have entering the picture the issue of trim; when you don't have a constant deadrise vee hull, it matters what the trim of the boat is at various speed, and therefore the amount of deadrise at different points on the hull. Generally speaking, the faster a boat goes, the flatter it will ride on the water.

We could, of course, design a boat bottom that is very pointy along the entire length of the bottom, but we'd have some problems with that. For one thing, as the boat gets going fast, the hull is going to rise up higher out of the water and attempt to ride on the apex of the vee. Then, if the boat is not perfectly balanced, our hull will flop over to one side or the other. Not good, so we don't do that. Instead, we have to choose hull angles that will give us both stability and a good ride. We can go with the constant deadrise vee, or choose a modified vee, depending on the performance characteristics we're trying to achieve.

We complicate matters even further by realizing that it matters where the weights are placed in the boat. From people to fuel tanks to engines, we have to have some buoyancy to keep all this afloat. When we go with very deep vees, we loose a lot of buoyancy aft, and with a pair of outboard motors hanging on the back, it's likely to sit low in the stern, so we have to be careful to get it just right.

We do that by compressing the top part of our vee inward a bit. The vee angle then increases but we end up with what is called a *chine flat*, an area around the perimeter of the bottom that has no vee angle at all. Chine flats can be very wide or narrow.

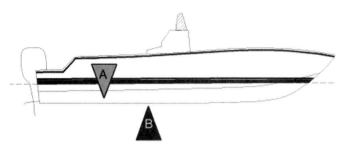

Fig. 2-14. Center of gravity (CG) and center of buoyancy (CB) are not in the same location in outboard boats due to engine location. The typical locations are shown above where B is the CB. This reveals why the trim of outboard boats can be hard to control. In this case, with CG aft of CB, the bow can always be trimmed with trim tabs.

We often find boats with heavily rounded vees - meaning instead of the vee coming to a hard angle point, it is rounded off. This will create more lift and cause the hull to ride higher. It also defeats the purpose of having a deep vee hull. The flatter bottom area it creates induces pounding.

What about bottom strakes, what is the purpose of those? That's a good question and one for which I'm not sure there is a good answer. Strakes, with their flat areas, certainly will create more lift and because of a flatter running surface, yet as with rounding a vee, they work to defeat its purpose. Again, the flat sections induce pounding and any benefit they may have can be achieved in other ways such as simply making the vee less deep. In my opinion, bottom strakes are useless and in many cases actually cause weakness in some bottoms.

And then there are slotted hulls. After much ado about nothing, most experts agree that putting transverse slots in hull bottoms accomplishes nothing worthwhile. Any speed gain is so slight as to be insignificant. They make boats more expensive and difficult to maintain.

Chine Flats

In the last 10 years or so, chine flats have been added to most vee hulls. A chine flat lies between the chine and the bottom, at the point where it angles downward, as shown in Figure 2-11(page 25). A chine flat is, well, flat. They serve three purposes. First, this narrow flat portion of the bottom provides extra lift, and in providing lift thereby reduces drag somewhat, probably in the range of 10-15%.

Second, chine flats help retard roll, especially in smaller boats like outboards where the engines aren't doing much in the way of ballasting except at one end. Chine flats will help some boats and not others, depending on hull design. The more weight that is located forward, and the more level the boat sits, the more chine flats will help stability. For a boat that sits with the bow up and stern down, chine flats will have little effect.

Third, when a designer desires to have a deep vee plus a wide beam, that vee is going to get awful wide across the base of the triangle, and thus the vee will end up becoming too shallow and cause too much buoyancy. By bring the ends of the base of the triangle inward, the amount of buoyancy can be reduced and the vee angle increased, so that chine flats simply become the byproduct of this design. Which is not say that that is the case for all boats. Only the designer really knows for sure why it's there.

Chine flats can have the negative effect of increasing slamming when they are too large, as they are, after all, flat to the surface of the water. A flat width of 3-4" is normal and not excessive.

Keel Boats

 Long before the deep vee hull arrived on the scene, most boats had keels, what appears as a long fin-like appendage that extends below the hull proper. Left over from the days of wooden boats, keels were actually the backbone of the boat, but they had the additional advantage of providing some protection in the event of grounding, plus keels will retard rolling moment. Keels also cause boats to steer very straight and make them harder to turn.

A few builders such as Shamrock still build keel boats. Boaters who operate in very shallow waters seem to like them. Another drawback is that when they do go aground, they're a lot harder to get unstuck as the keel buries itself in the bottom.

In recent years, we have not seen any outboard keel boats being built.

Stability

You may have heard that deep vee hulls are less stable than shallower, beamier boats. This is not necessarily true. It is true that the deep vee displaces more water, or at least sits deeper in the water, and therefore needs more ballasting. With inboard boats this is almost never a problem because the engines and fuel tankage, correctly placed, provide all the ballasting needed to make the hull plenty stable. No one who knows what they're talking about ever accused a deep vee Bertram of being unstable. In fact, they are much more stable than their wide beamed, relatively flat-bottomed counterparts. Here's why.

There are numerous factors that go into the make up of what we call a stable hull. Stability means the ability to remain upright, without rolling over. When boaters talk about stability, what they're usually referring to is how much the boat rolls, but rolling motion is not a direct indicator of stability. All boats roll. The question is how much and how fast. Of paramount importance is the "period of roll," which is defined as how fast the hull rolls from side to side. How many degrees a boat rolls is usually less important than how fast it rolls. A properly designed hull can roll a lot, but do so slowly and gently. Whereas a thoughtlessly designed hull (and there are a lot them) that may

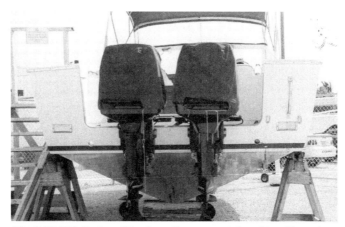

Fig. 2-15. This Bertram 26 outboard is representative of the older style cut down transom. The effective freeboard would only be to the top of the cut down in the transom were it not for the high-sided well forward of the motors. The scupper flaps reveal the cockpit deck level. The deadrise angle on this hull was measured at a whopping 26 degrees. It takes a lot of power and a lot of fuel to push this boat.

roll less, but do so much more violently. They develop a "whip-snap" action that tends to throw standing passengers right off their feet. They may roll slowly in one direction but then suddenly "snap back." Very wide beam boats with flatter bottoms are notorious for this.

An illustrative example of this would be the difference in motion between a rectangular wooden box with a flat bottom as compared to the same size box with a vee shaped bottom that is ballasted with weights. Place both into choppy water and note which has the more pleasant motion for passengers. The flat bottomed box would roll very fast, whereas the vee bottom box would roll more from side to side, but do so more slowly, being less likely to throw passengers off their feet.

Outboards and stern drive boats, because of all the engine weight hung off the stern, tend to roll with an oscillating motion. In other words, they roll in a circular motion because the boat is ballasted at the stern, rather than the center. Thus, the rolling motion will be less at the stern, and more at the bow.

Trim

It has happened on many occasions that a boat builder has taken a very good design of a naval architect, and completely subverted it by violating the rules of trim. This happens as the result of changing the arrangement of internal weights, throwing the boat out of a careful configured balance, such as putting outboard motors on brackets on a boat that wasn't designed for it. Trim literally means how a boat is balanced relative to how it is supposed to float, both while at rest and underway. Most people have a rudimentary understanding of this, but we'd do a little better if we understood it more thoroughly. For trim is one of the major factors that influence boat performance.

Designers have to consider both types of trim, dynamic and static. When at rest, ideally the boat should float level, yet this is not the ideal dynamic trim, which is to have the bow riding slightly higher, usually at an angle of around 5-7°. Were a boat to run completely level, it would perform poorly because the bow would dig in, causing it to steer poorly, as well throwing too much spray. As we discussed earlier, we want to minimize the amount of contact of the forward part of the hull with the water. Thus, a designer has a bit of a balancing act to perform in order to get the boat to float right at rest, and while underway, in order to optimize performance. The boat has to float right under both conditions.

There is a very important relationship between beam and waterline length. You probably have no trouble understanding why a 24 foot boat with a four foot beam would go much faster than one with an 8 foot beam: less drag and resistance by half. But there is another factor as well. This is a matter of buoyancy, and where on the hull the lift is coming from. The wider the beam, the more squarish the hull becomes. Consider the old Army Jeep vehicle, which had a nearly square wheel base that made that vehicle directionally unstable, resulting in an incredible number of crashes and casualties until they finally figured out what was wrong. The problem was solved by lengthening the wheelbase. A boat that has a squarish hull also suffers from both dynamic (directional) and static instability. Length increases directional stability. But like a large ship, too much water line length can mean that the boat becomes very hard to steer.

With fast power boats, we want to control directional stability with the steering system, not the hull, which is yet another reason we don't want our hull to ride level. If you look at pictures of fast powerboats underway, you'll notice that they ride on anywhere from one-half to one-fourth of the hull — and sometimes even less. This is what makes them very easy to steer; the hull is pivoting around the steering mechanism — be it rudders or an outboard drive system — giving it the ability to yaw, or perform sliding turns which are very smooth, efficient and easy to control. If the boat is not trimmed properly, then the hull tracks like a train on a track and the boat won't handle as well as it should.

Dynamic stability in a vessel means the ability to return to a level position after external forces have acted on it. That can be either waves or steering inputs. A most dynamically stable boat, for example, would be one with a single inboard engine mounted at or near the center of the hull, and as low as possible. Such a configuration makes a boat about as stable as it can get. An even better example is the sailboat with a ballasted keel, wherein even if you roll them over, they always pop back upright.

Balancing a boat is simply a matter of weights and levers. Every boat has a center of buoyancy and a center of gravity. The center of buoyancy is the upward force created by the hull displacing water (floatation). Gravity consists of the internal weights pushing downward. When the center of buoyancy and the center of gravity are aligned, the boat theoretically floats level. When these centers are offset, the boat will float out of balanced trim, but that may be exactly how we want it.

Trim is easy enough to understand because when you move to one side of the boat, the hull sinks deeper on that side. But when you move fore and aft, this is much less noticeable because there is a great deal more longitudinal buoyancy than there is transverse buoyancy; the boat is longer than it is wide. However, it is fore and aft trim that has the greatest effect on performance, and is the most difficult to influence or change.

The placement of weights in a boat involves levers. The easiest way to understand this is to consider picking up a bucket of water. Then try to hold that bucket out at arm's length. Unless you are extremely strong, you can't do it because the length of your arm constitutes a lever. The center of your body is the theoretical balancing point. If the bucket of water weighs 50 lbs. and is extended out three feet, then the amount of gravitational force created by this lever arm is 150 ft/lbs. (50 x 3).

While this may appear simplistic and obvious, a boat is like a balance scale. It has a balance point relative to how it should float in order to achieve the proper trim angle for the best performance. That balance point is not exactly either the center of gravity or the center of buoyancy, but somewhere in between and is dependent on hull shape. But, if a boat is not designed properly, it may float perfectly level while at rest, but not trim properly while underway. If that's the case, then it won't perform as it should.

You'll find more information on this subject in the chapter **Cockpits, Motors & Trim**.

Beam

The width of a hull is another factor that affects a boat's performance. To illustrate this, consider dragging a knife, sharp edge forward, through the water. The fine edge creates almost no resistance at all. Now rotate the blade 90 degrees and drag the flat side of the blade through the water. This, of course, creates a lot of resistance, and illustrates how the beam of the boat affects her performance. The wider the hull, the more flat surfaces of the hull are exposed to waves. The main effect on small boats is in terms of pounding, on whether the hull will slice through waves, or slam into them by presenting wider, flatter bottom panels to the waves.

In recent years, boat hulls have been getting increasingly wider as designers attempt to woo buyers with more interior space at the expense of performance. Unfortunately, many boat owner's aren't aware of the tradeoff they have made, and now find themselves stuck with a boat that pounds badly, even when going over very small waves. The rule of thumb here is the deeper the vee, and the narrower the beam, the better the hull will handle heading straight into the waves. Of course a *very* deep, narrow hull can be just as undesirable as a very wide beam, shallow hull. The longer, narrower and deeper the hull, the more it tends to track straight, and the harder it is to turn. The cigarette type hull can actually be very difficult to steer. Somewhere in the middle lies the intelligent compromise between interior space and adequate performance in the conditions that will be most often encountered.

Freeboard

The definition of this term is the height of the hull from the waterline to the top of the deck at any location on the hull. Freeboard is one of the factors of hull design that, in the interest of style, has been really taking a beating lately. Think, for a moment, on how boats used to be designed compared to the way they are today. Why were boats, and always ships, designed with high, flaring bows? To keep the water out, of course. So why do they design boats with low freeboard and noses that point downward? It's a style thing, of course. But is this the sort of design you want to go offshore with? Not me! If I wanted a submarine I would buy one. Boats with bows designed to ride *over* waves are preferable to bows that go *through* them.

There is a difference between effective freeboard and general freeboard. A good example of this is an outboard boat with a very low transom cut out to facilitate motor mounting. While the hull may have all-around good freeboard, at the stern it doesn't. Those high sides mean relatively little when water can come pouring in over the low transom to sink the boat anyway.

Effective freeboard means the lowest possible point where water can enter the hull. Another example would be an in-deck bait well that is open to outside water by means of plumbing. Thousands of boats have sunk because the builder failed to realize that the open bait well he designed reduced the effective freeboard to only a few inches. If you're concerned about your safety at sea, don't take it for granted that the designer got it right. Check for yourself the design of all hull openings.

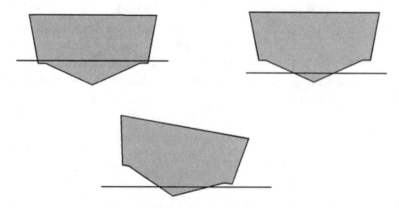

Fig. 2-16. This illustration shows how deep vee hulls can end up with transverse trim problems when hulls are too light and rise too high out of the water. It can't balance on the apex of the vee and so "flops over."

Wet Boat, Dry Boat

 The reference to a "wet boat" means that it tends to take a lot of water over the bow. All boats can and will take spray over the bow under the right conditions; some just happen to be worse than others, and some are so bad that they seem to be always taking spray under all conditions. That's what we call a "wet" boat.

There are many things a designer can do to minimize this. The primary means are bow flare; the more extreme the bow flare, the less likely to take spray. Conversely, what you get for that is a serious loss of deck space, so most designers try to achieve a happy medium between deck space and bow flare.

Another thing they can do is to add strakes or what we might call spray rails or false chines. Each of these has the effect of deflecting and directing downward the water that tends to run up the side of the hull, which then gets caught by the wind and blown back in your face.

In most cases, a buyer will never get the chance to actually test a boat for this. The best way to judge, short of actual sea tests, is by the amount of bow flare, plus the number or size of strakes or spray diverters molded into the hull in the bow section.

The Fuel Efficiency Issue

There is nothing anyone can do with engines that could improve fuel efficiency more than putting a motor on a flat bottomed boat which would have the least possible drag of all. To give you an idea of how much, a twenty foot flat bottom boat can achieve the same speed with a 50 HP motor as a deep vee with a 200 HP motor, a difference of four-fold. Of course, our flat bottomed boat is nearly worthless for what we want if for. Everything about a boat is truly a compromise and there are enough variations in the designs of the boats available to create difficulty in making these choices.

Judging by the amount of discussion that I see on the Internet forums, fuel economy is a major concern for a lot of boat owners. That's all well and good, but just be aware that you can't have your cake and eat it too. High speed, good rough water performance and fuel economy are conflicting characteristics You get one only by sacrificing the others. My recommendation is to lean toward better rough water performance unless you are certain that you'll be operating in very protected waters that don't get rough. It's just a hard fact of boating life that fuel consumption and costs are high.

Acceleration

Many people are disappointed that their boats don't make jackrabbit starts, complaining that their boats are slow to get up on plain. Boats don't accelerate like cars and one should not expect them to. As with any vehicle, slamming the throttles forward is not good for the engine and should be avoided. In my view, most of these complaints are unjustified.

How quickly a boat will get up on plane is dependent on many factors. This includes not only the boat weight/power ratio, but also the trim of the boat. Some boats are trimmed so far aft that you just have to live with slow acceleration and the bow rising high before it climbs up to planing attitude. Don't expect trim tabs to help this situation. Heavier boats will naturally accelerate slower because the weight to power ratios are lower.

Consider that a 24' boat weighing 5,000 lbs. with twin 200 hp outboards has a weight/ power ratio of 12.5:1, while a 32 footer weighing 12,000 lbs. with twin 260 hp inboards has a ratio of 23:1, exactly double the former. Naturally, it's going to take quite a bit longer to get going.

How fast should a small boat get up on plane? Probably not more than 15 seconds at a moderate throttle advance. The longer it takes to get there, the more fuel you burn. Fortunately, this is rarely a problem with the high horsepower that most small boats are equipped with.

What Is cavitation?

The root of the word is *cavity* , as in a hole in the water. Cavitation can occur for several reasons. Under certain conditions that are related to the attack angle of the propeller — the direction of travel relative to the water surface, as well as blade pitch — it is possible that the propeller can open up holes in the water. This is usually seen as a large stream of bubbles trailing off the blade tips if you were underwater looking at it. In other cases, the hull is actually causing a stream of air bubbles to be directed at the propeller. This causes the propeller and engine to overspeed because the blades are biting on air, not water, and why you often hear outboard motors over-revving when they're not trimmed right.

Over-revving is always the result of cavitation and means that the motor (or the boat) is not trimmed right. In the worst case, a propeller may actually be pulling water down from the surface, as often happens with an outboard that is way out of trim. This results in extreme over-speeding of the engine and there is no mistaking what is happening. You either correct it in a big hurry, or wreck your engines. It infrequently happens because something like a depth sounder transducer is directing a stream of air into a propeller. In this case, over-revving will not occur, but one merely experiences one engine that runs slightly faster than the other for no apparent reason. Usually the engine is suspect when that is not the cause at all.

This point is made because there are plenty of bad hull design/motor installation combinations that require some major work to get them straightened out. What we're looking to avoid here is taking delivery of a boat that requires major surgery and months of haggling with the builder and dealer to make it right.

While all of this may sound terribly technical and complicated, actually in the real world it's not. Getting a boat to sit right and ride right is pretty easy if the boat is designed right in the first place. Minor adjustments are usually easy to achieve. A boat that is badly out of trim may not be correctable at all. Our goal here is to educate you on what to look for so you don't get stuck with a turkey. Taking a test run will quickly point up any shortcomings since minor faults usually turn up major performance problems. All that is necessary for you is to know what to look for.

Torque and Transverse Trim

Both engines and propellers develop torque, which is the rotational force of a rotating body. Rotation of the earth is what drives our weather which, as we know, involves incredible forces. It's not much different with boat engines.

The direction of the force of torque is opposite of the rotation of the engine. For example, a single engine boat with a right hand rotation engine will tend to twist the hull to the left. This is a problem that is confined almost solely to single engine boats since twin engine boats have counter-rotating props, in which the torque directions offset each other. At least theoretically.

With twin engine boats, builders sometimes mount engines very close together. You shouldn't have any difficulty understanding why it is that the closer the propellers are together, the less transverse stability the boat will have. There are two reasons. First, the center of force is closer to the center of the hull, making for a much narrower "footprint," so to speak. Secondly, being closer together, the rotational forces of torque exert a stronger influence the closer the propellers are. This usually results in a handling characteristic which is "squirrelly," meaning that it is much more sensitive to steering inputs, and not infrequently developing a tendency to lay over on one side. This is discussed in more detail below.

Single engine outboards need something to counteract torque. This is most easily accomplished with trim tabs, be they electro/hydraulic or fixed type. Most motors have an articulating fin above the prop, but this often fails to achieve its purpose, requiring some stronger measures. Here again, trim tabs not only provide the ideal solution for transverse, but longitudinal trim as well. Tabs are usually one of the most useful options that you can add to an outboard boat purchase. The duo prop, with its counter rotating propellers, also overcomes this problem, although at considerable extra expense.

Rather than incurring the cost of adding trim tabs, why not just use the engine power trim? Because in doing so you change the propeller angle and reduce power efficiency, resulting in higher fuel consumption. The trim tab is more efficient at affecting minor trim changes.

What about propeller rotation on twin engine boats? Does it make a difference? The normal configuration is counter-rotating with starboard engine turning right, port engine turning left. This provides the maximum degree of stability as well as maneuverability. However, some people believe that inboard rotating props create more lift and higher speed, and while this may be true, it will decrease stability and make the boat harder to maneuver at slow speed.

Flop-Overs

One of the worst design faults is the boat that, at higher speeds, wants to lay over on one side and not ride level, often called "chine riding". It is a nasty performance characteristic that can be downright dangerous because the boat may become uncontrollable. This can occur for several reasons. One is the result of a boat that is too light in relation to its hull shape.

What happens is that the engines drive the vee hull up on the surface of the water so that it's riding too much on the apex of the vee. Of course the boat can't sit upright on a point, so it flops over. Any attempt to correct the condition usually results in the hull flopping over on the other side. Sometimes even a minor change in steering will do this. The placement and condition of fuel tanks will often have an effect. There are boats that basically handle okay when the tanks are full, but then begin to exhibit this tendency as the tanks empty.

Another is simply the result of bad design in which a variety of factors combine to create a hull that wants to ride along the length of the keel, with insufficient angle of attack. This creates too much lift on the hull and so it rises up too high, again to ride on the apex of the vee. Add trim tabs and power trim outboards or stern drives to the mix and the problem becomes even more complex, since the adjustment of these things will then have to be exactly right to keep the boat upright.

All small boats should be tested for this condition. If it demonstrates a tendency to lay over on its side, it's best to steer clear of that boat. This is not only a very annoying and inconvenient problem, it's also dangerous due to the potential loss of control it presents.

Chapter 3

Hull Construction

Nowadays, you can go out and purchase just about any automobile and be reasonably certain of getting at least a reasonably reliable product that won't immediately start falling apart on you. Unfortunately, this is not true of boats, for the reasons we discussed in the opening chapter. The sad fact is that there are a lot of poorly built boats out there. The purpose of this chapter is to help you avoid buying a boat with serious structural problems. If you are unfamiliar with many of the terms used here, you'll find them defined in the Glossary in Appendix A.

Many of the problems of the small boat class results from the fact that there are so many builders who are competing on basis of price alone. Check the newspaper ads and its price, price, price. The cheaper the better. While everyone should know better than to buy a boat and motor package just because it's the lowest price, the allure of a "good deal" is just too much to resist for many people.

This chapter discusses the elements of good hull design and construction, which will include the deck, other basic boat components, as well as related performance characteristics. Many people attempt to shortcut the process of learning about the nature of boats by trying to find information about the particular boats they are interested in, such as product reviews. Because there are so many different boats out there, this is not possible, as there are few such sources of information. No one wants to risk getting sued by publicly stating that a boat is badly constructed. The only way that you can evaluate the quality of a boat is by learning what constitutes good design and construction techniques so that you can evaluate it for yourself, or hire a professional to do that for you.

For thousands of years mankind has been successfully building good boats with no mathematics and no engineering whatsoever. There was no magic in this; they simply made them overly strong so they wouldn't fall apart. In modern boat building, things have changed. The impetus is to design a boat hull right down to the failure point in order to save on cost of materials and labor. Hand laid fiberglass has a certain degree of inconsistency of strength as all laminates are not uniform. Thus lacking a significant margin for error, hull failures can and often do occur.

While low cost may be in your best interest in terms of the initial price you pay for a boat, in the longer run you give up a lot for price in terms of durability. Ultimately, it's up to you as to whether you're willing to invest in a dispose-a-boat that is good for only so many years, after which it goes to the chopper. This chapter will give you many pointers on what to look for and how to avoid buying a lemon.

While it isn't really necessary that you have a thorough understanding of the materials that go into the making of a "fiberglass" boat, many people will find it helpful, and so it's been included here. If you want to skip the materials section, go ahead, but it is important that you understand the basic structural elements of a boat, so please do read this section.

Molded Fiberglass Essentials

The history of the fiberglass boat goes all the way back to 1936, but production fiberglass boat building got its start shortly after WWII and really took off in the late 1950's. By 1960, production fiberglass boat building was fully established. That means that the industry now has a solid forty years of history and experience under its belt, so there's really no excuse for building boats that fall apart. Unfortunately, defective boats abound, for the reasons already explained.

The full and proper name for a fiberglass boat is Fiberglass Reinforced Plastic, or FRP for short. In Europe they call it GRP for "glass reinforced plastic, but it's the same thing. The term "fiberglass" takes its name from the woven fabric that constitutes the reinforcement of what is in essence a plastic hull. Fiberglass is literally silica sand glass made into extremely thin fibers, thinner than a human hair, which is then woven into a variety of fabrics. Once transformed into a bundle of fibers, these tiny strands of glass become extremely strong, and the reason why it is used as a reinforcement for what is otherwise a very weak plastic.

Despite what you may have heard about fiberglass, particularly as respect to the blistering problem, fiberglass reinforced plastic is a near perfect material for boat building. Of course, as with all materials, that only holds true when the materials are used properly and with the correct engineering techniques. The material is easily molded into complex shapes. It is so easy in fact, that anyone with a little knowledge and a set of plans and a lot of spare time could build a small boat in his garage without a mold.

Fabrics

The fiberglass fabric comes in four basic forms, mat, cloth, roving and stitched multidirectional fabrics, which now come in a huge variety of types. Mat, or "chopped fiber" as

Fig. 3-1. At left, a stitched axial fabric; right, chopped strand mat or CSM. The one on the left is a structural reinforcement, the other is not, though far too many builders make too much use of it because it is cheap and easier to work with. CMS is also a major part of the cause of blisters.

it may be referred to, are short fibers simply pressed into a mat, which is how it got its name. It is commonly known by its acronym, CSM for chopped strand mat. It can be created by a machine that starts with a big spool of glass fiber thread, chops it into 3" pieces, mixes it with resin and then blows it through a nozzle with air pressure. This is called a "chopper gun." Boat builders like this stuff because it works easily into corners, whereas heavy fabrics do not and require more labor.

CSM also comes as a premanufactured fabric in rolls. It is not very strong and is used — or at least should only be used — as the layer that is set against the gel coat to prevent the texture of coarser fabrics for telegraphing through the gel coat. If you've ever seen a boat with a finish that has a pattern like a tweed coat, know you know why: not enough mat. The texture of the cloth has telegraphed through the finish layers.

Mat may also be referred to as "chopper gun," a term related to the machine. This is a method used mainly for manufacturing non-marine fiberglass parts and should never be used for boat hulls because of the weakness of the material. Unfortunately, it often is, and accounts for the poor quality of many boats, and also one of the primary contributors to bottom blistering because it can be extremely porous.

Woven fabrics are made in the form of very light cloth, on up in weight to what is called roving, which is nothing more than a very heavy cloth with flat fiber bundles 1/4" wide or more. Woven fabrics usually have a fiber orientation of 90^0 perpendicular angles. The interlocking weave makes for obvious strength, but is not the strongest type of fiber orientation available. Roving is or was the primary fabric used in most boat construction. It is quite strong and results in an acceptably strong laminate.

Fig. 3-2. Damaged hull side of Sea Ray boat built with Coremat. Note that there is only one layer of structural fiberglass showing here on the inside layer.

On the face of it, the random orientation of CSM fibers should make it stronger than others; this premise falls down simply because the fiber length is just a few inches. Oddly enough, it is the continuous length of glass fabric fibers that yields its ultimate strength, not unlike the cables of suspension bridges.

Unidirectional bias fabrics are usually used on high performance boats, and for purposes where higher strengths are needed. Unidirectional fabrics are considerably more diffi-cult to use, and so they are not often found in the average outboard boat, although it may appear in some of the more expensive fishermen or high performance boats. The typical ratio of glass fibers to plastic is 65/35 by weight. Thus a fiberglass boat is more glass than plastic.

Kevlar & Carbon Fiber

These two high tech, exotic materials have worked their way down from the aerospace industry to boat building, but not without some disastrous consequences. While both are known for their ultra high strengths, they also have characteristics that make them very difficult to work with, essentially requiring well-trained experts and designers. This adds far too much to the cost of ordinary production boats and so these materials are limited mainly to custom and specialty boats.

Resins

The very term "plastic" means a substance that can be formed into complex shapes, its definition rooted in the term "pliable." Refined from crude oil, plastic is versatile stuff indeed. It can be used to make anything from explosives (C4, Semtex) to boats. It comes in almost uncountable numbers of formulations, to which there is apparently no limit to its versatility. But the material has one serious fault: it is not very strong. Resin is the term for plastic in liquid form to which a catalyst, or hardener is added, causing it to solidify. Needless to say, a bit of precision is needed in the mixing of these chemicals or you may end up with a soft, sticky boat, or one that is excessively brittle. If you add

Fig. 3-4. A foam cored hull side. Note how it consists of small blocks of foam so that it bend to fit a contour. Even so, there was a failure to bond to the outer skin even though a special bonding agent was used (white material).

Fig. 3-3. A balsa core plug removed from the bottom of a boat.

too much catalyst, it can burst into flame or even explode from the ensuing chemical reaction that generates heat. Too little and it fails to harden and cure.

The process is known as exothermic, meaning that it gives off heat while curing. If too much catalyst is added, the amount of heat given off can result in heat distortions of the molded parts that usually shows up as waviness or a puckered appearance on the external surface. In most instances, this is only a cosmetic defect.

Resins come in three basic types and are, in order of their quality and price, least to greatest: polyester, vinylester and epoxy. These break down into dozens of differing "blends," each having different properties. Polyesters used in boat building break down into either orthopthalic or isopthalic resins. Orthos are the type that were responsible for the horrific blistering problems of the last two decades because ortho resin is an inexpensive, general purpose resin as compared to iso resins which are not prone to blistering, but are more expensive, roughly double the cost of orthos. Plastic resin chemistry can get very complex, and unless the builder has a plastics chemist on staff, he can very quickly run into trouble if he starts experimenting beyond the tried and true. Many builders do get in trouble because it is their nature to always be searching for the cheapest possible material.

Like shopping for a surgeon, price is not a good way to shop for resin. For most resins are not supplied by the big name chemical companies like Dow and Mobile. The big chemical companies are makers of the basic ingredients for plastic resin. People who are known as "formulators" then purchase the basic ingredients, mix them together and sell these as a huge variety of differing formulations for various manufacturing purposes, most of which are not good for boats. Thus, if a builder doesn't really know what he's doing, he can get in big trouble fast by fooling around with plastics.

The blistering problem became so painful to many boat builders (and boat owners) that most have either shifted to iso resins, or are using vinyl ester resin only on the outer layers of the hull in the hopes that this will prevent blistering. Certainly it will reduce the tendency, but its unlikely to completely solve the problem. Again, efforts to effect cost shortcuts result in less than satisfactory results as a few builders continue to have blistering problems. Most, however, have given this hell-pit a wide berth and have bitten the cost bullet when it comes to resin quality. And since resins are a major part of overall boat construction costs, prices have risen accordingly. Many have mitigated these cost increases by simply cutting back on the amount of resin used by making hulls thinner or using other materials such as cores.

Cores

A core is any material that is sandwiched in between two layers of fiberglass. In the past it was called "sandwich" construction, but often goes by the name of "composites" today. Composite simply means composed of more than one material, a term that also describes basic fiberglass. To say that a boat is built of composite construction really doesn't tell us anything we don't already know. The question we most want answered is, does it have a core? The most common cores are balsa, foam and plywood, and are employed for a variety of reasons.

The usual purpose of a core is to add strength to a flat or nearly flat surface such as decks or hull sides. Cores can add strength to flat panels similar to the way a roofing truss functions. However, when used on curved surfaces, a core can actually cause weak-

Fig. 3-5. Seven different core materials found in seven different damaged boats. Large piece at right is Coremat; the remainders are all spray-in putty types.

Fig.3-6 Top: a solid fiberglass laminate made with a vacuum bag. It is so dense that when dropped on a concrete floor, it sounds like a steel plate. Bottom, a foam cored deck section. Note the lack of bonding of core to upper skin at right. This came from a cockpit deck that was sagging because the composite was improperly designed.

ness. Cores should not be used in the bottoms of boats because of the potential for water getting into it. When that happens, the sandwich usually starts to come apart. On the smaller boats we're talking about here, the most common types of cores are foam or foam derivatives such as Coremat™ which is a type of fabric containing short fibers and a high percentage of solids. It sort of resembles that absorbent material one finds at the bottom of meat packages. However, plywood is still used in the decks of small boats, particularly cockpits.

Plywood is used at points where a laminate needs to be particularly strong, such as at points where mooring cleats or winches are mounted. It is not as common in small boats, except in decks of very fast boats such as the "cigarette" type boats where extremely strong decks are needed. Obviously, one big drawback of plywood is that if water gets to it, it will start to rot or delaminate.

Plywood is the most common material used for transom reinforcement to carry the weight of engines, and has proved troublesome over the years in terms of long-term durability. Within the last several years, a new material, an ultra high density foam-like material has come on the market and seems to be gaining rapid acceptance. This material looks like it may yield better long term results, though only time will tell. As of this writing, I know of no reported problems with it.

Balsa remains the most commonly used core material, but it too is usually found on larger boats. Balsa is remarkably resistant to rot, but even so it will deteriorate over time if it remains constantly wet.

Water getting into a core of any kind can lead to big trouble. Unfortunately, many boat owners are not aware of this and so they often drill holes in decks and such without understanding that what they are doing is allowing the core to become water saturated. Fortunately, the vast majority of outboard boats use no cores at all. For the most part, cores just aren't necessary. The lone exception is cockpit decks. It is always wise to find out before you buy.

Fig.3-7. This is disbonded tabbing of an inner liner to the bottom of a boat built in mid 1980's with DCDP resin.

Another core worthy of mention is NidaCore, which is a molded plastic honeycomb. NidaCore has the advantage of being extremely strong as well as resistant to deterioration. Its primary use is for decks as the material comes in flat sheets and does not take to bending. It is probably the best material for strengthening flat decks and is used for decks in commercial aircraft. Unfortunately, because of cost and difficulty of application, it will only be found in high end boats. Tiara/Pursuit is the only builder that I know of that uses it.

Putty Cores

Somewhere around 1992 putty cores (also known as "spray cores") were silently and secretly introduced into small boat building. I didn't discover this until after a minor hurricane in 1998 when I got the opportunity to examine numerous wrecked boats. Boats that were wrecked that shouldn't have been. There was a startling contrast between the condition of solid fiberglass hulls and putty core boats. Virtually none of the damaged solid laminate boats were broken up. I found it astonishing the number of boats that had broken up into pieces in ways that never happened with solid laminate boats, an event which convinced me of the weakness of this construction method.

What I call putty cores involve spraying a polyester-based filler into the hull after it's partially laid up, and on top of that other plies of fiberglass are laid so that what you end up with is a sort of peanut butter sandwich. These putties run about 1/8" to 3/16" thick, and by my own tests are very weak and brittle, resulting in a hull that is substantially weaker than a hull that is laid up of solid fiberglass. This is yet another cost saving effort by boat builders that remains to be seen how it's going to work out since most people are not even aware that this is how boats are being built.

In most cases, putty core boats are to be found in the so-called "price point" boats, predominantly family cruisers and runabouts, and usually only on the hull sides, not the bottoms. Sea Ray, for example, makes extensive use of putty cores. I have yet to find any putty cores in serious fishing or utility boats.

If you are beginning to get the impression that looking into buying a boat is something like opening up Pandora's box, you are not far off the mark. One trend that has become obvious in the last decade is that many builders have dropped all reference to the specifics of hull construction from their specifications and brochures. What was once referred to as a fiberglass hull is no longer mentioned. It's just a boat.

By contrast, we usually find that the builders of the higher end sport fishing boats will go into considerable detail about construction. The distinction here is that one builder feels proud or confident enough to state the particulars of his creation while others don't. Does this mean that putty core boats will fall apart? Not necessarily, though some have. When you're dealing with "price point" boats, chances are that you'll encounter this conundrum.

Ultimately, the reader's question is, "Should I buy one of these things?" The only answer I can give is that there are tens of thousands of these boats out there, that for the most part are doing well. Some few have experienced major problems with delamination, but the problem most likely to be encountered is extensive damage from minor collisions. Cases involving a minor hit against a dock have resulted in caved in hull sides, gaping holes and major fractures that should never have occurred, and wouldn't have with a traditional laminate. In relatively minor collisions with other boats, entire hull sides have collapsed and in more than a few instances we've seen entire bow sections broken off.

The bottom line is that putty boats are weak, vastly more prone to serious damage, and far more likely to develop serious problems as they age. If you're buying new, the aging problem is less likely to affect you, but in buying a used boat, one definitely needs to be wary of these structural issues.

Lay-up

The process of putting all these materials in a mold is called lay-up, or laminating. Laminates can be made of a variety of different fabrics, and since it is the orientation of the glass fibers that yields maximum strength, differing types of fabrics are often used in a single laminate. It is actually quite simple and straightforward, although it must be done with some skill and precision.

Here is where the problems start, for the lay-up process is very nasty, sticky, ugly work that only recently has been related to some rather severe health problems of workers. New EPA rules governing the use of resins and styrene emissions are having a considerable impact on boat prices. And because lay-up is such unpleasant work, there is a rather high turnover rate of lay-up workers, which further aggravates problems of quality.

Fig. 3-8. A pre molded structural grid in Jupiter 31. This all glass framing is laid up in a mold, then set into the hull and then manually glassed to the hull as compared to others which are glued with a bonding putty. Compare this with the glassed over plywood framing on facing page. Construction like this can pretty much take anything you can give it.

As you probably know, the outside finish of the boat, the gel coat, is sprayed into the mold. Yes, there is a reason for this. If one were to just put the resin and reinforcement into the mold, it would probably never come out. Gel coat is not nearly as adhesive as plastic resin, so it serves the dual purpose of making the part release from the mold easier, as well as providing the exterior finish all in one step, rather than having to paint the boat.

Before the gel coat is completely cured, one or two layers of mat saturated with the catalyzed resin is then laid into the mold, which is then rolled out with little rollers that look like small paint rollers, except they are metal. As mentioned earlier, the purpose of the mat is to prevent the pattern of the coarser roving that is laid in next from telegraphing into the gel coat. The purpose of the rollers is ensure that the resin is fully worked into the fiberglass fabric, leaving no air bubbles. Air bubbles or void spaces are bad news because these usually lead to the infamous blisters you hear so much about.

This process of laying in alternate layers of roving and mat goes on until the desired thickness is built up. Once this is completed, structural components like stringers, bulkheads and frames are then added and glassed in place. Pay attention to the next part here because it explains why some of boats fall apart.

Fig. 3-9. A 25 foot outboard hull under construction. Compare the size and spacing of structural members with photo opposite (Fig. 3-8). The white plastic tubes running down the sides are conduits for the control cables. Notice how they cut the outboard stringers by more than half, which are likely to fracture at these points.

While very simple in theory, the timing and precision of the process is critical because they are dealing with a material that is going to cure quickly, rather like fast drying paint. The atmospheric conditions must be right, there must be no contamination such as sawdust from the nearby wood shop in the air, and, most importantly, there should be no interruptions in the process. If it is interrupted, like its not finished before the weekend and everybody goes home, the laminate then cures and becomes hard. Now you have a situation where the laminating process that is restarted on Monday is not the same as it was on Friday. Instead of having the various layers fused together (because they were wet), you now have two layers that are simply glued together. This is because they're now putting a wet layer against a dry layer. This is called a *secondary bond*, which is nowhere near as strong as those laminations that are all put together when wet, or at least uncured. Laminations that are put together before they cure are called *primary bonds*.

You know from enough experience with paint that, unless the surface is clean and properly prepared, the paint isn't going to adhere properly and will probably peel off. To prepare it properly, it has to be sanded. Why? Simply because paint will adhere better to a rough surface than a smooth one. The bond is a mechanical one, not a chemical combination of two materials. The situation is much the same with the laminating process.

In the event that the resin does cure, all is not lost. In that case, a special resin appropriately called *bonding resin* can be used. It will adhere to a cured laminate much better than laminating resin. Do-it-yourself repair jobs often fail because the do-it-yourselfer wasn't aware of this fact and used the wrong resin. The stringers and frames of a boat are frequently laid in *after* the basic hull laminations have been cured. And just like our paint example, if they don't use a grinder and rough up the bonding surface, and use the proper bonding resin, then the bond is not going to be very strong and is likely to break apart.

Sometime in the early 1980's, a new low-cost type of resin was introduced, called DCPD for it's difficult to pronounce chemical name dicyclopentadine. This was called a "low profile" resin. If you've ever seen a boat with a checkered pattern to the surfaces, this is due to shrinkage of the resin during cure. The shrinkage causes the glass fabric pattern to show through. DCPD was supposed to solve that problem, but it created another one instead: stuck together parts had a bad habit of coming unstuck. After a laminate had cured, in order to bond anything else to it, it became necessary to grind the mating surface first. The problem was that nobody knew that.

Yet another problem developed, and that was due to this resin being rather brittle, with the result of a lot of cracked boat parts, including hulls. The more brittle resin meant that parts could not bend as much, and when gel coats were formulated using this resin, stress cracking in the finish coat could become extreme.

This is but one of many reasons why some boats started to come apart, and why after 40 years there are now more problems than ever in boat building. Obviously, all that

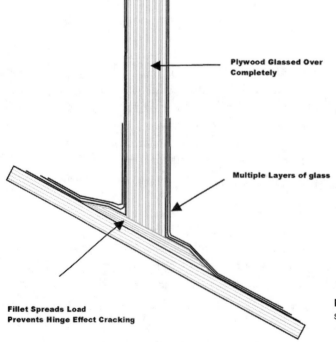

Plywood Glassed Over Completely

Multiple Layers of glass

Fillet Spreads Load Prevents Hinge Effect Cracking

Fig. 3-10. Traditional glass on wood stringer.

additional preparation work calls for quite a bit of extra labor. And the incentive to save money and increase profit by not doing it. It is also hard to keep good labor because the work is so unpleasant, with the result that quality frequently suffers from the lack of skilled labor. Other problems result from the desire to reduce cost of material, which makes boat hulls weaker, plus the never-ending incentive to rush the process. The pressure is always to get the hull out of the mold as fast as possible to increase the part rate. This motivates the builder to rush the cure rate, or to pull it out before it is ready. And so it goes, on and on, that these circumstances compound themselves into eventual parts failures that are very hard to determine what the original cause was when, in fact, it may be a multiplicity of faults.

While there have been endless attempts to automate the process, fiberglass boats still remain essentially hand made products that are only as good as the people making them. You can have the best designers and the best materials in the world, but if the people using them aren't skilled or well supervised, its all for naught. If the builder is going to ignore the basic rules and turn out parts as fast as possible, then there are going to be serious quality problems. The simple fact is that boats are hand made products, which are only as good as the people making them, on the *day* that they are made.

If you understand this, then you can understand why quality can also be highly variable from one boat to the next. Hull #203 may be built just right, while hull #204 is a disaster. Automobiles are mainly made by robots and other highly automated process. Thus, if there is a defect in one, they all tend to have the same defect. It's quite the opposite with a boat. With this in mind, the issue of warranties becomes rather important.

What all this boils down to is that smart builders are loathe to experiment with new materials; they tend to stick with the tried and true, being content to let others experiment with the new stuff. Hopefully, you get my drift here. When a builder starts advertising his use of the latest and greatest in "high technology," there may be good cause to be wary.

Some More History

Reinforced plastics are nothing new and have been around since near the turn of the century, getting its first applications mainly in the electrical equipment industry. Ever hear of Bakelite? This material was the first major use of reinforced plastic. The major advances have come with the evolution of plastics chemistry and the development of thermoplastics, plastics that remain in a liquid form until a chemical is added which causes the plastic to harden. As soon as the plastics chemistry was introduced, boat building took off like a rocket. But the beauty of reinforced plastic was not just its myriad uses and its application to boat building, but the fact of the ease with which it could be used. With a few hours worth of instruction, just about anyone could successfully use the material. It was no more difficult than mixing and pouring concrete.

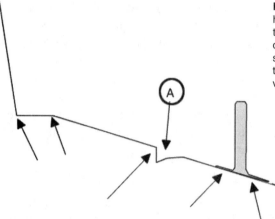

Fig. 3-11. Naturally occurring hinges points on a hull that require extra reinforcement. Note here the bottom strake is drawn "open" but the depression on the inside of the hull at point A should be closed off by glassing over. Otherwise, there is a triple hinge point here that becomes very weak and prone to cracking.

It was so easy, in fact, that a lot of people who had no business building boats quickly jumped on the bandwagon, turning out boats that were horrifically defective and poorly designed, so much so that many literally fell apart. I was the unproud owner of several examples, including boats built by Glastron and MFG, boats made by spraying chopper gun material into a mold, whose bottoms then split open and sank because the companies that built them knew nothing about boat building. They just saw an opportunity to make money and dove into boat building headfirst.

The status of boat building is certainly not as bad as it was back in the early 1960's, but its not a whole lot better either. You won't find as many boats whose hulls break open or otherwise fall apart, although there are still far too many after all these years. Today, the main problem is the lack of professional engineering sufficient to give many boats a reasonable service life. It's not so much the hulls that fall apart, but the rest of the boat that does.

Forces Acting on a Hull

An illustration that will drive the point home is to think what its like doing a belly flopper off a high diving board. Painful, even deadly. This illustrates the point that when a flat surface impacts water at high speed, that water no longer behaves like a liquid, but a solid. It's hard to image that water can be hard as concrete, but it can. That's because water, while it is fluid, it is also non compressible. A wide, flat surface impacting against water puts the water into its non compressible mode.

High speed boat hulls are subjected to these forces continuously. If there are any faults in the design or construction, they will usually start to show up rather quickly, first in the form of fatigue cracking, and ultimately in a failure. There are three primary forces acting on a hull which I will label (1) bending, (2) twisting, and (3) impact loading.

Bending refers to the fore and aft, or longitudinal force, like when you bend a stick over your knee to break it. The hull has to be strong enough lengthwise to resist these forces. When it's not, boat hulls can end up breaking in half. Like crumpling a card-

Fig. 3-12. Not often found, these large knees tie the transom to the hull stringers for extra support for the engines, a hallmark of superior design detail.

board box, the sides will buckle and other cracks and fractures will occur long before that happens. The bending force on a hull occurs in both directions — bending up or bending down — so that the structural design has to take this into account. This is why decks are usually a major part of the overall structure. Think in terms of a box beam or square tube and its easy enough to understand where these structures get their strength. The more a boat hull resembles a box beam, the stronger it will be.

Severe bending forces occur when the boat launches off a wave and when it comes down, only a portion of the hull hits the water, placing ALL of the load in one part of the hull. To understand this, imagine a boat flying off a wave and then landing on the back side of another wave. The impact forces are distributed unevenly, and so the hull has to be strong enough to handle this without bending or breaking.

Twisting is the torsional force exerted on a hull. Twisting occurs when a boat is put into a hard turn, and when a hull impacts a wave, shall we say, not squarely. An example is when only one side of the bow impacts a wave, causing the hull to twist. Box beams resist twisting somewhat, but are not all that good. That's the job of bulkheads which, when attached to all four sides including a deck, do an extremely good job of resisting twisting. What happens when a hull does twist? It tends to tear the deck loose from the hull, among other nasty things.

The problem for most small boats is that they do not have any full sized bulkheads. Why not? Well, because people wouldn't like to have to climb over them since they break cockpits up into small compartments. If we want unfettered, wide open cockpits, the structure has to be reinforced in some other way to make up for this. Sometimes designers forget these principles and fail to adequately stiffen a hull to the point where it twists too frequently and too much. At that point, things start coming apart.

Fig. 3-13. A cockpit liner before being installed in boat. Note that this one does not include the upper deck, which will be a third part.

Obviously, impact forces occur from slamming. In fact, bending and twisting usually results from the impacting of the hull against the water. The impact loading first occurs on the skin of the hull, and then is transferred through the framing and the hull sides, up into whatever structures are above it. As the old joke goes, it's not the collision that caused the damage but the sudden stop. As the boat hull hits the water, its downward motion stops instantly. The problem is that everything else in the boat, including the hull sides and the decks, do not stop as quickly, but keep on going down a bit.

Shooting a wooden arrow at a tree is a good example. You can easily break that flimsy wooden arrow over your knee, and yet the enormous impact against the tree does not break it. Why? Because the entire length of the arrow is perfectly in column, and cannot collapse against itself. If the arrow were slightly crooked, it would indeed collapse because the direction of forces are not traveling along a perfectly straight line in column. This illustrates why steel and concrete columns can support incredible loads. But put the slightest kink in that column and it will collapse because the forces are not being transmitted along a straight line.

Boat design works along similar principles. Designing a very strong boat hull is actually very easy to do, and there is absolutely no reason why any boat hull should ever fail. In fact, these principles are really so simple that even a novice can easily understand them. Of course, we know that they can and they do fail all too frequently. Our purpose here is to educate you sufficiently that you can begin to evaluate these things for yourself. If all builders made good boats, we wouldn't need to get into this. Unfortunately, they don't.

Basic Hull Construction

In order to be able to properly evaluate a boat, you need to know something about its essential elements. Fortunately, that's pretty simple. The parts all have names and every boat owner should be familiar with them.

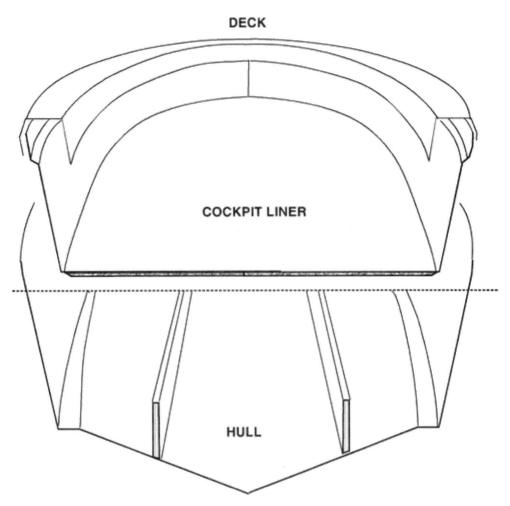

DECK

COCKPIT LINER

HULL

Fig. 3-14. The three major parts of a typical center console boat, consisting of hull, deck and cockpit liner. With some boats, the upper decks and cockpit liner may be one piece.

The skin of the hull is known by many names such as skin, shell, panel and plate. Many of these names come from the days of wooden and steel boat building and are still used. Never mind, they all mean the same thing. Few small boats today have true keels. A real keel is that appendage sticking off the bottom that runs the length of the hull like a fin. We still refer to the point where the two bottom panels come together as the keel. The chine is the point where the bottom and sides come together; the stem is the leading edge of the bow between the deck and the keel. A *chine flat* is a horizontal section of bottom between the chine and the point where the bottom angles downward. Strakes are those rib-like things you see running the length of the bottoms of many boats, although some boats do not have them. The transom is the back of the boat, although it is often called the stern, which really means the *aft area*, just as bow refers to the forward portion of a hull. Thus, bow and stern really refer to an area rather than an exact point.

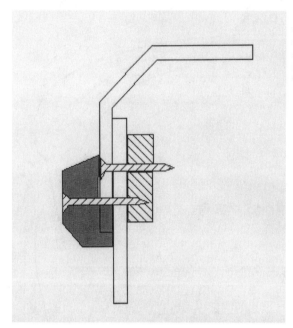

Fig. 3-15. The hull-to-deck join is a critical part of a boat's structure which needs to be made strong to withstand punishment. Here, the deck actually strengthens the hull sides. This method uses two sets of screws plus a backing strip on the inside.

Shortly after the lay up in the mold is completed and the resin sets or cures, the structural frames are then laminated into the hull. Sometimes builders are in a hurry to get another boat started, so they pull the boat out of the mold and then add the frames. If they do not set the fresh hull into a framing jig, then the hull is likely to go out of shape, because the resin is still somewhat soft. After which the frames are added to solidify the hull into a permanently misshapen form. That's why decks sometimes don't fit the hull so well. You end up with a boat that steers to the left, but you can never figure out the reason! The builder should be putting the boat in a special framing jig that will hold the hulls shape while the structural members are being installed. For outboard boats, the frames are usually plywood frames of various types. These consist of partial bulkheads, frames and stringers.

Stringers

These are the longitudinal frames that run fore and aft, bow to stern. The purpose of the stringers is to provide longitudinal strength to the hull so that the bottom doesn't bend or buckle. Stringers can be made of solid wood, plywood or fiberglass laid over a foam material. If a nonstructural material like foam is used, the only purpose is to provide a *form* over which to lay the laminations. It does not matter if water gets into this foam, and is unlikely to be harmful if it does. With wood cored stringers, its another matter entirely.

When wood is used for stringers, unlike with foam, the wood is not a core, but the major structural element. It is laminated over with fiberglass mainly to keep the wood dry, and thus the glass overlay must be complete and thorough to prevent water from

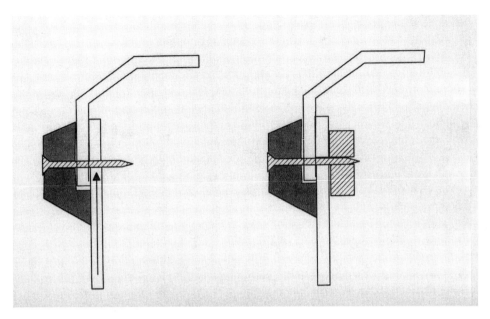

Fig. 3-16. Above left, the least satisfactory method of making the joint by using a single set of screws while attaching the rub rail at the same time. At right, a better method uses a backing strip on the inside. An even better method involves glassing the hull to the deck, a method that will keep it permanently in place.

getting at the wood. Though the glass does add strength to the wood, that is not it's primary purpose.

Some people believe that plywood is a poor material to use in boat construction. Actually, the main problem with plywood starts with use of poor quality plywood, improperly utilized. There are thirty year old Bertrams and Blackfin boats out there that have had wet plywood in them all their lives, and yet the wood has not rotted. That's the huge difference good quality plywood can make. Today, such high quality woods are extremely expensive, if not impossible to find. Regardless of the type of wood, it is critically important that it be thoroughly glassed over and sealed, otherwise water will get inside and cause the wood to rot. Especially in a fresh water environment which is much more conductive to rot.

Because stringers are the main girders in the hull, it stands to reason that they shouldn't have any holes in them, let alone big holes. As you can see in Fig 3-9 the builder has drilled 3" diameter holes in those stringers, which cut them more than in half. These are located at the point where the white plastic conduits pass through the outboard stringers. In all likelihood, those stringers will fracture.

The Bottom

The bottom of a boat hull is very similar to a bridge deck, except that the forces are working in the opposite direction, with the forces of the water pushing up, and a hull that is slamming down. In order to withstand traveling at high speeds, banging into

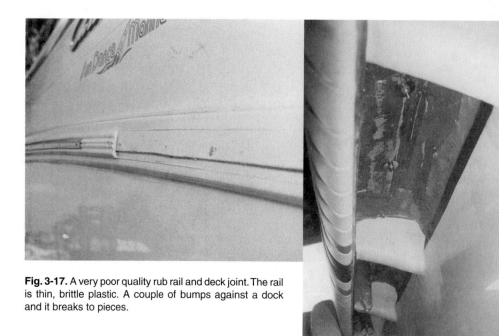

Fig. 3-17. A very poor quality rub rail and deck joint. The rail is thin, brittle plastic. A couple of bumps against a dock and it breaks to pieces.

Fig. 3-18. Looking up under the gunwale (side deck) of a high end CC boat. Here the deck joint is fiberglassed and there are these heavy frames on the underside of the deck which tie the inside face of the coaming to the hull side, thereby creating a truss.

the waves and even occasionally going airborne, a bottom obviously must be thick enough and be well framed. In order to survive these forces, the bottom panel between the frames must be sufficiently thick that it does not bend excessively. For while fiberglass is moderately flexible, it can only withstand so much before it starts to crack.

If the framing system isn't up to the job, then both the frames and bottom panels may bend too much. When this happens, there is not only a danger of bottom failure, but it must also be remembered that everything inside the boat is attached to those frames. Thus, if the bottom is flexing, one telltale sign of this is disturbance of the interior structures, such as shifting bulkheads and partitions, doors that won't close properly, and decks with a lot of cracks in them. Cracks will tend to appear at any point where there are hard angles.

Figure 3-11 shows the natural hinge points on a typical hull. On the outside edge or chine, the bottom is made strong by the vertical hull side. But notice right at the chine flat there is a natural hinge point. Also, that at any point where there is a frame, there is a "hard spot," a place in the laminate that is stronger than surrounding areas because of the frame. And because the surrounding area is weaker, the hinging action will take place near anything that prevents bending. At this point is where cracks can occur if the laminate is not properly designed.

On any boat with strakes on the bottom, Figure 3-11 illustrates how this can be a problem if the strake depression is not glassed over from the inside. Thus, it is important to check these points, and the outside strakes for signs of cracking.

How thick should a hull be? If we were to make a 20 foot boat that is generally 3/8" thick on the bottom and 1/4" on the sides, that hull could withstand tremendous abuse and show no effect, so long as it is properly framed. Instead, most builders will reduce those dimensions by around 50%, designing laminate thicknesses right down to the bare minimum, just slightly above the failure point. Naturally, when something is designed to within 10% of its failure point, it will not withstand any errors in its manufacture. Does this now adequately explain the situation of so many defective boats? All it takes is a few faults in the lay-up process and the hull eventually fails. This is what usually explains why a few hulls in a boat line fail, why many others don't.

Bulkheads

This structural element provides lateral stiffness to the hull and generally prevents the hull from twisting. A boat without any bulkheads tends to be like a flimsy shoe box that bends and twists. Small boats, however, often don't have *any* bulkheads and may rely on cockpit liners and decks to stiffen up the hull. Decks can act like horizontal bulkheads, but they won't perform the full function of a vertical bulkhead. Many, if not most, small boats are built of only two molded parts, the hull and deck, which includes the upper deck as well as the cockpit. Most of the structural elements, with the exception of the hull stringers, are built into the deck shell. The lack of adequate lateral framing can result in torsional twisting, causing failures of already weak hull-to-deck attachments.

So, having learned all this, you're probably asking why most boats lack these vital structural elements. That's a reasonable question and the reasonable answer is so that you can afford to buy them. To build a boat properly makes it quite a bit more expensive. Ultimately, the builder has to walk the fine line between cost and strength.

Frames

Frames are smaller transverse members intended to stiffen bottom and side panels to keep from them from flexing too much. They may or may not exist depending on the particular hull design. If there are any, they are likely to be located between the inboard stringers. You can take it on faith that any boat with a lot of frames in the hull is probably pretty well built. Figure 3-9 shows a rather typical small boat layout, although one that has a few major design errors.

Fig. 3-19. Built for high horsepower, this boat has two very large knees tying the transom to the hull stringers for maximum strength.

Hull Sides

It seems to be an unavoidable fact of boating life that builders see no need to put frames in the sides of the hull. Go into any dealership or boat yard and start banging on the hull sides with your fist and you're likely to be amazed at how thin and weak some of them are. Many will actually rattle, they are so weak. Think about when the hull slams down off a wave and you will realize why this can be a problem. A hull side that bends and buckles causes two problems.

First, it stresses the hull-to-deck joint and is often the cause of all those boats you see that have the rub rails damaged or falling off. That's because the hull and deck are usually just screwed together. The shock load is transmitted up to the joint, to which the rub rail is also fastened, causing the fiberglass to shatter around the screws. The net effect is like scissors cutting paper, only here the stress is applied to the screws and fiberglass that they penetrate. Then all the fasteners, including the rub rail, go loose.

It should be clear from Fig. 3-16 how easily this happens if the hull side is pushing up against the deck. There is a shearing action of the lap joint between hull side and deck flange. The second problem is that excessively flexing fiberglass panels cause stress cracking and fatigue. This usually shows up as stress cracks appearing in the outer finish, most often down along the chine. A properly constructed hull is one that doesn't bend and rattle when you bang on it.

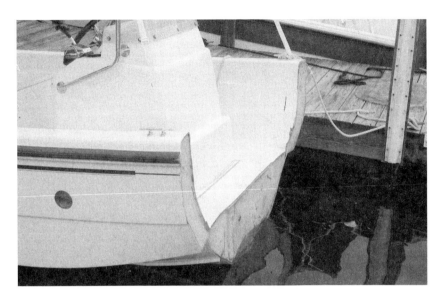

Fig. 3-20. Twenty foot Boston Whaler cut in half. Note that there are no stringers. The hull skin relies entirely on the foam for support.

Decks

More than just something to stand on, decks serve an important structural role in boats. Outboards, which are mostly open boats, will have a cockpit deck, small fore deck and side decks called gunwales. These are almost always molded parts that are combined together to make the whole boat. The cockpit molding is referred to as a shell or liner, which includes the inner sides and various components within the single molding.

Here, the cockpit deck does not add a lot to the strength of the hull, but the fore and side decks are critical. If you can imagine a boat with no decks, then you have a hull where the hull sides just end in mid air with nothing to stabilize them and they will flop around. Worse yet, the hull will tend to bend, so these decks provide some of the same functions as stringers, particularly in center console boats. We can think of decks as sort of horizontal bulkheads.

While the fore deck stabilizes the forward part of the hull, we need to reinforce the after section. Depending on the design style, this is usually done at the transom by widening the side decks at the point they meet the transom, particularly in cut down transom motor installations. Usually there are bait wells or some kind of storage box built into the corners that provide this added support. With the integral platform design, the faux transom and the platform deck itself provides a great deal of strength in this area. Thus, this design is much stronger than most other design styles.

Obviously, when a boat hits hard against dock pilings (and good boats should be designed to withstand moderately hard hits), there needs to be a degree of strength in the

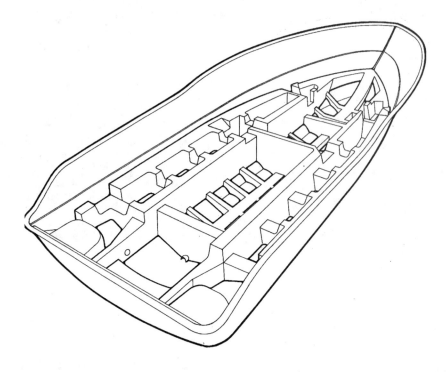

Fig. 3-21. The molded structural grid used by Triton Boats, which contains all the hull reinforcements. Illustration courtesy of Triton Boats.

side decks. Here the hull side and deck normally form an angle that is fairly strong. Unfortunately, some designers subvert or ignore this potential for making this area strong by fooling around with fancy designs.

Pictured in Figure 3-18 is an example of a very well designed and built gunwale on a large center console boat. Notice here that there are numerous frames between the hull side and the inner cockpit facing, which is the side deck angled downward. Here the builder has created a truss that makes the hull sides very strong, which adds strength to the entire boat.

Deck Joints

As discussed above, when the hull sides are not strong, then it is the deck joint that usually suffers. The larger the boat, the more important the deck becomes to the hull. For center console boats, the deck usually constitutes a substantial element of hull strength. Unless it is designed properly and built strong, the joint is likely to fail. Along the hull sides, the deck serves as one side of an angle beam or channel, making the point where hull side and deck are joined of critical importance. The ideal method is to fiberglass or "bond" the hull to the deck, and this is the way many of the better boats are put together. Another way is to use a wood or plastic furring strip on the

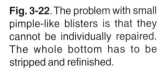
Fig. 3-22. The problem with small pimple-like blisters is that they cannot be individually repaired. The whole bottom has to be stripped and refinished.

inside of the joint as a backing strip, since wood and softer plastic holds screws better than brittle fiberglass.

It is the impact loads on the bottom that are transmitted up the sides of the hull that shears against the screws, causing the glass around them to shatter. This is why merely screwing the deck on does not work well. Something better is needed if you want a boat that is going to hold together well.

The worst method is to use pop rivets, which almost invariably fail. If you are looking at a boat that is put together with pop rivets, rest assured that you are looking at a boat that is poorly and cheaply made. The normal procedure is to put the hull and deck together first, and then add the rub rail. Some builders will attempt to join the hull and deck and install the rub rail all in one operation, all with a single set of fasteners. That means that deck joint and the rub rail all use the same set of fasteners. When done this way, the installer cannot see the lap joint as he is installing the rail and often ends up putting in screws that completely miss the lap joint. This is sort of like hanging a shelf on the wall with nails that miss the studs, nails that are only into the drywall. It's bound to fail.

Smaller, lower priced boats are usually the worst offenders in this regard, mainly because the price competition drives the builders to make them as cheaply as possible. However, there is no size limitation for shoddy construction, which can be found in all size boats.

Rub Rails

From the very first days of pleasure boat building, rub rails, that part of the boat that hits against pilings and docks, have always been a major problem. It is not reasonable to expect that boats never touch the dock. Thus, rub rails and deck joins need to be made to withstand fairly heavy impacts.

In recent years, the ideal material for rub rails has been found. It is a semi-hard, thick vinyl extrusion that is strong, UV resistant, and withstands impacts very well. It does not withstand abrasion against rough surfaces and for that reason usually a stainless steel molding is added to the outside edge to make for the best combination yet.

Anodized aluminum is often used and is a terrible material because it bends, gouges and corrodes easily. As shown in Figure 3-17, there are thin versions of vinyl rub rails that break easily.

Rubber or semi-hard rubber is another material widely used. Being flexible, it does not hold its shape well and often ends up looking wavy and making a boat look rather unsightly. Rub rails which have rope or other types of inserts are also a very poor choice for what should be obvious reasons: the inserts don't stay inserted very long.

The Transom

This is yet another critical element which must be very strong, for that's where the heavy engines will be hung. Typically double layers of plywood were used in conventional outboard transoms. Why plywood? Because of its obvious strength and because producing a 1-1/2" thick solid laminate would be very heavy and expensive. Once again, plywood being what it is, any water gets at it and the problems will start. Keeping that plywood sealed and water tight is of paramount importance, a factor which is sometimes overlooked. This makes the matter of drilling holes for mounting engines of equally critical importance. The bolt holes must be exactly sized to the bolts. If not, engine movement is likely to result, followed by water ingress into the core.

Fortunately, rot occurring in the plywood reinforcement of outboard boats is fairly rare, though when it happens it creates a huge problem. It occurs most often in stern drive boats because of the large cutout for the drive unit, which is then not properly sealed to protect the wood. However, outboard motors are bolted through the transom when the dealer makes the engine installation. Unless the dealer thoroughly caulks the motor mount bolts, this, too, can lead to water ingress and rot.

Boston Whaler

The boats from this builder are probably unique in that they advertise unsinkable boats with hulls that are completely filled with foam. While this seems like an excellent idea, their boats have not been without problems, one of which is that over time the foam has been known to become saturated with water. If it does, there's really no way of knowing short of drilling holes. Another is that there is no access at all to the inner side of the hull skin, so the only inspections that can be done are to the outside only, but this usually will not reveal much.

Figure 3-23. A premolded structural grid after being glassed into hull. At this point, the rough outer glass surfaces are being ground smooth, after which it will be painted. Photo courtesy Jupiter Marine.

With these boats, be on the lookout for serious cracking of the inner liners. One thing you'll notice is that there are no hull stringers in the boat shown Figure 3-20. Apparently they rely entirely on the foam for structural support. If the foam compresses, there's going to be a problem, which is why we advise being alert to any unusual cracking.

Liners

Decades ago, boats had fiberglass hulls, but the cockpit decks were wood that, of course, had rot problems. From this evolved fiberglass shells that came to be called liners, for these were nested inside the hull. For an outboard boat, the liner could consist of both the cockpit deck, gunwale, motor well and a fore deck. Or, these parts could consist of separate pieces.

The method of creating a framing system in a separate mold - as opposed to creating stringers and frames by means of laying fiberglass over wood in the mold - had been developed many years ago at Hatteras yachts. These were called "top hat" stringers because their cross section looks like a hat. After the stringers were laid up, they were pulled out of the mold and glassed into the boat hull.

There are three types of liners in use today. The first is the modular liner, in which are molded things such as internal cabin structures like a head compartment, bunks or galley, and in the case of outboard boats, the basic cockpit layout. The second type involved creating a one-piece fiberglass shell that contained all the structural hull reinforcements that was literally glued into the hull - as it's name implies - as a lining. This was termed "grid liner." Introduced only in recent years it has proved costly, problematic, and probably not a good idea. This type of liner is found in some Boston Whaler boats.

A third method, the structural grid, as its name implies, is grid that includes only the hull structural reinforcements as shown in Figure 3-21. The difference between the grid liner and structural grid is that the areas between the frames are open. The structural liner sort of resembles a French door with no glass in the little windows, whereas the grid liner has no openings between the frames. The structural liner is attached to the hull in the same way that top hat stringers are, by glassing with strips of fiberglass, a method called "tabbing." The grid liner cannot be glassed in because there are no open spaces to do so. Instead, a heavy, paste-like glue is troweled into the hull and the grid liner is then pushed into place with the hope that it will make contact with the glue and create a strong bond.

The pitfalls of such a method are fairly obvious; unless it is done just right, the method is likely to fail. Moreover, once the liner is set into the hull, there is no way of knowing if it has made a good bond because it becomes impossible to see it. The same problem with attaining full contact can happen as does with the use of foam sheets, as shown in Figure 3-4. Thus, from the buyer's point of view, a boat built with a structural grid would be preferable to one with a grid liner. Fortunately, the use of the later type is likely to be short-lived as not many builders have chosen this method.

The structural grid adds great additional labor costs to a boat, but it also creates a decidedly superior product. The amount of detail and number of frames shown figure 3-21 would be largely unnecessary to create a reasonably strong, lower price boat. Shown in Fig. 3-23 is a structural liner of considerably less complexity.

Cockpit Liners

Most small boats, such as open cockpit outboards such as center consoles, have full cockpit liners, a more recent addition to hull design. A cockpit liner is a molded shell that is set down inside the hull, usually resting on the hull stringers, and fastened to hull at the same point as the deck joint. The underside of the deck is usually glued to the tops of the stringers. The cockpit liner may or may not be part of the entire deck shell, but in recent years the design trend is almost exclusively toward a one-piece cockpit/upper deck molding. The primary advantage of this is economic, in that it reduces labor costs. But it also reduces construction errors and makes for a more water tight cockpit, if designed correctly.

Wood Framing -vs- All Fiberglass

Boat builders who build boats without any wood make a big deal about it in their advertising. It is well that they should, for the elimination of wood is costly and the resulting higher price makes their boats harder to sell. The question any budget minded new boat, or used boat, buyer will ask is whether the lack of wood is really that important. Or, conversely, should they avoid boats with wood in the hull construction?

Generally this question is relevant mainly to used boat buyers. Only the cheapest boats that use the lowest quality wood and shoddy construction are likely to end up with rot problems within ten years. After ten years, only the higher quality woods will endure. Thus, higher quality boats using wood will usually do well for up to twenty years, but you definitely have to watch out for "price" boats as they age. An all fiberglass boat is great if you can afford one, but for the "average" boat buyer I wouldn't recommend "no wood" as a primary criteria.

Blisters, New Boats and Warranties

We have been dealing with the issue of hull blisters for nearly a quarter-century now, and all we can say about them is that there is no excuse for this. It has always been known that low quality plastic resin, combined with poor wet-out of the mat behind the gel coat is the cause of blistering. For the first ten years of small fiberglass boat building, hull blistering was quite rare. The reason for this was simply that good resin cost proportionately much less in those days, so builders didn't have much incentive to cheat and make boats with cheap resin. Then the price of oil went up dramatically, and so did the cost of resin. In recent years (the period 1980-1994) with increasing volumes of mass production, all that has changed, and dozens of builders were putting out boats that blistered like crazy.

A boat that develops blisters is an inferior and defective product. Blistering of small boat hulls is a more serious problem than for large boats, and the reason is that small boat hull laminates are proportionally much thinner than a larger boat. This means that blistering has a much more serious effect on a small boat, and in some cases extensive blistering can seriously weaken a hull. If you are looking at a late model used boat that has blisters, you should think twice about buying it. It is likely that they will only get worse and end up costing you big money to repair. It will also be more difficult to sell.

If you are looking at a new boat, we would warn you that there are some builders now who are claiming that their warranties *do not cover blistering*, and some warranties say so outright. We have no reservation in stating that blistering constitutes a defective product, since the problem is 100% preventable. If they could make boats that didn't blister 30 years ago, why not today? Before even considering a purchase, perhaps one of the first things you should do is to get a copy of the warranty and read it - seriously read it, even though you may have trouble interpreting legalistic gibberish. Don't rely on simply asking the dealer whether the warranty covers this problem. The salesman's word means nothing since the builder provides the warranty, not the dealer. Or, if you're going to take his word, bring along a tape recorder and a couple of witnesses.

Some of my clients have come to me with stories of the most outlandish warranties and boat builder excuses to avoid making good on blistered boats. Some have even made such absurd statements (in one case, directly in the owner's manual) that the owner should never leave the boat in the water for more than two weeks! Imagine that, a boat that shouldn't be left in the water.

Another builder stated that the owner must seal the bottom with a certain kind of wax every several months. Others have even stated that it was the owner's responsibility to have a very costly "barrier" coating applied to the hull. Outrageous statements like this will give you an idea of the integrity of some of the boat builders out there.

Yet other builders have taken blistered boats back and attempted to repair them, only to have the repair fail and the builder then says, "Sorry, that's all we can do."

Many people have asked me what they can do to avoid buying a boat that blisters. My answer is very little, unless you're willing to do some rather extensive research to find out how a particular builder's products are holding up. If a builder is using more expensive isopthalic , or even vinylester resin in his hulls, chances are he's broadcasting that fact to the heavens. Very few make such claims in their brochures and advertisements so you have to assume that they aren't. If they do, that's one answer.

The warranty may give you a clue if it's written in such a way that it looks like the builder is trying to weasel his way out of making good on defects. If there's too much legalese or twisted language in the warranty, you had better be prepared for what you get if you buy the boat. If the warranty provides guarantees against any and all types of hull defects, without a lot of escape clauses, at least you have a good starting point. A warranty that is written in unequivocal language is a good sign.

The best advice I can give you is to spend some time researching the boating forums on the Internet where you will find discussions of boat builders that do have such problems. Find out which ones and avoid them. Don't waste your time making posts asking about certain boats. Many people who have problems aren't willing to admit to them. Others attempt to defend their choice of purchases, and some may have little knowledge but talk a lot. Pay attention to those who have voluntarily posted their problems, and have described the problems intelligently.

Chapter 4

Evaluating Boat Hulls

This chapter provides a rough outline of how to make a basic evaluation of a boat hull. It does not propose to make an expert surveyor of you, but you can use it as a guideline to try to decide if you even want to invest the money to have a boat surveyed.

Checking Out a Used Boat

One of the major advantages of a used boat, other than price, is that it has been tried and thoroughly tested. If a boat isn't made as well as it should be, there's going to be evidence of that. The evidence is usually not hard to find if it exists. Chances are, anything that doesn't look right, probably isn't.

If the boat is on a storage rack or a trailer, you have an ideal situation. Start with the outside first and look for stress cracks or any other flaws on the bottom. It's pretty common to find a few paralleling the bottom strakes, deep in the corners. Just a few is usually not indicative of a serious problem. But more than just a few, and particularly cracks across the strakes, should give pause for further consideration. Cracks that appear in wide arcs, or in any kind of pattern are even more ominous, and at that point you should either call a surveyor or reject the boat.

Note: *Stress cracks are a frequent occurrence in boats. Because of this, I have included an entire chapter devoted to the subject which describes where and why they occur. Read Chapter Seven,* Stress Cracks, Finishes and Surface Defects *in conjunction with this one.*

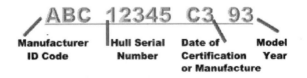

Fig. 4-1. How to interpret the hull number codes.

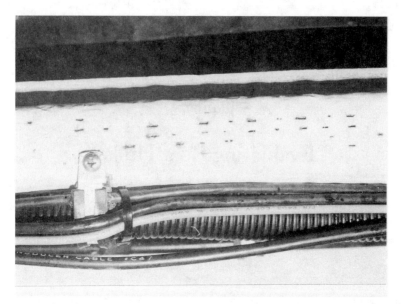

Fig. 4-2 Stringer rot. Looking down on stringer: What looks like small staple heads is actually brown fluid stains resulting from rotted wood in this stringer. Brown water trail stains on sides of stringer are another telltale of this condition.

Boats with painted bottoms tend to show up stress cracks even more prominently than nice, glossy gel coat. Wet painted bottoms tend to conceal them, so if wet, allow it to dry. As it is drying the cracks will soon start to stand out, if there are any.

Many, many boats have very weak hull sides and deck joints that often result in need-less damage caused by even the most minor bumping against docks. This is really very easy to check. You do it by going around the hull and banging on it with your fist. If its flimsy and shudders when you hit it, then it is excessively weak. If it rattles when you hit it with your fist, imagine what it's going to do when hitting waves.

Check the Rub Rail

This is a good place to start, for if the rub rails are loose and falling off, there are likely to be more serious problems to follow. The hull is usually joined to the deck behind the rub rail. The one thing you don't want to buy is a boat in which the deck is fastened to the hull with the same fasteners with which the rub rail was installed. Another thing you do not want are boats where the hull and deck are joined with pop rivets. Both Sea Ray and Bayliner have been known to use pop rivets on their smaller boats. How can you tell? Find a place on the inside where you can see the joint and whether rivet heads are present. If the two parts (deck and rail) are individually fastened, you should see double sets of fasteners. The spacing may not be close, but they will appear in odd groups. If singly fastened, it should be clear that there is only one set of fasteners.

Check whether the rail is starting to come loose in places. Bring a screwdriver with you and check the fasteners. Does the rail pull away from the side? Are the screws loose and

Fig. 4-3 A rub rail that looks like this with many screws backing out is a sure indication of a serious problem, namely that the deck is coming loose from the hull because it is not attached properly.

do they spin without tightening up. If you find a lot of these, then that means that the whole deck is loose and the best thing to do is to start looking for another boat. If the rub rails are all loose and bent up, with a lot of stress cracks on the deck above the rail, you have a boat with a very weak hull/deck joint, and one that is best left for someone else to deal with.

The use of black rubber rails are common. This is a material that is easily damaged and subject to distortion. Often times, these rails look wavy, and a bit of probing may reveal that the fasteners have pulled right through the rubber. There are two types of white plastic rail moldings found, one is hard vinyl and is excellent, the other is a much more brittle ABS plastic that is prone to cracking and breakage. Again, the signs of potential trouble are unevenness, looseness of fasteners and gaps between rail and gunwale.

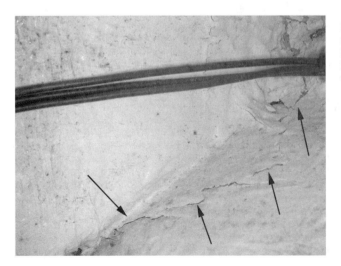

Fig. 4-4. This photo reveals very sloppy workmanship and poor bonding of a stringer to a hull. So poor, in fact, that it is breaking loose and will eventually result in a hull failure.

Fig. 4-5. When a bottom hasn't been properly sanded prior to painting, it usually ends up with loose, flaking paint. Correcting it is either very hard work or an expensive yard bill.

Internal Hull

Inspecting the internal hull is usually quite a bit more difficult, and you'll probably need a flashlight and mirror to do it. You simply have to open up every available hole and hatch and look inside as best possible. If you have any access at all, what you're looking for are signs of cracking, breakage, loose/broken frames and possible evidence of water or rot in stringers or frames. If you don't feel comfortable doing this, you should hire a surveyor.

One should be extra cautious about old boats, particularly the price boats which are sold on the basis of very low price.

Many boats simply have no access at all, so now you're stuck deciding if you want to buy this kind of boat. As for myself, I am very skeptical of completely enclosed bilges. Why? Because I want to be able to look at the structure and be sure that it's holding together. But there are other good reasons too. Like taking a look to see once in a while just to make sure that there isn't a lot of trapped water down there. Or if I want

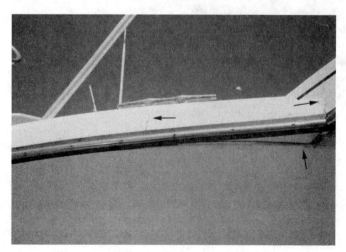

Fig. 4-6. This bow pulpit was stuffed into a wave, which caused lifting of the pulpit, cracking and tearing loose from the deck join. Check pulpits carefully from inside and out whenever possible.

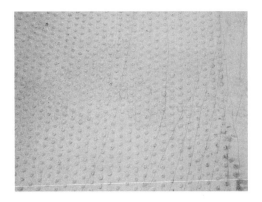

Fig. 4-7. Above: Stress cracks in deck like these are a sure indicator that something is wrong.

Fig, 4-8. Below: The design and installation of this console was done wrong, first being screwed into a cored deck (note screws backing out) and secondly, it is not adequately supported, causing the deck to sag.

to string some wires or run a hose to a piece of equipment I want to install. If the bilges are completely sealed off, I can't do any of that.

The only judgment you can make about it is from what, if anything, you can see on the exterior. Checking the inner liner or whatever kind of decking it has may provide clues. If you see a great deal of stress cracking in the deck, or there is a pronounced hump or unevenness, this is cause for alarm, at which point you should contact a surveyor or take a walk.

In recent years there have been increasing complaints about problems with deteriorating hull stringers, which are usually glass laminated over plywood. Problems develop in two ways. First, incomplete glassing of the stringers can allow water to get at the wood. Since plywood tends to be highly water absorbent, this can mean that large sections of the stringer get wet. Once this happens, it may never dry out and it starts to rot. This is particularly serious in fresh water boats (salt tends to be preservative of wood), but is a problem with salt water boats too, since rainwater in the bilge may be involved.

The main thing to look for is unevenness of the surface of the stringer, such as distortions or delaminations. Are there any strange dark stains? Look for any signs of fluid leaking out of the stringer at any point, and which will likely be dark brownish in color. If you can tap around with your screwdriver handle, so much the better. A hollow, thin sound

Fig. 4-9. Aluminum tank sitting on plywood deck only two inches above bottom of hull. Wet plywood against aluminum will ultimately cause tank failure.

usually means delamination of the glass from the wood, or possibly that the wood beneath is rotted away.

Wet stringers are also caused by failure to seal the limber holes, which are the drain holes that allow compartments to drain should they fill up with water. These can be quite difficult to see, so you'll need to look closely, and is where the mirror comes in handy. Also look for any point where holes have been cut in the stringers to route hoses, or places where screws have been run into them. If water is leaking down from the deck above, even an opening as small as a screw hole can result in the stringer absorbing water.

Finally, check the stringers at the point where they attach to the transom. There should be no cracks here. If there are, it probably means a problem that you don't want to deal with.

When There Is No Hull Access

Many, if not most, outboard boats will have virtually no access to the interior hull, a situation that is very much going to leave you feeling in the lurch. In that case, all you are left with is the external appearance. If you have examined the bottom very carefully for evidence of stress cracks, and have found none, then at least you have a reasonably fair chance that the hull is not going to fall apart anytime soon, at least with reasonable and careful use. Beyond this, there is nothing further you can do except to accept it as is, or take a pass and move onto on boat hull that can be inspected.

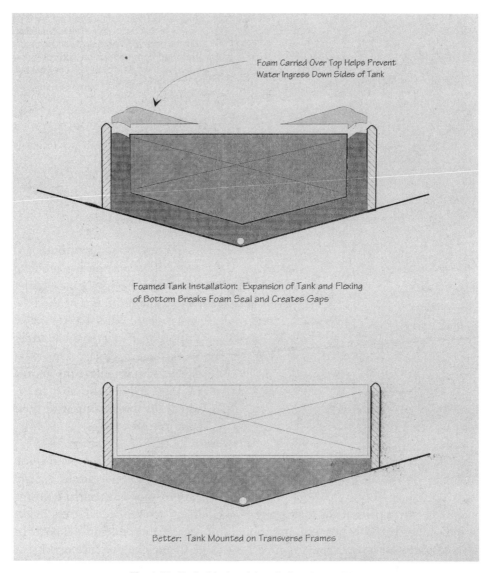

Foam Carried Over Top Helps Prevent
Water Ingress Down Sides of Tank

Foamed Tank Installation: Expansion of Tank and Flexing
of Bottom Breaks Foam Seal and Creates Gaps

Better: Tank Mounted on Transverse Frames

Fig. 4-10. Typical fuel tank installations in small boats.

Hull Sides

The advent of putty cores (sprayed in polyester filler) has led to some pretty serious delamination problems. Most often used in hull sides, but not bottoms, this material is very weak and often facilitates a poor bond with resin. Serious ply separation on boats with putty cores often results in widespread stress cracks appearing on the sides.

Go around the hull and bang on the sides with your fist. The sides should feel reasonably solid. If they shudder and shake, you probably have a poorly made boat. If you hear a clacking sound, most likely there is a ply separation and what you hear are the two plies smacking together when you hit it.

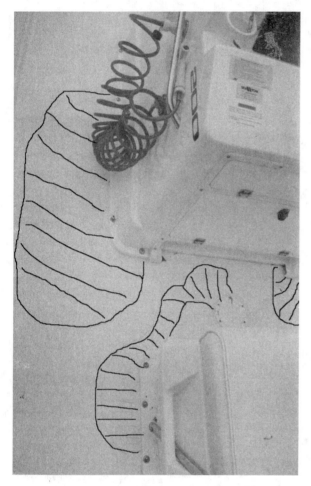

Fig. 4-11. This console and seat are both screwed to a balsa cored deck. Sounding out the deck with only a screwdriver handle revealed core separation and rot in the areas marked. This boat was one year old.

External Bottom

Inspecting bottoms of outboard boats often poses a big problem when they are sitting on a trailer or a cradle. So much of the bottom is obscured that a reasonable inspection is not possible under these circumstances. One possible option is to have the marina (if that's where the boat is located) lift the boat up with their fork lift truck.

Stress cracks are the main thing to look for. They are as equally easy to spot on painted bottoms as unpainted because paint tends to magnify cracks. The existence of a few stress cracks are an indication that all is not well, but should not necessarily condemn the boat. In this case it usually takes an expert to properly evaluate them. The presence of a lot of stress cracks usually means a serious problem.

Trailer boats and boats handled with fork lifts frequently get chips, scratches and gouges on the bottom. Just because the gel coat is damaged doesn't mean that water is going to enter the laminate and cause blisters. If the hull is made with quality resin, it's not going to blister. Water goes right through most gel coats, so a few chips here and there does no harm. Thousands of boats with loads of chips and gouges on the bottoms prove this point.

The Transom

Regardless of how the engines are mounted, the transom (literally the back of the boat) should be closely inspected. If it is a standard motor well type transom, first sight across the width from side to side. What you are looking for is any bowing outward

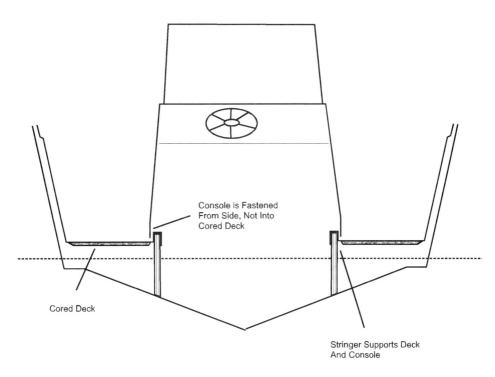

Console is Fastened
From Side, Not Into
Cored Deck

Cored Deck

Stringer Supports Deck
And Console

Fig. 4-12. The proper way to attach a console to a cored deck so that screws don't have to be run into the core.

caused by the weight of the motors. Next, check all around the mounting points, and particularly the corners of the transom. You are looking for cracks. A few small ones may signify nothing more than minor stress. But if they are numerous and tend to be deep and large, then there is probably a problem with structural weakness. This is definitely something you don't want to mess with because repairing structural weakness in any kind of transom is a major job.

Use the handle of a screwdriver or the butt end of a pocket knife and tap around on the transom, particularly around the mount brackets. Does it sound hollow or thin? If so, you may be looking at delamination or deterioration within the transom reinforcement. To repair this often exceeds the value of the boat, so it's worth looking at very closely. Check the motor mount bolts. You should see caulking oozing out from the bolt heads on both sides of the transom. Watch out if you see gaps around the bolt holes.

For fiberglass or aluminum brackets bolted to the transom, you basically do the same thing. Here you look for gaps between the mounting surface of the bracket and the flat transom. You are looking for evidence that the transom is bowing outward, that the bracket itself is distorting, or that the mounting bolts are loose. And it's not unusual that the mounting bolts may not be properly backed up on the inside and are starting to crush the transom and pull through. Look for evidence on all these points. If there is

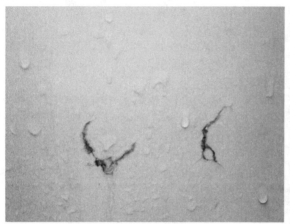 

Fig. 4-13. Cracks like these are an almost certain sign of rot or damage in a plywood cored transom. Note the brown water trails from the cracks in both photos.

crushing or cracking around the bolt heads, this is a sign of trouble. Either reject the boat, or get a professional evaluation.

Hull Integral Platform Mounts

So far, we've seen very few structural problems with this type of engine mounting arrangement. The convoluted shapes of these designs tends to make them stronger than the standard flat transom mount. Generally, you should inspect the mounting much the same as you would for the other types described above.

The Cockpit Deck

The cockpit deck may or may not have a core in it, but most likely it does. Generally check the deck for signs of cracking or unevenness. If there is humping or distortion, this is likely either caused by a defect in deck design, or a hull structural problem that is being transmitted up through the deck. Look for stress cracking or any other irregularities that look like they shouldn't be there.

You can check for delamination or bad core material either by banging on it with a screwdriver handle, or stomping around a bit with your feet. If you are wearing spongy soled athletic shoes, this won't work; you need harder soled shoes at least like deck shoes. Any softness you feel is indicative of a problem. The deck should feel solid and not springy. It should not crackle or make any kind of noise when you walk on it.

Pay close attention to how center consoles are attached to the deck. Frequently, they are attached with screws. If so, the screws are likely to leak water into the core, causing deterioration. Test the screws by turning them to see if they hold, or if they just spin. Screws that spin are a sure sign of trouble. Are there any soft spots or delamination around the base? Figures 4-7 & 4-8 will give you a good idea of what to look for.

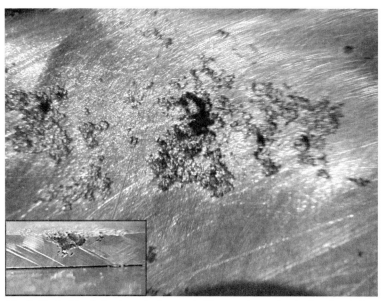

Fig. 4-14. Inside of aluminum tank corroded from water contamination. Inset shows depth of corrosion pits after cross-sectioning.

In recent years most builders have learned not to screw consoles to a cored deck. Instead of putting an attachment flange on the bottom of the console, they now put the attachment flange in the deck molding so that the screws go horizontally through non cored parts. This is easily discerned by determining whether the attachment screws are vertical or horizontally installed. If the later, all is well.

Also closely inspect the points of attachments of T-top legs where they meet the cockpit deck. Any cracks or distortions are usually indicative of a problem.

Fuel Tanks

Why fuel tanks in this section? Well, because in outboard boats the tanks are usually located under the cockpit deck. And it doesn't take much imagination to realize that if the deck leaks in any way, the tank is going to get wet and probably stay wet.

Most small boats have aluminum tanks set in the hull between the stringers and foamed in place. This method of installation has had mixed results. It works fine so long as no water ever gets between the foam and the tank. The reason why this can be a serious problem is a complex issue, but I'm going to explain it in detail anyway because you need to understand it.

Aluminum is an unusual metal in the way it corrodes. Actually, aluminum is not corrosion resistant. What happens is that aluminum corrodes very readily but, like Corten steel, it develops a layer of oxide on the surface that then protects the metal from future corrosion. Thus, you can take a marine aluminum tank and wet it down with salt water for years and nothing will happen to it. The reason that it will not corrode is because there is plenty of air getting to it. In order to develop that protective **oxide**, it needs lots of oxygen, and as long as the protective oxide develops and is not disturbed, the metal will be protected indefinitely.

But take that same tank, and put it in a boat hull and foam it in place, and bad things can happen if it continues to get wet. The reason why is that, now foamed in place under the deck, and surrounded by foam, it no longer has a good source of oxygen, and is no longer able to develop the protective layer of oxide. It can then develop what is known as crevice corrosion. Also known as closed cell corrosion, it works like this. Whenever there is a place where water is trapped against the aluminum, the corrosion or oxidation process chemically removes all the oxygen from the water. This causes the water to become acidic. Now, instead of having oxidation corrosion, which is self-limiting with aluminum (so long as there is plenty of oxygen available) we now have an acid attack on the aluminum that can advance very quickly and eat holes right through our tank.

Here are some of the reasons why this happens to foamed in place aluminum fuel tanks:

First, since aluminum tanks are fairly thin, as they fill up and empty, the tank will expand and contract under the weight of the fuel. Plus you can imagine the pressures on the tank as the hull is slamming off of waves. The foam is supposed to adhere to the side of the tank and prevent water from making contact with it. This is great in theory, but if the tank is frequently ballooning out every time it is filled up with fuel, it's probably going to break that seal with the foam. When that happens, there is now the chance that water is going to get into the void between tank and the foam. Once that happens, not only is there no air flow to evaporate that water and it is going to stay there indefinitely, but there is also no oxygen source to form the protective oxide to

Fig. 4-15. In some cases the fuel tank may be actually seen, as shown here. In this boat, the tank is sitting on a plywood platform within an inch of the hull bottom and is almost always in contact with bilge water. This is the perfect environment for closed cell (crevice) corrosion to occur. This tank cavity is not protected from bilge water as it should be.

protect it. Remember that it is the initially corroded surface of the aluminum that protects it from further corrosion.

What ultimately happens is that the water which is in contact with the tank turns acidic because it is starved for oxygen. It is no longer merely water corroding the aluminum, but an acid that dissolves the aluminum, eventually causing a hole in the tank. Technically, this is called crevice or closed cell corrosion, and is one of the most destructive forms of corrosion. Shown in Fig. 4-13 is a photo of the *inside* of an aluminum tank. Here, it only took a few large droplets of water to cause the deep pitting. How did this happen? Well because the tank, being full of fuel and the fuel has no free oxygen in it. This same condition occurs to the outside of tanks, only to a more serious degree when in contact with water.

It should be pretty obvious that, if the deck and tank installation are designed in such a way that it is never going to get wet, then there won't be a problem. Unfortunately, not many builders are very attentive to this detail, and decks are designed, and tanks are installed, in such a way that they often get wet and ultimately fail.

There are lots of reasons why tanks get wet, but the most common of these are that the builder puts one of those plastic inspection ports in the deck which is necessary to access fittings like the fuel gauge sender and hose connections. These things frequently leak. Another reason is that the deck itself is not water tight. Very often there is a large hatch or removable deck plate over the tank that will facilitate the tank's removal. This is a good thing if you ever have to replace the tank because it means that you don't have to cut the deck out to do so.

It's less of a good thing when the deck plate seams are located directly over the fuel tank, so that if the seams leak, the water once again causes the tank to get wet. If the deck plate is substantially larger than the tank, then the leaking seams won't wet the tank. In looking at a new or used boat, you really don't know how big the tank is, but if you can determine the stringer spacing, then you will get a fairly good idea how wide the tank is, since the tank will closely approximate the stringer width minus about 4 inches.

It should be rather apparent then, that if the deck plate approximates the stringer width, and if there are a lot of open seams or bad caulking of that deck plate, then you have good reason to suspect that the tank is getting wet. Try removing the inspection port and see if the tank top is wet, or if you see corrosion on it. If so you may be facing a dangerous and expensive problem. If the deck seams look to be well-caulked, and you don't see a lot of extra caulking smeared all over the place, and the tank top is dry, and none of the screws are loose or missing, then this is a much more positive sign. If any of these signs exist, then you need to be wary.

Even so, that does not preclude the possibility that water isn't getting at the tank by some other means, such as from the under side, or that the boat sank once. Another thing to consider is that the fuel tank cavity must be sealed off from the other sections of the bilge. Most often there are floor frames front and back of the tank. If you see them, you should find a small hole through the frame in the bottom of the bilge. Usually they glass a PVC pipe between the two frames to allow water to drain from one compartment to another. Check whether this drain pipe exists, and whether there are any cracks around it that may be allowing water into the tank compartment.

The most common age for tank failures to occur in salt water is approximately 6 - 10 years, so if you are looking at a boat this age, fuel tank corrosion is something that must be considered as a possibility. If you can actually remove the deck plate and take a look at the tank too, so much the better.

Another problem that we frequently run across is that the builder uses a foam that is unstable and, over a period of time continues to cure and expand. Perhaps you've had one of those Igloo coolers that did this - where the foam insulation continued to expand and caused the whole cooler to self-destruct, literally forcing the whole thing apart. Foamed in place fuel tanks can do the same thing. This condition is very easy to spot because you'll find the deck or cover plate is heaved up.

How to Check

In many cases, the builder has given you no access to the tank at all except for maybe a six inch port in the deck. If you see a fuel gauge sender that is heavily corroded, then you know for sure that water is getting at the tank. About the best you can then do is to just assume that a tank failure is going to occur at some time.

If you can see the tank at all, look at the interface where the foam meets the tank. Check to see if that foam is wet by digging into it with your fingers. If it is, then once again, the only wise judgment is to assume that the tank is corroding and will fail.

Replacing Tanks

The potential for facing the need to replace a tank soon after the purchase of an older used boat is fairly high. Fortunately, aluminum fuel tanks are not expensive, typically in the $400 to $500 range and neither is the cost to get them in and out so long as you don't have to cut the boat up to do so. Most later model boats will have a removable deck section to facilitate this. The cost can be well under $1,000 on a do-it-yourself basis and around $1,500 to $2,000 when done by a yard.

There are three major tank manufacturers in Florida and several in the MidAtlantic states. I don't recommend that you have a tank fabricated by anyone other than a professional. Because of their size, the cost of shipping will be rather high, depending on your proximity to a manufacturer. Otherwise, it is a fairly simple matter to have a replacement tank fabricated based on the dimensions of the existing tank. Proper installation is possible by anyone who is reasonably skilled at this sort of thing.

Plastic Tanks

Unreinforced plastic fuel tanks were tried and outlawed many years ago. They have once again been reintroduced but their use at present is so limited as to have no track record by which to gauge their performance.

Blisters on Used Boats

Should you buy a used boat that has blisters? I have some very definite opinions about that, but you are likely to hear many opinions that are contrary to mine. I would point out, however, that my view is based on 30 years of looking at boats on a daily basis, including many years of dedicated research on this problem.

First, I would recommend against buying a boat that is only 1-3 years old that is developing blister problems, since the only expectation that you can reasonably have is that the blistering will get worse. And because you will be paying much higher prices for a late model boat, it really doesn't make good sense to buy a boat that demonstrates the potential for a widespread problem. Blistering on late model boats is far more likely to affect resale value than on older boats, so this should be a serious consideration.

Second, if the boat is 5 years or older, and it only reveals a few blisters, then the odds of ending up with a severe blistering problem decreases dramatically the older the boat is. Many boats develop blisters only in some limited areas, which suggests that the cause is due to isolated workmanship deficiencies, in which case on an older boat is not likely, or at least less likely, to blossom into widespread blisters all over the bottom.

Third, hull blistering in larger boats rarely causes significant structural weakening of the hull. The main reason is that the hull is sufficiently thick that the damage caused by the blister doesn't affect the strength very much. This is less true the thinner the hull skin is. And since small boat hulls are naturally thinner, the potential for causing serious weakening is greater. While the number of boats that have actually experienced blister-related weakening is quite small, you still should be aware of this possibility.

A few larger blisters cause more damage and weaken the hull laminate far more than hundreds of small pimples. Consider dime-sized or smaller pimples as being more acceptable that quarter-sized blisters or larger. Very small blisters have little effect on hull laminate strength. Having inspected thousands of boat hulls, I have never seen or heard of one single case of extensive pimple rash (our term for a hull with hundreds or thousands of pimple-sized blisters) that resulted in a hull failure. In fact, I only know of three cases where even large blisters resulted in catastrophic hull damage, but there are probably quite a few more. On the other hand, a few larger blisters are rather easy to repair.

Forth, there are no absolute rules. One of the most common and frequent factors involved in the sudden appearance of blisters, or a sudden increase in the number of blisters, is the moving of a boat from colder waters to warmer waters. This occasionally happens when, say, boat owner in Michigan moves to Florida. A year later his boat, which only had a few blisters, now has hundreds of them. Higher water temperatures are known to have an effect on blister development.

Fifth, for older boats, say seven years plus, consider blistering as being relatively less important, if only because the value of the boat is so much lower, and is neither going to affect resale value as much, nor the integrity of the hull. By the time a hull has reached this age, the laminate has pretty much stabilized and has done whatever it's going to do. If it's only developed a few blisters, it is likely only to develop a few more. It is very unlikely to suddenly develop a bad case of acne if it presently hasn't any. But, as I said, there are no absolute rules and all bets are off if you move it to warmer waters.

Repairing Blisters

I am continually being bombarded with the question of whether blisters on small boats have to be "fixed." Let's start with the fact that there are no known guaranteed fixes. A very high percentage of all attempts to repair the problem have failed. Add to that the relative high cost versus the boat's value and it becomes rather impractical.

Should you do it yourself? I suggest not for several reasons. Unless you are versed in the proper techniques and materials, and have the skills and tools to do the job properly, you are likely to end up with a boat bottom that looks worse than the original problem. And you will have wasted all that time and effort for nothing. Unless you are particularly skilled at this sort of thing, you'd probably best leave it alone.

Chapter 5

Power Options

This chapter has been included in a book on outboards so that you can get an idea of whether an outboard boat is really the right choice for you. This because outboard boats seem to be getting bigger and bigger, and therefore more amenable to other power options. Once boats get up to around twenty feet or so, the wider the range of power options you will find available.

Why outboards? The outboard motor was originally created for the purpose of portability for very small boats like dinghies. Over the course of the last eighty years, they've grown and grown. Portability is no longer a major consideration, but trailerability plus the additional interior space outboards provide over inboards or stern drives becomes the major consideration, among many others.

There are only three basic choices for power options, outboard, stern drive and straight inboard engines. That there is much debate about which option is best, it is my view that most of that debate is inspired by manufacturer advertising, and not real world performance. The following is my take on the pros and cons of each, based upon several decades of observation and operation of boats of all descriptions.

Stern Drives

It is incontestable that the stern drive power option is the most troublesome and ultimately costly to own. While it is the lowest priced initial power choice, mainly because manufacturers have managed to sell these drive systems to builders in volume, the reliability factor of stern drive boats, particularly in sea water, remains unacceptably low.

I have no doubt that any manufacturer or dealer would hotly contest that statement, but all you have to do is take a tour of the repair shops to prove the point. There, in most instances, you will see dozens of damaged units laying around that are being cannibalized for parts. Travel around to the small boat yards and you will see the same thing: dead and abandoned boats because the owners can't afford to repair or replace drive units that have expired prematurely.

There are two basic problems with stern drives. First, they are made of cast aluminum, and are connected to a cast iron engine block. This combining of these two different metals, along with the steel and stainless steel used in other parts, causes galvanic corrosion. Moreover, aluminum is extremely sensitive to stray current from your boat's electrical system. It only takes about ½ volt or so of current escaping from the boat's system to be causing severe corrosion.

The second problem results from all that complicated machinery being submerged in water. A stern drive unit has a three-way joint to allow it to rotate in three directions. In addition to that, there are cable controls, drive shaft, the exhaust system, tilt and trim mechanism, and water pumps all located in or on the submerged drive.

Yet a third problem results from marine growth in sea water. The stern drive unit cannot be retracted from the water, so that one of the worst mistakes an owner can make is to leave his boat in the water and neglect it. Barnacles and oysters attach themselves with the strongest glue known to mankind. And while you can knock the barnacles and oysters off, the shell bases will remain attached. The only way to get the heads off is by grinding which, of course, damages the finish on the drive.

My view is that stern drives are a poor choice for any boat that is going to remain afloat in sea water. If you have even the slightest inkling that you may not be able to foot the bill for the frequent maintenance needed, then you now know what kind of drive system not to buy. This is a better choice for boats that are going to be dry stored and used more or less infrequently. And finally, the track record for stern drives is considerably better in fresh water than salt.

Having said that, your next question is, "Who makes the best drive?" As with just about any other product you can think of, there are the most widely sold brands, and the most expensive brands. I have been a long time critic of Mercruiser, and from what I have seen in over 20 years of investigating stern drive failures for insurance companies, I find it impossible to recommend this manufacturer's products. The rates of failure have for decades been exceedingly high. This company has been changing their models rather frequently in recent years, which makes it inappropriate to make any broad brush statements about a fairly wide model range, beyond what I have just said.

One would think that with a product that has been on the market for so many years, that the parts prices would eventually decline to something more reasonable than what they are. One of the reasons that we see so many dead stern drive boats in storage lots is that the owners can't afford the cost of replacement parts. By way of illustration, I recently replaced a complete engine in a car for considerably less than it costs to replace one of Mercruiser's smaller drive units. The price you pay for replacements is way out of proportion to what you paid for the boat originally. This makes it entirely appropriate to question whether the manufacturers are subsidizing low cost initial sales with huge markups in replacement parts prices later on. In many cases, the cost of a drive replacement is more than half the cost of the entire engine package to the builder.

Recent offerings by OMC and Volvo are obviously superior products. That's obvious just by looking at them. Equally obvious is the higher price.

Outboards

Outboard motors are also made almost entirely of aluminum, but there is a major difference: they are not attached to a cast iron engine block, and outboards can be raised up high enough that they are not always immersed. In terms of corrosion problems, there are substantially fewer problems than with stern drives.

The decision to go with outboard power is often based on shallow water operation. While it's true that outboards can be operated in shallower water, the difference in draft is hardly enough to warrant this choice over others. It is true that when running aground or hitting underwater objects is likely to result in less damage to an outboard than a stern drive.

On the other hand, both outboards and stern drives have very weak water pump systems in the lower units that are easily damaged as a result of picking up sand, silt, sea weed and other debris. Because the water intakes are on the sides of the lower unit, picking up a plastic bag on the unit can completely block off the water supply. The sudden loss of cooling water, and the failure to immediately recognize this, frequently results in catastrophic engine damage. Because they have aluminum engine blocks, outboard motors are extremely sensitive to overheating.

The obvious advantage of outboards is that being hung on the back of the boat frees up cockpit space. Another is that the systems are quite a bit more simplified, and easier to maintain, than a dual stern drive installation where the engines may be so tightly packed together that it is very hard to maintain them. You certainly don't have that problem with outboards. And unlike inboard engines, there are no internal exhaust systems to be maintained. Outboards have no exhaust system problems whatsoever.

On the downside, outboards are considerably more expensive, and have a lot more electronic controls that are more costly to repair or replace. They are more or less engineered so that only dealers can service them, and there are relatively few shade tree mechanics in the outboard world.

In recent years there has been quite an effort to promote the myth that outboards are fuel efficient. This is utter nonsense since outboards have no internal lubricating system, and have oil mixed with the fuel for oiling. This, among other things, makes internal combustion less powerful and results in considerably higher fuel consumption.

While this is true for carbureted engines, DFI (direct fuel injection) engines do offer substantial gains in fuel efficiency over carbureted engines. However, with the possible exception of the Yamaha HPDI engines, there is a lot of evidence to suggest that these engines have yet to be perfected due to large numbers of complaints about breakdowns of both Mercury and OMC engines.

Even so, the outboard engine remains the engine of choice for small boats in no small part due to the better conditions for trailering, as the vast majority of all outboard boat are kept on trailers.

Straight Inboards

Hands-down, the straight inboard is the most reliable, economical and easy to repair and maintain power system. That's because the engine is inside the boat and only the propeller, shaft and strut are outside the hull. Inboards, like most stern drives, utilize marinized automotive engines, the parts for which are plentiful, far less expensive, and are more easily repaired. The engine designs are also more simple. You don't have to have computerized diagnostic equipment to work on these engines, and most don't even have computerized components except for those with electronic fuel injection.

Inboards are very much out of fashion these days for smaller, open boats, and there are several reasons for this. The obvious one is that the engine ends up smack in the middle of the cockpit and people don't like that. The exception is the center console boat where the engine is placed under the console. The other difficulty is that it is rather difficult to accomplish a twin engine installation on a boat with a narrow beam. To accomplish a satisfactory twin engine installation, the boat needs to have at least a nine foot beam and be about 24 feet long.

My view is that the single engine inboard is a very underrated and unappreciated power option these days. I have owned four of them and would never even consider the other options for a single engine boat. The benefits of reliability, performance, ease and low cost of repair greatly outweighs all other limitations.

Performance wise, the inboard is superior in almost every respect. With the engine close to the center of buoyancy, the hull all around performs better and is more sea kindly. The weights — engine and fuel tank — are located so as to ballast the boat properly, resulting in a greater ease of motion, and far better rough water performance. They get up on plane faster, stay there longer (at lower speeds) and there are no serious throttle range limitation as there are with both outboards and stern drives. There is no drive housing being dragged through the water, nor propellers with large hubs.

It is true that single engine inboards are more difficult to dock, as they do not steer in reverse at all, and will often only turn to one side when backing due to propeller torque.

While you don't have aluminum gear casings submerged in water, you do have to keep the propeller and rudder clean.

Trailering is a bit more difficult owing to the weights being more toward the center, but this is overcome by adding a more powerful trailer winch. There are also fewer trailer options available, since the trailer crossbeams have to accommodate the propeller shaft. Most trailer makers can easily accommodate this at little additional cost if they don't offer such a trailer standard.

Advice for Newbies

 At this point you may be thinking that the selection of a power option is a daunting task. Actually, it should not be because what has happened here is that, for a newbie, I have given you too much information that has confused you. If you have none, or very little experience with boats, this is about like buying a PC: without much hands on experience, you can read all this and it may not mean much to you.

I can spare you much of the indecision by saying that as a beginner, you have little choice but to jump in feet first and begin learning. To help ease the burden a bit, I have laid out the pros and cons of the various power options in a simple listing. From this you can pick and choose those advantages that will most suit your apparent needs. I say "apparent" because at this point you don't really know from first hand experience. That's why it is a good idea to approach your first boat as an experiment, and be prepared to make some mistakes. And why it's also a good idea to start small.

Stern Drives

      Advantages:
            Lower initial cost
            Better for trailering
     Disadvantages:
            Highly susceptive to corrosion.
            Difficult to maintain.
            Generally poor reliability record.
            Frequent engine damage caused by failed exhaust risers.
            Takes up more cockpit space.
            Very high repair cost.
            Frequent poor handling characteristics.
            Frequent trim problems.

Straight Inboards

This drive system has some benefits worth considering.

Underwater metals are not sensitive to corrosion like outboards or stern drives.

More seaworthy due to better balance and trim.

The least initial cost of all drive systems.

Easy to maintain.

Low maintenance and repair costs.

Highly reliable drive system.

Longer engine service life

Few trim and performance problems.

Inboards also have the following disadvantages:

Inadequate space in small boats for dual engine installations

Loading on trailers is more difficult.

Engines are centrally mounted in cockpit and requires either a motor box, or must be located under a center console.

Poor single engine handling.

Outboards

Advantages:

Takes up least amount of cockpit space

Better trailerability.

Better single engine handling.

Drives tilt up out of water.

Minimal corrosion problems.

Generally low maintenance.

Disadvantages:

High initial cost.

High repair costs.

Substantial computerization means less do-it-yourself repairs

Sensitive to overheating.

Frequent trim and engine torque problems.

Shorter service life than inboards.

Often won't cruise well at mid-RPM ranges.

Higher fuel consumption.

I have rated the most desirable characteristics in the table, scored from 1 to 3, for each drive type, with 1 being best, so that the lowest score is the winner. Not everyone is going to see it this way because some will place more emphasis on one feature such as trailering. From this, you can prepare your own rating based on your own priorities, and maybe add a few that I haven't thought of.

While the straight inboard scores the best for most circumstances, its two main draw-backs are that small boats don't support twin engine installations well, and they are considerably more difficult to get on and off of trailers because the engine weight is amidships. However, the inboard is inescapably the overall best choice when measured in terms of overall cost of ownership, reliability and performance. That they are less popular has mainly to do with trailering and massive promotion that the other two drive systems get that inboards don't get.

I point this out because I think the inboard has been given short shrift for the lack of advertising, and because many people do not trailer their boats, but have ended up with costlier and less reliable systems when the simple straight inboard may have best served their interests.

	Stern Drive	Inboard	Outboard
Longest Service Life	3	1	2
Lowest Maintenance Cost	3	1	2
Self Serviceability	2	1	3
Overall Reliability	3	1	2
Drive System Reliability	3	1	2
Lowest Initial Cost	1	2	3
Least Corrosion Problems	3	1	2
Better for Trailering	2	3	1
More Cockpit Space	3	2	1
Best Ocean Handling Characteristics	2	1	3
Least Trim Problems	3	1	2
Best Performance Characteristics	3	1	2
Best Single Engine Handling	2	3	1
Best Twin Engine Handling	3	1	2
Best Fuel Efficiency	2	1	3
Best for Long Term Staying Afloat	2	1	3
Total (Least Score is Best)	40	22	34

The Two-cycle, Four-cycle Debate

An outboard engine is a two cycle engine, meaning that the pistons fire every time the crankshaft makes a complete revolution. With a four cycle engine, the cylinder fires every other revolution. All things being equal, a two cycle should develop more power than a same sized four cycle engine because the four cycle engine drags the pistons around for a complete revolution without a power stroke. For outboard motors this does not hold true by reason of the fact that the fueling intake system is very inefficient.

The fueling system is via the crankcase with a mixture of fuel and oil. As the engine is exhausting on its power stroke, it is also taking in fuel at the same time. This results in some raw fuel being discharged through the exhaust. The fact that it is also burning oil has an effect similar to using a lower octane fuel. Therefore, these two factors combined mean that while the outboard should be more powerful than its four cycle cousins, it is not.

But there is also a third factor that comes into play here, and its name is torque. Torque is another measure of engine power. This involves the kinetic energy that builds up within a rotating mass of metal, and accounts for why engines have flywheels. It accounts for why a diesel engine can have a lower horsepower rating than a gas engine, but actually be more powerful in terms of pulling and pushing power. When we talk about power, we should be talking about what kind of power to do what? Horsepower alone is not an adequate measure of all kinds of power.

For example, an outboard motor horse power rating is always rated at near the maximum RPM of the engine. Were the rating to be obtained at a much lower speed, say 2000 RPM instead of 5000 RPM, the horse power rating would be much lower. Both the diesel and cast iron block automotive engines develop more power at lower RPMs and are thus more efficient at powering heavier boats.

So it is that outboard engines are very good at moving small, light weight boats at high speeds. But they're a lot less good at moving heavier boats because of their low torque. Thus, there is a good reason why you should not try to power a big heavy boat with outboard engines when another engine type would be more suitable. Similarly, people get into trouble when they attempt to use diesel engines to make boats go very fast when what the diesel does best it does so by turning slowly.

Bottom Line: Big, heavy boats benefit most from heavy, slower turning engines. Small, lightweight boats benefit most from high speed, lightweight engines. For boats that fall in between large and small, heavy and lightweight, we have the gray zone where it pays to err on the side of the engine most suitable to pushing heavier loads.

What's that got to do with two cycle, four cycle? Well, this: The native power advantage of the two cycle outboard is lost through necessities of outboard engine design. The new four cycle engines capitalize on this fact, giving them a power efficiency that the two cycle does not have. These engines will be, at least in theory, better at pushing heavier loads at lower speeds. They are clearly not as spontaneously powerful as the two cycle in terms of burst power, but they ought to do better at powering heavier boats at reasonable speeds. Only time will tell as we get to see more and more of them in operation on a wide variety of differing boat types.

Chapter 6

Cockpits, Motors and Trim

The subject of Cockpits, Motors and Trim has been included here as a separate chapter because it is so important that the uninitiated understand that the design of a boat, and how it is trimmed, has a tremendous affect on its performance and seaworthiness. It is a three part subject because all three are inter-related. This chapter is not about engines per se, but how outboard engines affect the performance and sea worthiness of a boat beyond just propelling it.

There is a very prevalent misconception amongst novices that, because the builder built it that way, it must be okay. I've already gone to great lengths to explain why this isn't true, so please don't automatically assume that all boats are seaworthy. Some aren't, and some may have serious deficiencies.

Many readers aren't old enough to remember the Chevrolet Corvair. A lovely little rear engine car that was the technology leader of its day. It only had one small problem: at high speed, or when roads were wet, it wouldn't steer. Why not? Well, there quite simply wasn't enough weight in the front end to keep the wheels on the ground. At certain speeds and conditions, the car wouldn't steer. I owned one, and I loved it, but that car almost did me in one day. A silly design mistake, although a very deadly one.

The Definition of Seaworthiness

While I'm at it, let me give you the true definition of seaworthy, which is actually a legal term, one that has its root in maritime law. A vessel is seaworthy only for a particular voyage (in your case a day of boating), meaning a particular body of water, at a certain time of the year, under the normally expected conditions, with a competent operator, crew and all necessary supplies and equipment. In other words, the seaworthiness of a boat is dependent on who, what, where, when and under what conditions. There is no definition of seaworthiness for the vessel alone, divorced from the circumstances in which it is operated.

Fig. 6-1. This photo is a good illustration of some of the problems that brackets can cause. This motor is cantilevered 30" off the transom. Note that the scum line (water line) seen at left and on bracket, is three inches higher than the painted water line. Arrow denotes location of scupper. The deck of this boat is normally flooded with one inch of water. It doesn't sink because there are no openings in the deck.

So what the devil does this have to do with cockpits, motors and trim? By itself, a boat cannot be seaworthy; conversely, by itself it can be unseaworthy. Sound crazy? Then consider the following.

Only in the last few years have outboard boats been redesigned so as to eliminate one of the worst and most grievous of problems: sinking. Over the years, the typical outboard boat has been notoriously prone to sinking at the dock . . . . all by itself without any owner/operator error to help it along. In many cases, all it takes is a heavy rainfall to put the boat on the bottom. There are several reasons for this. Having a cut down

Fig. 6-2. This bolt-on bracket is designed to provide floatation so that it does not severely alter the trim of the boat.

transom and motor well reduces effective freeboard. Many builders somehow just could not resist cutting holes in the motor well to route such things as control cables, or to place access ports at the bottom of the well to be able to access things like bilge pumps below the deck. This can mean that the hull has only to sink a few inches further in the water for it to start taking on water. That is, the water that it is floating in.

Perhaps it seems ridiculously obvious to you that the purpose of a hull is to keep the water out of places you don't want it to be. The purpose of the motor well is also to keep water out of the hull. Yes, the concept is supremely obvious, but the reality of complex designs is not. It is easy to loose sight of the forest for all the trees. These problems occur because people get carried away with other ideas and inadvertently end up violating the obvious principle that a boat hull must be water tight. I will use the analogy of a bucket to illustrate.

Whatever else one does with it, the purpose of a bucket is to hold water. The principle for a boat is the same: whatever else you do with it, the purpose of a hull is to keep water out. A bucket with a hole in it leaks; so does a boat. A boat is not as simple as a bucket, even though the principle is the same. It would be an absurd notion to put a hatch in the side of the bucket so that you could put a mop in it easier. Yet, doing similar things with boat hulls is not perceived as being absurd. The difference here is that there is nothing else on the bucket to distract you from the simplicity of the purpose of the bucket. You don't make holes in the bucket because that would obviously destroy its purpose.

The complexity of a boat and conflicting ideas are what gets in the way of adhering to the principle of a water tight hull. Start with the idea of hanging a motor on the outside of the boat, and already we're well on the way toward violating our hull principle. Yet, now there is a big industry devoted to doing just exactly that. Attaching the motor to the boat is just one way different principles can conflict.

Fig. 6-3. Older style motor well design

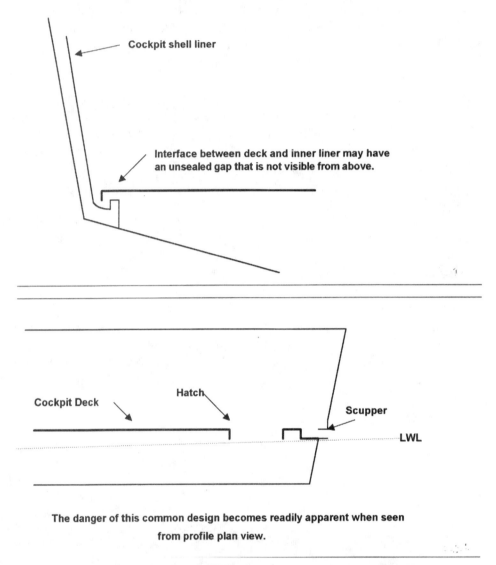

Cockpit shell liner

Interface between deck and inner liner may have
an unsealed gap that is not visible from above.

Cockpit Deck

Hatch

Scupper

LWL

The danger of this common design becomes readily apparent when seen
from profile plan view.

Fig. 6-4. Cross section and profile illustration of how low self-bailing cockpit
decks can end up sinking the boat.

What is a motor well for? Well, to keep the water out of the rest of the boat, that's
what. And if it fails to do that job, then its rather hard to consider such a boat as
seaworthy. Of course, a motor well occasionally fills full of water, and so we have to
have a provision to drain it. So we make some drain holes to facilitate that.

Next we have to have a way to get the control cables, fuel lines and battery cables from
the engine into the boat. We don't want these things draped all over the outside of the
boat, so what do we do? You got it, we make some more holes in the motor well. Now

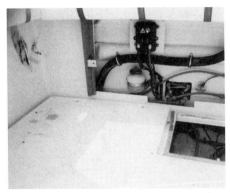 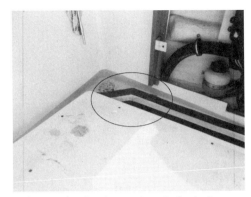

Fig. 6-4, 6-5. The illustration on opposite page and photos above make clear how serious design faults occur and go undetected. This is a boat with twin outboards on a bracket. In this case, the scuppers are hidden under a removable cockpit deck (left). Above right, the deck is moved to reveal that water floods up through scuppers and into hull because the deck is not water tight. This condition was photographed with only the photographer in the boat.

we've got a bucket full of holes. Then what often happens is that debris such as leaves, or candy bar wrappers end up in the well and plugs up the drain holes. Then, water sloshing over the low transom fills the well up with water which then runs into the hull through the control cable opening that the dealer couldn't resist cutting in the wrong place.

But our holy enterprise does not stop there. In order to reach our bilge pump down in the bilge, we have to put some kind of access back there. Now we make a BIG hole in the form of a hatch which, because of cost issues is made of plastic, is cheap and doesn't seal well. So what we end up with is one very leaky bucket, except that this happens to be a boat.

Ultimately, someone comes along who says, hey, motor wells take up lots of space in the boat, so let's eliminate it completely. Now we end up with a boat that has a door opening in the transom, but no door. This is the no motor well design. Waves can freely wash into the cockpit. That's not really a bright thing to do for reasons that should have been glaringly obvious. But, designers and marketing people being what they are, were not to be hindered by mere principles.

You've heard me say that uncountable thousands of boats have sunk because of this, so you're probably wondering how such a thing could go on so long. In a word, the answer is insurance. People had insurance on their boats, and when their boats sank, they simply fell back on that, rather than making a big legal stink about it. Insurance companies paid the claims and everyone was happy except the insurance company. And so the builders and dealers had no incentive to change their ways. Until insurance companies were swamped by sinking claims and started asking guys like me to find out why these boats were sinking. And when nasty guys like myself started saying that it's because the builder made holes in his buckets, insurers started calling their lawyers and

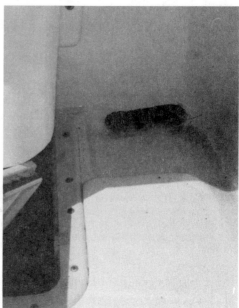

Figs. 6-6, 6-7. This deck is at best only 2-1/2" above the water line with no passengers aboard the boat. Note that in photo above right, there is a hatch within inches of the scupper, a plastic hatch cover that was shown to leak.

the lawsuits started flying. Soon, a few boat builders were going down along with their boats.

Then we had some incentive toward avoiding making holes in the bucket, and it wasn't too long before some happy changes were made which I'll discuss in a moment.

But won't the bilge pump take care of this problem, you ask? Sure, if the bilge pump never fails due to corroded wire connectors, a stuck float switch, or the batteries never go dead. Dead batteries? Who ever heard of such a thing! With the pump failing to operate, the hull begins to fill with water, and since the transom opening is already so low, it doesn't take much water to finally sink the boat. And, of course, there is only one bilge pump in the boat, with no back up.

So it is that marketing considerations frequently take precedence even over common sense and safety.

A Bit of Design History

In recent years, starting around 1992-93, the design of most outboard boats began to change with many incorporating the integral combination swim platform/mounting bracket that, for the most part, eliminates the leaky bucket problem. I call it the "platform extension," for lack of a better name (see Fig. 6-11, 6-12). Although we've seen several builders who have utilized this design and still managed to defeat the additional safety such a design can provide, it's an all around better design.

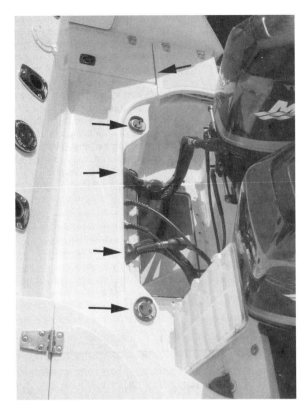

Fig. 6-8. This is an example of an exceptionally bad design. This is a platform extension with a deep motor well that is unnecessary. It has a large, leaky hatch in the bottom of the well plus two cable openings. The flimsy plastic hatch does not seal at all. Then they put the batteries under the hatch seen at upper left. The oil reservoir fillers, shown at point of arrows, also frequently go underwater. If the cap leaks this will probably wreck the engines if the boat doesn't sink first. You get all this with only one ill-considered design.

Our boat is still like a bucket, and if you put holes in the wrong places, it's still going to leak. On these pages you will see the wide variety of transom designs displayed for comparison. These run the gamut from the traditional motor well design to the bracketed engine installation. Each has their own strengths and weaknesses.

The purpose of a bracket or extension is simply give you more unfettered cockpit space. Although I've heard claims that bolt-on extension brackets improves performance, this

Fig. 6-9. This is why water tight integrity of the motor mounting area is absolutely critical.

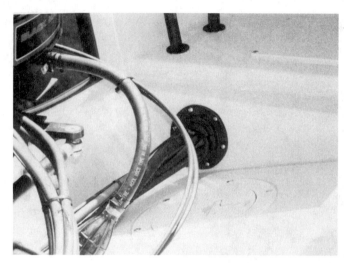

Fig. 6-10. This no motor well design has an open transom and shallow recess to accommodate the motor mounts. Note that not only the control cables penetrate the side of the recess, but there are pie ports in it as well. Water sloshes over the transom, fills the recess and enters the hull through the control cable opening. Although there is a little rubber boot around the cables, that does nothing to keep the water out. This boat sank twice in six months.

is nonsense. In many cases, brackets are known to actually hinder performance by causing severe squatting.

Because of the weight of outboard motors being located so far aft, actually as far aft as it can get, outboard boats naturally tend to have trim problems. The trim of a boat is affected as a function of the engine weight times the distance from the center of floatation in feet. Think of it as a balance scale: the farther from the balance point the weight is, the more effect it has in terms of foot/pounds — weight times distance. Add to this the fact that the traditional motor installation uses a cut down transom, plus the desire for so called self-bailing cockpits, and you have the reason so many older style outboard boats sink.

The latest designs essentially solve this problem by moving the transom forward, so that the motor well is outside the major floatation part of the hull. The down side is that in moving the transom forward, you end up with a smaller cockpit, smaller even than a boat with a motor well. To compensate, builders simply make the boat longer. Of course, this means that your 20' boat is now a 22' or 23' boat and carries a higher price tag, so the improved design comes at a considerable price premium.

Since there are still millions of boats around with the older designs, we'll give a brief discussion of each type so that you'll know what to look for.

Basic Design Types

Standard Motor Well

Once the only design, it has become outdated and is disappearing, though there are still many of them around. Properly designed, this arrangement was effective so long as no one filled the motor well full of holes, as was/is often the case. It generally fell out

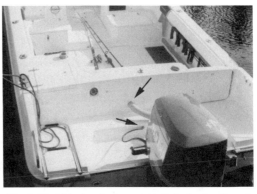

Fig. 6-12. This one is done right. Note the location of the control cable pass-through. The fuel line pass-through in well is water tight.

Fig. 6-11. Even though the integral platform design, when properly executed, can completely eliminate the sinking hazard, its safety can still be defeated as it was in this boat: the cable entry is at the bottom of the small well!

of favor because of the drawback that it took up a lot of cockpit space, plus you had to climb into the well to reach the motors for servicing, swimming and diving.

Is this type of boat absolutely to be avoided? No, so long as there are no holes where they shouldn't be. If it does have holes, they need to be closed up and made water tight. These boats should have a skilled and knowledgeable owner who is aware of certain dangers while at sea, dangers that are rather easily avoided.

The No Motor Well Design

Beginning in the 1980's, builders started eliminating motor wells in favor of a design which carries the cockpit deck all the way to the cut down transom. Most of this type had a very shallow well simply to allow space to accommodate the motor mounting bracket and steering. The idea was to make the deck water tight so that if it did flood, it wouldn't be a problem.

This design was fraught with problems since it was darn near impossible to make the deck water tight. There was always the problem of how to get at things like bilge pumps, valves and fuel tanks. Because of the necessity for deck hatches and access ports in the deck, there were numerous ways that the water coming over the transom, or heavy rainfall, would find its way into the hull in large amounts. Then there's always the problem that owners forget the need for water tight integrity, and start making holes in places they shouldn't be made.

There is also the problem of stopping the boat at sea with the stern toward the waves (see photo 6-9). This could prove to be rather dangerous as there was nothing to stop a large wave from washing right into the cockpit, literally flooding the boat. Many such

Fig. 6-13. Although not completely water tight, this type of fitting does a much better job of keeping water out of the cable pass-through. Even so, it should not be placed at the bottom of a well.

cases as this were reported where the boat went down in only a matter of seconds, catching the occupants completely off-guard.

If that didn't sink the boat, leaky deck hatches or holes drilled in the deck or cockpit liner for controls, wiring and fuel lines often did. It was really amazing how often builders, dealers and boat owners failed to realize that, lacking a transom, drilling a hole in the cockpit deck, or low on the side of the liner close to the waterline, was putting the boat in jeopardy. The effect was nearly the same as if they had drilled the hole or placed the hatch in the side of the hull. For without a transom, sooner or later the water would be sloshing over it. Photos on nearby pages illustrate some of these problems and will help you get a better idea of what to look for.

Bracketed Installation

Motor brackets, motor mounting frames, or other constructions bolted onto a full transom also made their appearance in the early 1980's. At first, many of these were steel or aluminum, so you can imagine what happened to them. Corrosion took its toll if they were steel, some wasted away and motors suddenly fell off. The problems with these things soon became apparent to everyone and it wasn't long before the boxed aluminum, and then the molded fiberglass bracket appeared to replace these clumsy arrangements.

There are two major problems with brackets. First, most boat hulls were not designed for placing the motors two or three feet further aft; they were designed for motor placement on or at the transom. Or they were originally stern drive hulls changed over to bracketed installations. Putting the motors so far aft caused major trim and handling problems, such as causing the bow to ride very high, cavitation, and causing the motors to go underwater when the boat slowed down, when the stern wake closed in over the

Fig. 6-14. This bracketed motor installation presents a problem that should be obvious to even a novice. A 3" hole for the controls is located only 6" above the water line (arrows). This boat is patently unseaworthy. The same boat is shown in full view in photo 6-15.

motor. With wakes or waves washing right over the engines, they tended not to last very long. Motors don't run so good underwater.

In many cases, add-on brackets are attached to boats that weren't designed to handle the weight and leverage created by these brackets. If you're looking at a bracketed boat, be sure to check whether the bracket is starting to pull away from the transom, or has caused any damage or distortions.

Further, a lot of builders (never bothering to employ a naval architect) didn't know that trim change is a function of distance from the center of buoyancy in feet times weight. Thus, two engines weighing a total of 1200 lbs., moved two feet further aft from the transom on a bracket creates a whopping 2400 ft/lb. effect on trim. (1200 lbs. x 2 feet). And when you have a self-bailing cockpit, literally with holes in the transom to let the water run out, and a deck only inches above the water line, it's easy to see why so many of these boats sank in a big hurry. Indeed, it is very easy to overlook the fact that water that runs out can also run in.

Then along came the OMC SeaDrive, which essentially placed the engines in the same position, with what was essentially a bracket incorporated into the motor mounting system. These were mounted on boats originally designed as inboards or stern drives with the same ill-considered effects. Sea Drives came . . and they went, another great idea down the tubes, at the consumer's expense.

As these boats sank by the hundreds, the builders slowly learned the errors of their ways — although the boat owners usually paid the price for their mistakes — and closed up the transoms so that cockpits are no longer self-bailing. Unfortunately, there are still a few of these boats around, having been dry stored most of their life so that the sinking problem was never discovered by the owner. Most often these boats usually sank when left afloat and a heavy rainfall was the coup de gras.

Add-on brackets also frequently resulted in squirrelly handling problems. By that I mean that steering could be greatly affected, as well as causing peculiar handling char-

Fig. 6-15. With brackets locating motors this far aft, it's not hard to understand how this upsets a boat's trim and can result in sinking. In this case there are two plainly visible water lines (drawn in for clarity) that are far above the self-bailing cockpit. The scupper is near the platform support.

acteristics such as uncontrollable porpoising, slow speed maneuvering and docking difficulties. It can be fun to try to back one of these beauties up. If you're looking at one of these, pay close attention to how it handles. You may end with a dolphin disguised as a boat.

Bracketed installations are still being offered, and there are plenty of used boats around with this type of motor installation. Very often they are to be found on boats that formerly were stern drive powered but have been converted to outboards. We often find straight inboard boats similarly converted by boat owners. These need to be approached with some caution because in all likelihood the conversion was made by an amateur, to ensure that (1) the transom alteration was done properly, (2) that the boat doesn't come with a built-in sinking hazard (see Figure 6-4) or, (3) serious trim and performance problems.

Hull Integral Platforms

As shown in Figure 6-11, I refer to this type as the integral platform design. For the most part, this design should completely eliminate any sinking hazard. This really is a good idea and a good design. Unfortunately, in researching this chapter, I went to a number of dealers and marinas and found a number of boats where even this good design was defeated by filling the hull integral platform full of holes! Again, the holy bucket. What else can I say except that there are a lot of builders and dealers out there who are sadly lacking in knowledge and expertise. This isn't astrophysics, folks; this is basic, fundamental boat design as it has been done for thousands of years. Care must be taken to keep the water out.

The most common error was, once again, simply drilling holes in the platform for the cables, which would also allow water to enter the hull, plus hatches and ports to reach bilge pumps. While there is no excuse for this, you should check over the installation very carefully. In most cases, if installation errors exist, they can be fairly easily corrected.

Note: High quality, water-tight couplings for engine controls have recently come on the market. If you're looking at a boat with breaches in water tight integrity due to improperly routed engine controls, it usually won't be a difficult or costly proposition to have the problem corrected. The cost of the correction should be born by the seller.

Despite the fact that you lose a couple feet of cockpit space, this newer design has a lot of advantages, starting with the fact that you have a built in swim platform, plus you can walk right out to the engines and reach them more easily for servicing without having to pull the boat or stumble around in a motor well. That is, of course, if it is intelligently designed. Some aren't.

Perhaps most importantly, the additional floatation back aft usually means that there is no trim penalty, or at least much less of one. Integral platform boats generally don't have any of the trim problems associated with bracketed installations. The engine housing will be situated much higher up, helping to keep the engines out of the water, meaning that they should last longer. And because these platforms are higher up, the risk of waves crashing over the stern are greatly reduced, especially if you have a full door that fits in the bulkhead or transom opening, which most of them do. Altogether, this is a much better, much safer design.

A few of these new designs come with a bulkhead or transom opening which has no door. If you have small children, and the boat you are looking at does not have a closing door, we recommend that you have one installed or look at a different boat. It's far too easy for little children to walk out onto the platform and fall overboard. Or even fall backward as the boat accelerates. A lift-gate type door makes this nearly impossible, and is inexpensive to have installed.

Cockpit Decks, the Weak Link

Self-bailing cockpits have an inherent potential for trouble because, once again, we have holes in our hull. If decks could be perfectly water tight, this wouldn't be a problem. But decks aren't perfectly water tight because of the necessity for hatches which, unless they are made of heavy cast aluminum with multiple, heavy dogs, are not going to be water tight. Particularly since most hatches and ports are made of flimsy plastic that can't possibly seal well. Thus, the relationship between cockpit deck height above the water line becomes all important. And with small boats, this is almost always at least a borderline problem.

Most of the platform extension boats do not have cockpit flooding problems because most are sufficiently high up that water will not back up through the scuppers. Regardless, this is a point that should be checked out anyway. Bear in mind that there are still platform boats out there where the cockpits are too low, where water enters through the scuppers, and may sink the boat. It is critical that you pay close attention to this, a point which can only be checked with the boat afloat.

The idea of self-bailing cockpits means that water entering onto the deck, either through heavy rains or water sloshing over the transom, will drain off through the scuppers. This concept often fails because:

(1)   The boat is so poorly trimmed, and the drain scuppers are too low to the water line, that the water doesn't run out, but instead runs in.

(2)   The deck has hatches or other openings that leak.

(3)   In addition to this, there may be holes drilled in the cockpit liner or other openings that completely defeat the water tight integrity.

If you want to find out how much a deck leaks, simply stop up the scuppers and cover the deck with water from a hose and see how quickly the water runs into the bilge. This will leave you with no questions as to how water tight that deck is. If all that water goes into the bilge in a hurry, you'll know there is a problem.

These are points that should be carefully considered before buying and heading out to sea in a small boat.

Deck Height Above Water Line

For any boat with a self-bailing cockpit, the height of the cockpit above the water line is a critical feature. For most boats, I recommend that the scuppers need to be at least 4" above the water line to be safe. The ABYC standard reads as follows: "......*not less than .....0.02 times the overall length .....but not less than eight inches. EXCEPTION: Boats with watertight cockpits.*" I find very few boats that meet this standard. The key word there is "watertight." That presumably does not mean cockpits with leaky hatches.

Fig. 6-16. The no motor well design needs to have an absolutely water tight cockpit.

You can quickly judge this for yourself by having one or two people go stand at the aft end of the cockpit. If the scuppers go under, then it only takes the weight of those two people to sink the boat. Water weighs 8 lbs. per gallon, so if the two people weigh 300 lbs., 37.5 gallons equals the same weight, and that amount of water in the aft bilge will begin sinking the boat. 37 gallons isn't much water, so you can see that reliance on a single bilge pump and a battery puts the boat in a rather precarious condition.

Unfortunately, the decks of a lot of boats are nowhere near 4" above the water line, and with a full load of fuel and equipment (like that big cooler full of ice and drinks) it may be even worse. Coupled with leaky deck hatches, it's not hard to see why a lot of boats sink. Of course you want to find out if the boat you are looking at has a propensity to sink before you buy it. That's why it is essential to demand of the seller to see the boat afloat, and not just buy it on a trailer or from a showroom floor.

If you're looking at an older boat, one that does appear to have this problem, probably one with a standard transom mount without a motor well, there are several ways of dealing with this. The first is you can close up the scuppers, thereby eliminating the self-bailing aspect. If that's not practical, you can clean and seal all hatches and ports with silicone sealer. This is a cost-effective solution. However, hatches have to be resealed every time you open them, which is inconvenient. But a lot less inconvenient than getting a phone call from the marina informing you that your boat is sitting on the bottom.

The other danger you want to avoid is the no motor well boat described earlier that's going to sink, or at least become endangered of floundering if it takes a wave over the stern. Take a look at the boat shown in Fig. 6-17 below and you will see exactly what I mean. This is not the kind of boat you want to throw an anchor over the stern and not expect waves to come crashing into the cockpit. They can and they will. You may want to take a pass on boats designed like this if you're a novice or open water boater.

Fig. 6-17. This design can make for a precarious situation in open water.

Dynamic Trim

Trim is a term that refers to how the boat floats. There is transverse trim and longitudinal trim. There is static trim and dynamic trim. The static trim is the trim of the boat when not moving and will differ from dynamic trim. The attitude at which the boat travels at higher speeds is called dynamic trim, or angle of attack. Planing hull boats are not intended to ride on the water completely flat, but at a slightly stern down, bow-up angle. As I've mentioned in other chapters, the faster the boat goes, the less the percentage of the hull will actually be in contact with the water because the amount of lift to the hull increases with speed. Needless to say, if the hull ran completely level, there would be a tendency for the bow to dig in to the water, causing acute steering problems.

The correct trim angle depends a lot on the shape of the hull and will vary accordingly. As a general rule, the larger and heavier the boat, the greater the trim angle will be. Most outboard boats will run about $3-5^0$ of trim at high speed. But trim angle is also greatly dependent on where the weight is concentrated in the boat, weights such as motors, fuel tanks and boats with cabins up forward. For completely open boats, this is rarely a problem because the motors on the stern usually provide for more than enough weight aft.

Shape and depth of the hull also has a major affect on trim, so as you can see, this subject can become rather complex. All you really need to know is how to evaluate whether a boat has correct trim or not.

Pay attention to this point: As it affects performance, it is best to have too much trim aft rather than too little. In other words, it should have more of a stern down, bow up attitude. If the boat is bow heavy, the only things that can be done to correct it is to shift something like the fuel tank further aft, or add more weight aft. Moving fuel tanks can be expensive, and adding weight just slows the boat down and decreases fuel economy, so it's best to get it right from the beginning.

A boat that is slightly stern heavy can always be trimmed out with the addition of trim tabs; a boat that is bow heavy cannot. A well designed boat takes into account the boat may have to carry heavier loads of people, as well as fact that the owner may add some heavy additional equipment. If there is no room for trim adjustment, then the owner is stuck with a problem for which there are only bad solutions.

Single or Twin Engines

One factor that causes many trim and performance problems is whether a boat has been designed for single or twin engine installation. With large motors weighing up around 600 pounds, and if the motors are hanging far off the stern, there can be a world of difference in how a boat will perform. The questions we have to ask are these:

What was the boat designed for? Single engine, twin engine, or both? And will it perform properly for both, or just one or the other? Obviously, the only way to find out is to get a test run in a demo.

Trim Tabs Versus Power Trim

There are two ways to trim the boat, with the electric power trim of the motor(s) or trim tabs. Changing the trim angle of the engines is not the best way to adjust hull trim because this changes the attack angle of the propellers that may result in cavitation. The motors should be trimmed for optimum engine performance, but you should understand that optimum engine performance and optimum hull trim are NOT the same thing. The former involves optimum propeller angle, the later hull attack angle. Occasionally these will coincide and slight adjustments in motor trim will achieve a correct hull trim angle. On the other hand, it is just as likely that it won't, and the cause is merely a matter of coincidence. Then, too, the way YOU use a boat may not require trim tabs because you never load the boat up, but another person with the same boat would find trim tabs essential.

Ultimately, there's no definitive answer as to whether you should or should not have trim tabs. It's just a question of whether you need them. That question gets answered by whether or not you have to rely heavily on the engine trim to correct hull trim. Then there are other factors such as the waters in which you operate. Increasing trim angle is a good way to deal with heading into a steep chop to reduce pounding. This is one instance where having considerable aft trim can be of great help because only with a lot of aft trim can you trim the bow up a lot. Remember that trim tabs only trim in one direction — bow down. To trim in the opposite direction, you have to rely on the heavy aft trim, or use the engines. In other words, when you push the switch that says "bow up," the boat is merely resuming its normal trim.

Most experienced boat owners would prefer to set trim stops on the engine mount bracket at the ideal level, and then to only use the tabs and not have to touch the power trim.   That's the simplest and easiest way of dealing with trim.

Should you order a new boat with trim tabs installed as a matter of course? Well, that's just one more instance where getting a demo ride can help answer these questions.

Two types of trim tabs are available; mechanically adjustable and hydraulic. Needless to say, you can't adjust mechanically adjustable tabs while the boat is running, so these are not a very convenient solution. Hydraulically operated tabs typically run $600-$1,000 installed, but are one of the most useful options you can get. But don't make the mistake of getting them only to find that they have no effect and you have to add weight to make them useful.

If you are completely new to boating, all of this is going to be a bit hard to understand. The best suggestion I can make is to read some, go out and do some looking around, and then come back and read some more. Just as civilian aircraft pilots have to be critically concerned with trimming their aircraft, so do boaters if they expect to get a boat that performs properly. With so many newcomers to boating, there is a great deal of ignorance on these finer points that, at first, may seem insignificant, but mean the difference between buying a good performer or a dog. It's a heck of a lot easier to learn from the experience of others than to learn the hard way . . . . . and a lot cheaper, too.

Chapter 7

Stress Cracks, Finishes and Surface Defects

Finishes

Rather than being painted, nearly all FRP boats have a finish called a gel coat. A gel coat is simply a highly pigmented plastic resin that is first sprayed into the mold, after which fiberglass fabric wetted with plastic resin is laid directly on top of the gel coat. Thus the finish and the molded part become one. Many people ask why they don't paint boats instead of using gel coat which, as anyone with a little boating experience knows, is a rather poor finish. The primary answer is that the gel coat ensures a proper mold release. Without it, a hull or deck would probably end up permanently stuck to the mold. And for that reason, we are stuck with gel coat.

Secondly, as we all know, paint finishes can chip. Gel coat can chip too, but not nearly as easily, and because it is bonded to the surface, it does not flake off like paint can. Gel coat is thick, and it will tolerate a lot of abuse, without scratches going through the surface to reveal the darker surface beneath. So while gel coat doesn't hold a shine well, it does have other advantages that painted surfaces do not have.

If you are familiar with boats at all, you are probably aware that gel coat does not hold that bright, shiny new finish for very long. The material is highly vulnerable to sunlight, despite the best efforts to create a gel coat that is durable. It will oxidize and become chalky. If you're also wondering why boats are almost always white, it's for the same reason why the finish on dark color cars, particularly dark blue or black, fade more rapidly than other colors. Basically, gel coats do what all plastics do in the sun: deteriorate, albeit at a much slower rate due to the high concentration of pigments.

When the gel coat does become chalky, that's because the plastic on the surface, after being bombarded by ultraviolet rays from the sun, has disappeared, leaving only the pigment. Fortunately, this is only the surface layer, and if one polishes it away, at least some of the original shine can be restored. How much is a function of the quality of the gel coat.

Many folks want boats with colors other than white, but experience over the years shows that colored gel coats are a mistake. They will fade and discolor very rapidly, and once it does, that finish cannot be restored. The boat will forever after have a faded, chalky finish that can only be remedied by painting with a costly urethane finish. And yes, there are numerous bottles of magic goo on the shelves of the marine store, but be assured that none of those potions lasts any longer than the gel coat shine will. Like all those miracle car waxes where the only miracle was your falling for the advertising shill. So, as much as you might detest a white boat that looks like every other white boat, there is a very high price to be paid for color. Only if you plan to keep the boat in inside storage should you consider any other color.

Stress Cracks

Because gel coat is a hard, fairly brittle material, it is subject to cracking. Cracks can appear on the exterior surface of a boat for a variety of reasons. You probably know that painted wood cracks because the wood absorbs water and swells; then it dries out and shrinks. Thus, the foundation to which the paint is attached is changing shape, which is mostly what causes the cracking. The situation is much the same with gel coat, except the cause is usually the result of the laminate bending or receiving shock loads.

The cause of the cracking is usually specifically related to the area where they appear. Stress cracking in gel coat may or may not indicate a serious underlying problem, so you need to know where they occur and why.

Gel coat cracks most often appear on the gunwale just above the guard rail as a result of the stress caused by hitting up against dock pilings. How many and how severe they are

Figs. 7-1. This severe transverse cracking is caused by improper bulkhead installation. Failure is imminent.

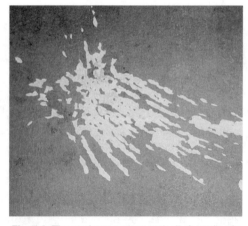

Fig. 7-2. The starburst pattern typically foretells of a hard spot on the interior. In this case the cracking is serious enough to indicate that the stress needs to be relieved to prevent laminate failure.

Fig. 7-3. An open strake design caused these stress cracks. This bottom is beginning to look suspiciously weak with too much cracking for comfort.

is usually an indication of the weakness of the hull/deck joint. The lack of stress cracks on an older boat is pretty good evidence of adequate design and strength.

Unlike a painted surface, gel coat is fairly thick, about 1/32 to 1/16" or 30 to 60 mils. A mill is one-thousandth of an inch. And because it is brittle, it is not very tolerant of bending. In fact, the underlying fiberglass laminate can bend far more than gel coat without cracking. Thus, when fiberglass bends, the gel coat finish can crack *without meaning that the underlying laminate is also cracked or damaged.*

Stress cracks can also be related to shrinkage, shrinkage of the gel coat, or shrinkage of the underlying substrate. These types of cracks appear on boats built throughout the 1980's that often utilized a plastic called dicyclopentadiene resin, or DCDP for short. One unfortunate thing that happens when resin cures is that it shrinks a little. When that happens, the fabric pattern of the fiberglass may show through the surface, which is cosmetically unpleasant looking. DCPD doesn't shrink, which was the reason for its development, but it does cure rather brittle, which is what results in gel coats made with this resin cracking excessively.

How do we know if a boat is made with DCPD? We don't; there is no way to tell at all, although we can speculate that a boat which has an excessive number of stress cracks all over which appears unexplainable, may have been made with this resin.

Stress cracks frequently appear on decks and around cabin structures for no apparent reason. For example, cracks that appear on inside corners are usually the result of a corner that wasn't designed right. It is a principle of fiberglass construction that inside corners should have a fairly large radius, say about one inch. Cracking is apt to occur at any point where there is a sharp, 90 degree inside corner. If you go around and look at a number of used boats, the pattern of this cracking, that is, the locations in which it occurs, will rather quickly become obvious.

Fig. 7-4. Despite fouling and heavy paint build up on bottom, these stress cracks are highly visible right through the grime. Paint tends to make cracks more rather than less visible.

Very well designed and well made boats are capable of remaining free of stress cracking. The average boat is likely to have some small degree of cracking, while poorly made boats tend to have an excessive amount of cracking. How much cracking exists on a boat is a measure of the quality of design and construction. There are, however, other reasons why stress cracks can occur. Here are some tips and clues what to look for.

Most stress cracks appear as very fine lines. In new boats, or boats kept under cover, they can be very hard to see. The fineness of a crack generally indicates how much the surface is bending. The wider the crack, the more cause for concern there should be. On newer boats where there is an indication of many cracks that are hard to see, I simply wet a finger, rub it in some dirt, and then rub the dirt into the affected area. Or you can rub some pencil lead over the surface, and then smear it around with a wet finger.

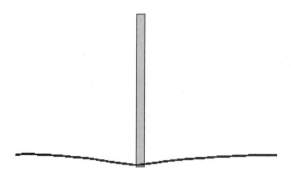

Fig. 7-5. Hard spots are created when a somewhat flexible panel such as hull or deck meets resistance against a frame, bulkhead, deck support or other member.

Fig. 7-6. A good example of catastrophic bottom panel failure in progress. This was the result of a too thin laminate.

Obviously, this means dirty cracks show up much better than clean ones, so you can take it from here that old boats show cracks better than new ones because the cracks get dirty.

Another reason cracks appear is when the gel coat is either sprayed on too thick, or it is catalyzed too quickly, causing it to over cure and become excessively brittle. This is often indicated by cracks appearing on open spaces or flat surfaces, such as the middle of a deck. It is fairly common that textured, nonskid surfaces end up with a gel coat that is too thick and ends up with large numbers of random cracks for no apparent reason at all. The cracks will often appear in odd patterns. Gel coat should be about 30–40 mils thick, or slightly over 1/16" thick. When it's more than that, the finish will tend to crack in high stress areas.

Star burst patterned cracks appearing in decks, cracks that radiate out from a common center, typically indicate that there is a hard spot under the deck that causes the deck to dimple upward slightly. You can tap around and locate the hard spot just like locating a stud in a wall. When there is a hard spot, it will quite logically sound harder than the surrounding area. Sometimes star burst cracks are caused by dropping a heavy object on the deck like an anchor, although this is fairly rare.

Sets of closely spaced, parallel cracks anywhere indicate that a hinging or bending action is occurring, such as what you would find on the gunwale, toe rail or at the point where the deck meets the side liner of a cockpit. This is rarely a serious problem on decks, but is always cause for concern on the bottom of a hull.

Stress cracks often occur at the points where hardware is screwed to the deck. The cracking pattern usually radiates outward from the piece of hardware or fastener point. If there are a lot of cracks around hardware attachments, it's usually because the gel

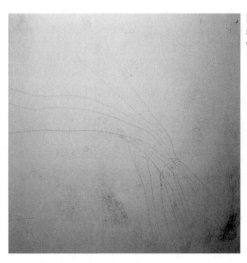

Fig. 7-7.   Radial cracks appearing on bottom or hull sides are an indication of oil canning, or excessively weak and flexing panel (laminate).

coat is too thick, or that the pilot hole for the screw was drilled too small. It does not usually indicate a structural weakness at this point. One exception may be railings. Push against a railing and see if the deck to which it is attached moves.

Cracks appearing in the corners of a transom, or anywhere around an outboard motor mount should be cause for concern. In all likelihood the transom is weak. This is especially true for later model boats where cracks appearing early in its life is likely to be signaling a serious problem. For older boats, a few minor cracks can be ignored, but not if they are numerous or obviously very deep, combined with an obvious bow in the transom. The thing to do here is to sight across the transom and see if it is bowing. If so, then the structural integrity of the transom becomes subject to question.

To summarize, surface cracking at these locations are cause for concern:

- Transoms in way of motor mounts
- Severe cracking around deck hatches
- Severe gunwale cracking without evident impact damage
- Unexplained large cracks in decks
- Around bow pulpits
- Hull sides and chines
- Bottoms

Common areas of cracking that are usually considered as "normal":

- Inside corners of cockpit liners
- Along gunwales at impact points
- Light cracks at hatch corners
- Minor cracking at hardware attachments

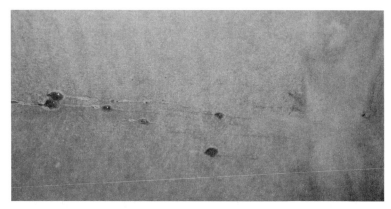

Fig 7-8. Ordinary parallel stress cracking caused by laminate hinging off of a stringer. Fluids and residue weeping out indicates water is migrating through the cracks and that they are more than just superficial and likely penetrate into laminate.

Stress Cracks on Hull Bottoms

Anytime stress cracks appear on the bottom of a hull, the structural integrity of the hull should be considered as suspect until proven innocent. There should not be any cracks on the bottom or sides of a hull, and appearance of the cracks is telling you that something is wrong.

Most often stress cracks indicate that the bottom laminate is flexing or "oil canning" between the frames. Longitudinal cracks, usually appearing in parallel rows, indicate that the panel is hinging off the stringers.

Cracks appearing transversely to the length of the hull are the most serious of all, indicating flexing off of a bulkhead or frame, and are the type most likely to result in a bottom failure, i.e. the bottom laminate actually beginning to fracture. Anytime you see pieces of gel coat flaking off around the cracks, the problem is particularly severe. If you find multiple cracks appearing across, or perpendicular to a bottom strake, as shown in figure 7-1, this may indicate a serious structural defect.

When there are single line cracks appearing in radius of the bottom strakes, this condition may or may not indicate a problem. If that's the case, you should have a professional evaluate the situation to determine if the cracking is serious or benign. Much depends on how the boat is built as to whether they indicate a structural problem or not. When there are multiple cracks appearing in the radius of the strake, there is a likely structural defect. Star burst cracks usually indicate a hard spot caused by something on the interior. In most cases, the hard spot can be eliminated, but in any case, it should be corrected.

Fig. 7-9. Excessive cracking around this stanchion base suggests more than normal stress. In this case, a plywood core is completely wasted so that the laminate has been badly weakened.

Gel Coat Voids

Gel coat voids often scare people, particularly when they are fairly large. Fortunately, these are actually pretty harmless and are easily repaired. Anything more than just a couple of them, however, are an indication of poor workmanship. Voids occur when there is an air bubble between the gel coat and the first layer of fiberglass reinforcement. You'll recall that I described the lay up process as one of laying in sheets of fiberglass fabric wetted with resin, and then rolling out the entrapped air bubbles. The layup crew failing to get all the bubbles out is how most of these voids occur.

There are instances in which very large numbers of voids and even incomplete ply bonding occurs. This is the result of a condition known as "outgassing" wherein something has gone wrong with the resin/catalyst mix and the curing resin creates gas pressure within the laminate. This causes bubbles as well as ply separations. This is fairly rare. The symptoms include large numbers of voids and circular cracks along with visual unevenness, sometimes similar to large, but very flat blisters.

Depending on the thickness of the gel coat, these voids may go on unnoticed for years. Then suddenly pressure is applied to exactly the point of the void and it breaks open, exposing the void that had long been hidden. Very often, voids begin to show up as crescent shaped circular cracks. If you press on them with a sharp instrument, they will usually break open. Older boats will seem to have more voids than newer boats. It's not that old boats have more, but that more voids have broken and become exposed over time.

Aside from flawing the appearance, voids are relatively harmless and can easily be fixed without making a mess of things. Since so many people do make a mess trying to repair them, I will tell you how to do it right a little further on.

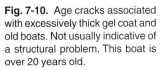

Fig. 7-10. Age cracks associated with excessively thick gel coat and old boats. Not usually indicative of a structural problem. This boat is over 20 years old.

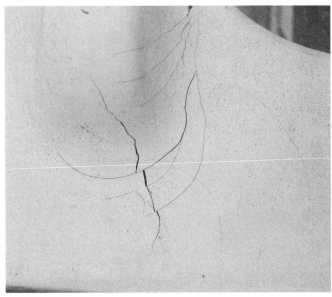

A Common Question

Many people ask whether stress cracks and voids are allowing water to enter the laminate and cause blisters. The answer is that, yes, these things are allowing water to enter the laminate, but there is no evidence that this causes blisters. Millions of boats have stress cracks without there being any blisters in the area of the cracks. Water enters the laminate through the gel coat anyway simply because it is naturally porous, but there's no evidence that these conditions are damaging to the structures.

The lone exception is when wet seat cushions or deck carpeting keeps the laminate wet for a long time, then blisters can and usually will form.

Should Stress Cracks be Repaired?

My answer to that is no. First, most attempts to repair the cracks fail, with the cracks just reappearing again because the root cause of the problem was not corrected. Second, attempts to repair them usually end up creating an unsightly mess because restoring the original contours and the finish is very difficult, not to mention costly.

It is possible to repair stress cracks with the proper materials and methods, but the main problem is with restoring the gel coat finish. Over time, the original finish fades and changes color, and to attempt to match the changed color is nearly impossible. Even repairs made early in the boat's life usually end up blotchy looking. Therefore, it is usually better to leave them be.

Fig. 7-11. Less than a year old, this black painted hull now has the texture of a washboard due to heat distortion of the laminate.

Damage Repair

When damage occurs, it is the unfortunate nature of all finishes that they are very difficult to repair without complete refinishing. You know about this experience with auto body damage. A large scratch in nearly new finish can be touched up more successfully, while one on an old, faded finish cannot. That's why when auto body damage is repaired, they will often paint the whole fender, but then the different coloration will stand out because the rest of the car is faded. We have the very same problem with boats, only it is a bit worse.

When it comes to scratches and abrasions, the repair can be worse than the damage. People who understand this often opt not to attempt to repair scratches and dings, particularly if they cover a larger area. If the scratch does not penetrate the gel coat, it's often best just to leave it alone. If it appears in a highly visible area, such as the middle of the hull side, and you want to have it repaired, it would be best to turn to a professional.

Gel Coat Crazing

Sometimes we find boats where the finish is best described as "crazed" rather than merely stress cracked, similar to that which you see on ceramics. What we're dealing with here are not normal stress cracks, but cracks appearing for a different reason than stress to certain points in the laminate. Crazing means an irregular cracking pattern which is usually the result of a defect in the application of the gel coat, or an unstable substrate. It can be that the gel coat is either too thick, or that it was improperly handled or catalyzed. This condition usually does not begin to appear until a boat is five years or older. In either case, there is probably nothing you can do about it except not to buy a used boat in that condition. Or be prepared to live with it. If a boat is plagued with this type of defect, it is best to walk away from it.

Dark Colored Boats

Another reason why boats should not be made with dark colors, aside from the fading problem, is what happens when the dark finish absorbs heat from the sun. Heating up,

Fig. 7-12. These highly irregular cracks result from an improper repair. Gel coat was applied over a fairing material that shrunk with age.

the plastic, which was once a liquid, will often continue to cure. And as it cures, it may continue to shrink. I've measured the temperature of dark blue and red surfaces at temperatures of over 200°. The end result is likely to be that the lovely red or dark blue boat that had such a flawless finish on the day you bought it, a year or two later may end up suffering from post-cure shrinkage, cracking and blistering. What happens is that as the plastic continues to cure as a result of heat, it shrinks and begins to take on the coarse pattern of the reinforcing fiberglass cloth beneath the surface.

Blistering and cracking is a common problem with very dark surfaces, such as black and navy blue that is often used for trim features. As a general rule, these colors should never be used because the sun can heat them up to near the deformation point of the plastic. Boats with hulls painted these colors are often found with very large blisters on their hull sides which are the result of heat-induced ply separation.

If these colors are to be used, they must be used in conjunction with what is called high heat distortion resin, a resin specially formulated to resist the problem. If a builder has used this very expensive resin, chances are high that he will have touted this in his brochure.

Blotchy, Discolored Finishes

As mentioned at the beginning of this chapter, sometimes parts stick in the mold. When that happens, pieces of gel coat will tear off the part and remain stuck to the mold. This can happen for a variety of reasons, most often the result of an old, worn out mold. Molds are only good for making so many parts, as molds gradually degrade. Every part pulled out of a mold is not as good as the one before it, until the mold reaches the point where the quality of the part is unacceptable.

It is fairly common that parts get damaged during mold release. Because of the size and cost of the part, such as a hull or deck, damaged parts are not rejected and discarded, but repaired. The repair is fairly successful because the builder is (hopefully) using the same exact batch of gel coat to make the repair, and the finish isn't aged, so there isn't much of a matching color problem here.

However, there is a problem with uneven aging and fading of the repaired part (Fig. 7-14). After a period of a year or two, perhaps even longer, the repaired spots are going to start to show up as discolored areas. While there is no structural problem involved with this, it can be a bit unsightly and there is nothing you can do about it unless you want to paint the whole boat.

This is problematic from the standpoint of evaluating used boats since gel coat repairs made by the builder look just like damage repairs years later. If you can look at the area from the inside, this may tell you whether it's a finish or a damage repair. If it's serious damage, you will see the repair from the inside.

Longevity of Finish

The highest quality gel coats that are most resistant to losing their luster and chalking are very expensive, and few builders, even of large yachts, use them. My review of numerous boat brochures shows that many of them trumpet high quality gel coats for "long lasting finish". Experience shows that few live up to this promise, and that they end up just as faded and chalky as all the others.

I get many questions from people asking what they can do to preserve the finish. It is, of course, easier to keep a finish up than to try to bring a faded one back. If the finish

Fig. 7-13. Stress cracks appearing on a hull side indicates serious structural problems. Notice how the painted stripes make them show up better.

will not hold wax, and turns dull and chalky very quickly, then you have a poor quality finish that cannot be preserved. If it fades without heavy chalking (run your hand over it to see how much comes off), then frequent waxing and occasional compounding with a buffer will probably keep it up fairly well. There's really no way to tell except by experience.

What about some of these commercial preparations being sold that offer miracle solutions? I have seen a few of these and the result was not exactly encouraging. At first, it can make the finish really shine, but when that miracle goo itself begins to fade, the result can be a finish that looks worse than ever, becoming streaked and blotchy. It's like putting Armoral on plastic; it shines good for a week, after which it looks worse than ever. Then you can't get the stuff off easily without using a very abrasive compound or solvent. I haven't seen any that I'd recommend. My view is that compounding and waxing is still the best method, and most maintenance experts agree.

Repairing Chips and Dings

More often than not, minor chips and dings are better left alone, mainly for the same reasons I described about repairing stress cracks. The cure is often worse than the disease, just as it is with auto finishes. Unless you are skilled at this kind of thing, I would recommend that you either hire a professional to do it (minor chips and scrapes aren't all that expensive to repair) or just leave it alone.

What about chips or gouges that penetrate into the laminate? Won't water get into the laminate and cause damage? Usually not, but if the area is unsightly, it is a good idea to repair it. Deep gouges or chips that made a deep hole (also gel coat molding voids) should be filled with two part epoxy first, before applying the gel coat finish. Merely filling the void with gel coat will usually result in cracking and an unsightly appearance later on.

What about damage on the hull bottom? Won't that cause blisters by letting water in? In all my years of surveying, I have never seen blisters appearing around bottom scrapes, so my presumption is that breaches in gel coat will not cause blisters. Conversely, so called "barrier coating" will not prevent blisters by keeping water out. It is next to impossible to avoid breaches in the finish. It's like trying to keep your car tires clean. For trailer boats and dry stored boats, dinged up bottoms from handling are considered as normal wear and tear.

Repairing Small Dings and Scratches

To fill a void or deep gouge, use a marine two-part epoxy. DO NOT use the kind for use around the home. You will probably have to buy a quantity 100 times more than you'll need, so don't be tempted to purchase one of those very small epoxy kits from the

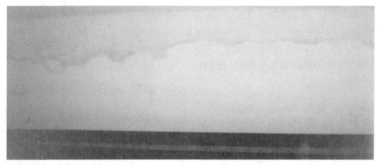

Fig. 7-14. This is what a typical aged gel coat repair usually looks like years later when the two finishes fade and discolor at different rates. It's the reason why it's often better to leave minor scratches unrepaired.

hardware store. While you're at it, pick up a pint of acetone. Dig out all loose material in the area to be repaired, and make sure that it is completely dry. Use a flat plastic or rubbery applicator of the type commonly found in auto parts stores. If the applicator is too big, use scissors or a knife and cut it down to the right size for the job. Apply the mixed epoxy to the hole, pushing it down to make sure of good adhesion.

Use the applicator to scrape away all excess epoxy so that there is epoxy only in the cavity. Using the soft applicator, try to level the epoxy in the scrape to just below the level of the gel coat. The idea being that the remaining unfilled area will be leveled with gel coat. Running the applicator down the length of a scratch will usually do the trick. Use the acetone and a rag to clean away all the excess on the surrounding surface. If you don't do this, you will end up with an ugly spot, so be sure to get it all off.

You want the surface of the epoxy-filled hole or scratch to be slightly lower than the surrounding surface. The reason being that you are going to apply a thick layer of gel coat after the epoxy has cured. Use the corner of the applicator to remove the excess so that the fill is about 1/32" or so lower. You will have either purchased a standard white gel coat repair kit, or the builder supplied some with the boat. Before applying the gel coat, lightly scuff the cured epoxy with sandpaper. Following the instructions on how to catalyze it, you will pile the gel coat into the repaired area which still has a slight depression. You pile it on until it stands just slightly above the surrounding surface, keeping in mind that it will shrink a bit during curing. When fully cured, sand the excess off with nothing less than 300 grit paper, and finishing off with 600 grit.

Finally, allow at least a week, preferably more, for the gel coat to completely cure. Then you can use some fiberglass compound and polish the sanded surface by hand. And that's it. On an older boat, the area where you sanded and polished is going to show a blotch for a while, but it will age back to the surrounding color, while the new gel coat you put in the hole will not.

Cleaning

Many people use abrasive boat cleaners or just plain scouring powder to clean their boats. You know what would happen if you used these materials on your car, so why would you use them on your boat? It's one thing to use abrasives on hard-to-remove dirt on nonskid deck surfaces, but you certainly don't want to use it on any other parts of the boat. Remember that any cleanser is going to remove the wax, if any. If simple brushing won't remove those dark water stains, try a little petroleum based cleaner such as Fantastic or 409. If that doesn't do it, you'll have to use the abrasive such as Bon Ami, but remember that the abrasive is scratching the surface, which now will get dirtier, faster. Do not use petroleum based products, or products that contain bleach on large areas as these are very damaging to anodized aluminum, plastics and other material.

Should Older Boats be Painted?

A professionally applied linear urethane spray finish can make an old boat look darn near like new. It is, of course, expensive, but expense should be considered relative to the cost of a new boat.

Ninety percent of the cost of a paint job is in the preparation. The only way to get professional results is by using a professional who knows what he's doing. The preparation and use of this costly coating is not for amateur use. While expensive — usually figured at around $125 per foot — having a boat painted is a very viable option in buying an older boat and making it look new, especially if you are capable of doing the prep work yourself.

Many people consider the cost and decide that it is too expensive. If you are in the market for an older boat, consider including the cost of painting in the financing. Tell your lender what it is that you intend to do, and that you want to work out an arrangement to finance the boat and have it painted with the financing. Painting can substantially increase the value of the boat and some lenders will be open to this option, particularly the ones that specialize in boat loans.

Maintaining the Finish

As I mentioned earlier, gel coat oxidizes rapidly because it has a very high ratio of pigments to plastic. Restoring the dulled finish is mostly a matter of removing the surface oxidation, but also a matter of burnishing the plastic, which is where the shine comes from. Therefore, just hand waxing a faded, chalky finish rarely produces the desired results.

Unlike paint on a car, gel coat being much thicker, allows for numerous compoundings before the gel coat completely wears away. But when it comes to older boats, it's a good idea to pay attention to how much gel coat is left. When the gel coat is getting too thin, the result is much like a car finish; you'll see the substrate start to show through on the high spots, edges, corners and occasionally even on large flat surfaces. When you see this, it means that every time the boat is compounded, the appearance is going to get progressively worse. Then the only solution is to paint the boat.

To fully restore the finish, you need to perform a two-part process, compounding and waxing. And for this a serious buffing machine is the right tool to use. Please note that the inexpensive ones made for cars isn't going to fit the bill very well, for these are not designed to work in all the nooks and crannies of a boat, nor do they operate at high enough speeds. A light duty angle grinder with buffing pads is the most versatile.

Depending on the degree of oxidation, use a light to medium grit buffing compound. It does not matter if it is specially formulated for fiberglass, but it does matter what color the compound is. DO NOT use anything but WHITE compound as it may discolor the gel coat.

When compounding, you must be very careful not to burn the finish by pushing too hard, or leaving the buffer in one place too long. Get a feel for the right amount of pressure by working on a few test spots, buffing first, then applying a coat of wax to see how it looks. The trick here is to avoid a blotchy looking finish as the result of over and under buffing from area to area. This will be less of a problem on the top sides than on the hull sides where you want to use a smooth, sweeping movement of the machine to achieve a consistent degree of luster.

Work on a test area about 4 - 5 feet long. Buff it out, then apply the wax. If it looks blotchy or you see too much swirling pattern, go over it again, this time more lightly, until it looks right. Use a very light pressure on the machine to minimize swirls, and move it quickly and evenly across the surface. Eventually you'll get the feel for how much pressure to apply, and how long to buff. When working with the machine, be very careful to not work with the edges of the pad. You want to tilt the machine about 2 degrees so that the pad is contacting the hull at a point about midway between the center and edge of the pad. If you hold it perfectly flat, you're going to end up with a pronounced swirling pattern and the buffer will bounce around.

On the hull sides, work from top to bottom, side to side, in long rows, as if you were working on a series of rectangles. Because gel coat is so very porous, generally two coats of wax are needed.

If there are stains that won't come out, you can try dabbing on a little chlorine or oxygen bleach. This may or may not work depending on the nature of the stain. Bleach will not work for grease or oil stains. For the bleach to work, you must wash off all polishing compound and oil. It's best to apply the bleach to the stain before compounding. For rust stains, try a rust stain remover, but be sure to use both these products very judiciously, a little bit at a time. It's best to try a test spot in an out of the way location, just in case things go wrong.

Chapter 8

Details & Design

Ultimately, the quality of a boat, the satisfaction and enjoyment that you get out of it, comes down to a matter of dozens, even hundreds of small details. The importance of good, thoughtful design in boats can't be overstressed, but is frequently overlooked, particularly by those with little experience in boat ownership. Is a door hinge made of stainless steel or plastic? Are the deck hatch hinges recessed into the deck so that you don't cut your bare feet on them? Are electrical switches and other apparatus located so that they don't get wet? The list can go on and on.

In this chapter, mostly by means of photos, we explore some of the good, the bad and the ugly aspects of the details of design, hardware and other important aspects. I'll show you how to determine whether a boat has been thoughtfully designed by an expert with a lot of experience, or whether it's been hastily conceived by an amateur or just someone who doesn't really care about the quality of their product.

Ergonomics

Some people don't mind spending a lot of time in a boat with very cramped quarters; others find cramped and cluttered layouts to be intolerable. I am of the later type, and there's nothing I dislike more than a boat that is hard to move around in. When you figure you may spend entire days on a boat, it becomes very tiring to have to be constantly bumping into things, or trying to get around other people because, every time you turn around, some one is in your way. There's nothing like having to say, "Excuse me," 57 times in one day.

Regardless of the size of the boat, it can either be intelligently laid out or not. Just because a boat is small doesn't mean that it has to be cramped. One of the big problems of interior design that has always existed is the tendency to put too much into a boat, thereby making it crowded or ergonomically uncomfortable. But when it comes to outboard boats, which are naturally small, having good, ergonomically designed interior becomes critically important to those who demand a little elbow room. Shown on the following pages are a variety of different designs that make varying uses of interior space.

The center console boat, long considered by many as a fishing boat, has been notable for its lack of seating, mainly by reason of the fact that fishermen prefer open, uncluttered spaces. Many designers have turned the center console boat into a multipurpose boat simply by adding more seating, adding a cuddy cabin up under the deck, or making the center console very large and creating cabin space therein. All of these things have a profound impact on cockpit area elbow room.

Moreover, the faux transom provides the opportunity, by making it very wide, to create space for tackle boxes, storage, and conveniently positioned bait wells, and other goodies, again at the expense of deck space. Depending on how you plan to use the boat, keep in mind that for everything extra you get, you also end up loosing open space.

Integral Platform Designs

There is a huge variety of differing platform designs. By its nature, the integral platform creates a false transom which creates new opportunities for design and add-on goodies. In fact, almost no two seem alike. Platform design should be an important consideration for people who engage in water sports such as swimming, diving and even water skiing. Platform design, depending on what the designer had in mind, can make it very easy to get into the boat from the water, or very difficult. Intrepid center console boats have one of the more unusual (and useless) platform designs, pictured below, right. Here is a boat that basically has a very large motor well with two very

Fig. 8-1. The integral platform is a radical change for the better in outboard boats by doing a far better job of keeping water out of the cockpit. It either makes the cockpit two feet shorter, or the builder adds a couple of extra feet to boat length, usually the later.

Fig.8-2. Not really an integral platform, this is a modified motor well design that incorporates tiny, built in platforms on each side that are not large enough to facilitate getting in and out of the boat from the water. It's not a good design for water sports enthusiasts.

Fig. 8-3. The above boat is a 30 footer, and although it has a walk-in console, the boat is large enough that the cockpit has plenty of space to move around in.

Fig.8-4. One complaint about the walkaround design is the way it narrows the forward cockpit area. On this boat, it is a squeeze to get between the two helm seats. Note that the integral platform, although it has a large well in it, is large enough to facilitate easy entry from the water.

small platform areas on each side of it. Imagine trying to climb onto that from the water. It's very hard to do.

The opposite extreme is a boat with a platform that has a very narrow, shallow well, one that is only large enough to facilitate mounting the motors, but provides the maximum amount of flat deck space. Note that the well in this case is the depression that allows the motors to be mounted over the edge of the transom. These can be either very large or small. Some large wells exist as a necessity to allow the motors to tilt up, but this depends entirely on the basic transom design.

The advantages of the flat deck design are many. It allows plenty of space for swimmers or divers to easily climb aboard, or to put their scuba tanks aboard, as well as allowing a fisherman to walk around back there while attempting to keep a fish away from the lower units. And not only that, but this makes it a lot easier to work on the motors without worrying about twisting your ankle while stepping into a deep well. However, this has to be done intelligently, without wires, cables and hoses being strung all over, creating tripping hazards. I've only seen a handful of designs that are very well done, while most seem quite thoughtless.

It's nice that large walk-in consoles afford some sheltered space for storage, a head, or even just a place to get out of the rain. The obvious down side is that large consoles gobble up deck space. The question is whether or not the loss of deck space is worth it. Shown in Fig. 8-3 is a large center console boat that has only an ordinary size console. The nice thing about this one is that it is literally possible to run from the bow of the

Fig.8-5. Islands can be pretty handy as long as there is adequate space for them. You have to decide whether the sacrifice of deck space is worth the extra utility.

boat to the stern without hitting anything. This is the type of layout that divers and fishermen will appreciate most.

For parents with kids, this would be a far less important consideration, where seating and a means to escape from sun and rain becomes more important. And speaking of kids, pay attention to the faux transom and door, if it has one. Some boats have no transom door, while for others, the height is very low. It is very easy for kids to fall overboard from the transom. It should have a door and be of sufficient height to prevent them from falling overboard when suddenly accelerating.

Motor Well Designs

For about the last 6-8 years we saw very few boats offered with motor well designs. At the 2001 boat shows several turned up such as the Proline walkaround shown below. This unusual offering has seating on each side of the well. Among the pros and cons of the internal well are that it can offer you these additional fixed seats, as opposed to the

Fig.8-6. An internal well design with seating on the sides of the well.

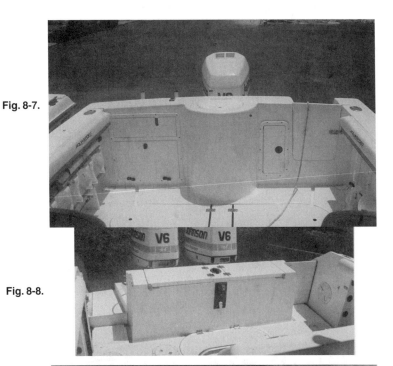

Fig. 8-7.

Fig. 8-8.

Fig. 8-9. The false transom/platform extension opens up many new design opportunities. These can either be very simple or complex, have one or two doors and house a variety of options.

fold-out seats of other designs. Perhaps the biggest drawback is the feel of the boat. The seats are not at gunwale height, thus one cannot brace oneself against the gunwale for support, an important consideration for fishermen. Also, unless it's a four-stroke engine, not many people would want to sit right next to a roaring two-cycle engine!

On the other hand, there is very little difference in overall cockpit space between internal well boats and integral platform boats.

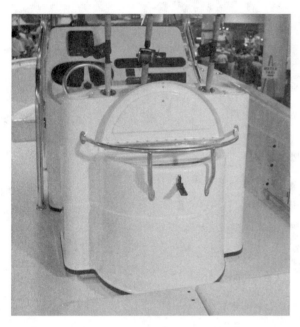

Fig. 8-10. This creative design uses a semi-circular bait well set into the helm seat back combining a rocket launcher. The stainless handrailing is superbly well positioned.

Walkarounds

The walkaround boat always comes with a cabin, and has a recessed deck with only a step up or two that allows easier access to the fore deck area. Personally, I have found this to be of questionable benefit since a cabin cruiser or express boat can also have an equally or larger sized cabin without the walkaround facility. The great drawback of

Fig. 8-11. The same Triton CC shown above. Placing the bait well behind the helm freed up all this space in the Faux transom, the most important of which is the large center door that provides excellent access to all the equipment located under this area.

Fig. 8-12. The under side of a center console revealing an ugly and very unprofessional mess of wiring created by a boat builder.

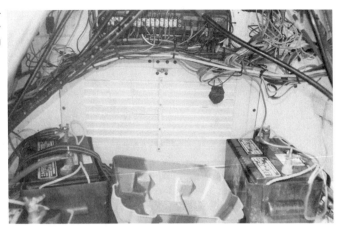

this design results from the narrowness of the forward cockpit area that, in many cases is so narrow that it becomes hard to even squeeze between the two seats.

While under way, passengers always gravitate toward the windshield, but in this type of boat, it's a crunch for even two people to occupy this area. It's also difficult for even the owner/operator to get in and out from behind the helm. As a family boat, it can leave a lot to be desired. If you are interested in this type of boat, I'd suggest you consider your needs very carefully.

Islands

In recent years, all sorts of islands have been devised for center console boats. The most common of these is the combined helm seat/island. These can contain anything from a tackle center to a wet bar, replete with sink and refrigerator, or a simple rod rack. These all have the disadvantage of gobbling up large amounts of deck space that

Fig. 8-12. A sure sign of a poorly designed electrical system is this very large number of wire splices and inline fuses. Each one of these crimp-on wire nuts creates a little cup which can trap water, causing the connection to corrode, fail and possibly start a fire..

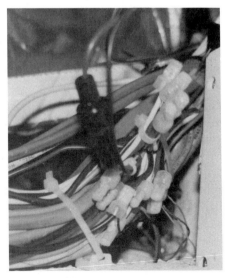

Fig. 8-13. It pays to look under the hood ....or rather the deck. This is the way important plumbing, controls and electrical are installed in a new, well-known name brand boat that has a reputation for high quality. Or at least some people think so. This boat sells for $110,000. Would you pay that kind of money for a sloppy mess like this?

might best be left open for other needs. Fortunately, most of these islands are sold as optional equipment. When it comes to diving and fishing, most owners would agree that you're better off without these space eaters.

One of the more interesting designs that I've seen was on an Intrepid 322 CC boat which had a large seat or lounge that pulled out horizontally from the front of the console, and thus was could be completely gotten out of the way when not needed. On the other hand, this design eliminates all possibility of using the inside of the console for storage.

Interiors and Soft Goods

The boats that have the most problems with interiors are runabouts and deck boats and this involves the use of plywood, upholstery and carpeting. Anyone should be able to understand why it is a terrible idea to glue carpet or vinyl onto plywood. After all, this is a boat, not a house, and it will frequently get wet, and then stay wet, eventually causing the plywood to rot.

Seats, cabinets, decks and upholstered decorative trim are items that are frequently upholstered in this type of boat. Because of this problem, most of the industry has abandoned the use of plywood for these structures which are now either made of molded fiberglass and other types of plastic. Naturally, this has driven up the price of boats considerably. However, there are still numerous low price builders that continue to use these materials which are easy enough to identify.

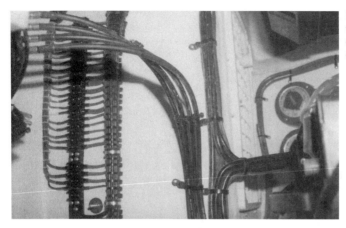

Fig. 8-14. The importance of neat, well secured wiring cannot be overstated though it is often overlooked.

Although you may not be able to see any plywood, structures made of it are almost always angular with flat surfaces. Usually the plywood is completely covered over with vinyl, so look for the staples. Next, take a look at the seat cushions. What you don't want is vinyl stapled to plywood as this will rot very rapidly. Better quality construction uses poly plastic for cushion bases.

Those slick looking bucket seats commonly found in runabouts are also build on a plywood frame. They are indeed buckets and will fill up with water, rot and fall apart very fast when left exposed to weather.

Carpeting does not belong on the exterior of a boat. Wet carpeted decks can retain water for weeks before it eventually dries out. In the meantime, it can cause leaks, gel coat blisters and problems with cored structures.

Runabouts that have back-to-back seating units are almost always made of plywood. The only solution for this is to keep the boat covered when not in use.

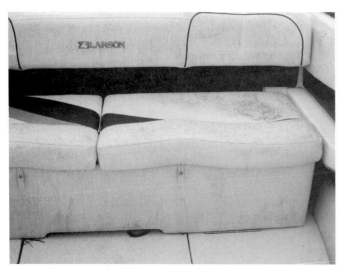

Fig. 8-15. These seats are made of vinyl and foam rubber stapled onto plywood. Only three years old and left exposed to weather, they are rotting and falling apart.

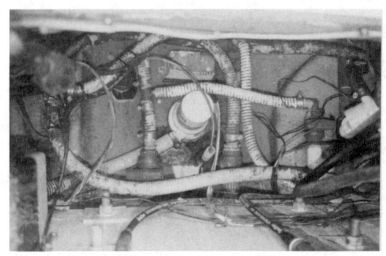

Fig. 8-16. Here's another example of the sort of thing we don't want to find in new boats, an unintelligible mess of plumbing and wires. This photo was taken looking down through a hatch three feet above. The space is only 16" wide, so none of this stuff can be reached for service or repair. This is substandard and unacceptable.

Faux Transoms

It often surprises me how badly designed some of these are. It happens when the designer attempts to do too much with this very useful space. What usually happens is that both a bait well and fish box is designed into the top of the faux transom, thereby making all the rest of it unusable because, with wells at the top, the only place left to put cabinet space is at the bottom. It's not too cool to have to get down on your knees to open a storage cabinet. In addition, so many of these cabinets are not designed to keep water out, so everything put there gets wet. Figure 8-7 (Aquasport) shows one creative design solution by creating a round live well that stands out from the transom.

One drawback of all faux transoms is that they can make it very hard to service bilge pumps and all the other stuff that needs to be placed in the aft hull. When looking at boats, you may want to check this aspect out carefully. In the case of at least one large boat I saw recently, it was almost impossible to reach many items that needed to be reached for servicing.

Electrical Stuff

The electrical systems on most outboard boats are so simple that there are rarely any system design problems. Most problems that do occur usually result from a failure to protect against water damage.

More and more in late model boats I'm finding sensitive electrical equipment installed in places where it gets wet. This ranges from switches to wiring to batteries and instrument panels. As for the later, it is common to see engine instruments and switches sitting out exposed. After 35 years of surveying boats, I can assure you that there are no

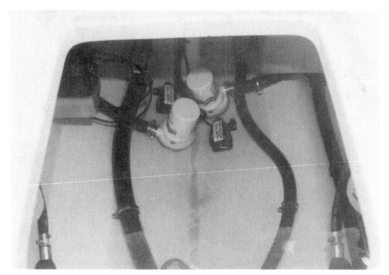

Fig. 8-17. Contrast this photo with that on the preceding page. These are both the aft bilge areas of comparably sized boats. The care taken by this builder is obvious, not only in the neat, clean installations, but also the dual bilge pump installation.

gauges and no switches that are water proof. When you leave them exposed to sun, rain and spray, these things are going to get wet and damaged. If you left a Rolex Submariner watch out in the hot sun, let it heat up, and then pour cold water on it, you can be sure that it too, will leak.

Electrical apparatus and systems need to be protected from water. When it comes to instrument panels, this is not hard to do, even though most designers will leave them exposed. Praise the designer who puts them under a Plexiglas cover with a properly designed lip.

Switches of any kind should not be located on the face of the faux transom because of the obvious problem of being constantly doused with spray. The designer who puts them there doesn't care about you, so you shouldn't care for his boat either.

Neat and Secure

If you want to understand why systems in boats can be so amazingly unreliable, you need look no further than the manner in which these systems are often installed. First, understand that boats do a lot of slamming and are subjected to high G-forces. Anything that is not solidly secured, particularly wiring and plumbing, is going to be bouncing around and likely become damaged.

Figure 8-14 & 8-17 shows how some of the top, high end boat builders do their best to ensure reliability. This is not merely eye candy, but keeps wires and connections from becoming damaged, and also makes things much easier to repair when repairs are needed. The use of terminal blocks makes it much easier to replace equipment as it

Fig.8-18. This boat has no foot cove. Notice how the cockpit inner liner is not merely vertical, but slopes inward slightly. The end result is that one cannot comfortably stand close to the gunwale.

eliminates unreliable wire splices. Figure 8-12 illustrates a builder whose primary interest is price. If you find wiring and plumbing looking like a disorganized rat's nest, chances are that you're going to have problems with systems like that.

Speaking of wire splices, check over the electrical system. If you find numerous wire splices plus many inline fuses, what you are looking at is a very poorly wired boat. Unfortunately, there are a lot of them. What's wrong with that is that every crimped wire splice is an opportunity for corrosion to either cause high electrical resistance, or a broken circuit altogether. A very small boat with minimal wiring is one thing, but larger boats with extensive electrical equipment that also has poor wiring, is a prescription for disaster. Because we are dealing with outboard motors which are made of sensitive aluminum, we do not want to take any chances with shoddy electrical systems. It only takes a bit of stray current to cause extensive corrosion damage to lower units.

Plumbing also needs to be well secured. A hose that is full of water and is hanging from a plastic through hull nipple — well, guess what can happen to that when subjected to serious pounding.

Electricity on Outboard Boats

Electricity and water don't get along very well, and on boats, particularly outboard boats, when electrical current escapes from its directed pathways, this can lead to disaster to the aluminum outboard motors.

Small outboards rarely have problems in this regard because their electrical systems are small and simplistic. That is, so long as no one makes any serious mistakes in making changes, repairs or alterations. But as boats get larger, the size and complexity of

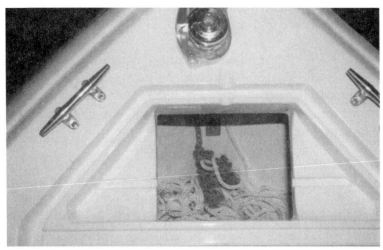

Fig.8-19. A rope locker with a beautifully designed guttering system, plus provision for convenient storage of the anchor. This will prevent water from going into the hatch.

electrical systems grows geometrically. It only takes 1/4 volt of stray current to destroy an outboard lower unit in a very short period of time.

The most serious problems arise when we start adding shore power systems and battery chargers. Because shore power systems end up grounding the boat to the dockside ground, we have now made the boat dependent on the dock ground, and have changed the boat's electrical potential to that of the dockside ground. Moreover, every different dock that one goes to and plugs into is going to have a different potential, a situation that bodes ill for motors.

Essentially, what can happen is that if the dockside ground is energized, say from any device that has a power leak, that can back feed into the boat's system. To overcome such problems, devices called ground isolation transformers are used which control the direction of flow of current in a grounding circuit. All boats that have shore power systems should have these devices. Beware that many new boats are sold without them, so be sure to check.

If you buy a boat with a shore power system, I strongly recommend that you keep the engines fully tilted up and out of the water anytime the system is connected. With the lower units out of the water, most of the potential danger is eliminated.

Batteries

Batteries are almost always installed in a bad spot in small outboard boats owing to the lack of adequate space to install them in a convenient location. Sometimes builders install them in truly unfortunate locations. Another problem is that outboards almost always come with automotive quality batteries which tend to be of universally poor quality.

It is important that batteries be mounted in a dry location, and especially that terminals not get wet and allowed to corrode.

Many people feel the need to have a three battery system with a twin engine boat, with the third battery running the "house" side of the system. This means everything except the engine starting function. Certainly it's nice to have a third battery, though I'm not convinced of the necessity for it. Most outboard boats do not have so much DC equipment that it is unquestionably needed.

In lieu of a third battery, having a battery paralleling switch installed is a darn good idea. All a parallel switch does is to join two batteries together. It is true that engine charging systems tend to fail rather frequently. The parallel switch will overcome the problem most of the time and get the engine started when the failure is with just one side of the system, which it usually is. Battery paralleling is often "built in" by the use of master switches that have positions marked, "1", "2", and "All." The problem with this is that if you leave it on the "all" position and the batteries discharge, both batteries go down and you're out of luck. With the parallel switch, the batteries are always separated unless the switch is pressed and held, thus making it more reliable.

Battery Chargers

The subject of battery chargers is a complex one that few people fully understand, yet these are very necessary devices for most boats, especially those that are kept afloat and are used infrequently. For boats maintained on a trailer or storage racks, battery chargers are much less necessary. Batteries will not hold a charge indefinitely because they generate power by means of a chemical reaction that cannot be precisely controlled. Even when charged and then disconnected from a system, the battery will eventually discharge. But when you consider that most electrical systems develop current "leaks," the problem of keeping batteries charged becomes even more difficult.

Batteries tend to be very short lived on outboard boats for several reasons. First is the primary reliance on engine alternators to do the charging over fairly short periods of time. Aside from battery quality, the thing that most affects battery life is the *depth of discharge.* The more a battery or bank of batteries is allowed to discharge between full charges, the more this reduces it's life span. It naturally follows, then, that larger batteries, or more than one battery in a bank, is going to last longer than smaller batteries.

The next most important thing is *rate of charge.* The problem with reliance on engine alternators is that the engine usually isn't run long enough, or at high enough speed, to bring the batteries up to a really full charge. What typically happens is that when an engine is first started, it will charge at a very high rate, but as battery power starts coming up, the regulator starts reducing the charge rate dramatically until the batteries are at around 75% of full charge, when the charge rate drops off to only a few amps to avoid cooking the batteries. This causes the need to charge for much longer periods.

Fig. 8-20. Notice how this hatch gutter connects to the margin gutter (drain scupper visible at upper right.)

How much longer? Well, that depends on the alternator capacity and number of batteries and size. This is where it gets really difficult to determine whether your batteries are going through a full charge cycle or not. If you are running the engines for 2-3 hours continuously, the odds are good that the full charge cycle is being achieved. But if you're running the boat for an hour and then shutting down while using electrical equipment, you're engaging in a charge cycle that is incomplete, a situation that seriously shortens battery life.

When it comes to outboards, we are limited as to alternator *and* usually battery size. It would certainly be of benefit to increase battery size and thereby reduce total discharge rates between charging and thereby improve battery life. But to do this, we also need to increase alternator size which we cannot do.

The only solution is to add an AC battery charger that will bring the batteries up to full charge when the boat is not in use. That would be a simple enough proposition but for the problem of bringing high voltage on board. To do that, we have to install a proper system according to ABYC marine standards. Just stringing an extension cord and plugging a charger into it is not acceptable for a variety of reasons, not the least of which is that the charger and the circuit will have no circuit protection. A lot of fires, shocks and corrosion damage has been caused this way.

When purchasing a new boat, and shore power and battery charger is offered as an option, it is well worth the cost to have it. To add it to a used boat requires a marine certified electrician and requires the following: marine shore power cord, receptacles, circuit breaker panel, ground isolation transformer and the battery charger. The cost

Fig. 8-21. The problem with pop-up cleats is clearly illustrated here where even a small 1/2" line will not fit well on the cleat. Unless the line has a eye splice, a line cannot be made secure to this cleat as it's size does not permit a sufficient number of hitches.

would be around $1,500. Or you can just live with the problem of short battery life and frequent replacements. The real problem arises when the engines fail to start at a location other than your home port.

Fuel Systems

One of the more common problems with outboard boats is water contamination of fuel. Though it is widely attributed to condensation in the fuel tank, very often the source of the water is through the tank vent line due to either improper location of the vent, or poorly designed vent fittings. Frequently these fittings are either chrome plated zinc or plastic that corrode or crack. Or the fitting is mounted wrong, so that the vent channels water into the tank instead of keeping it out.

When looking at a boat for sale, be sure to locate the vent fittings and check them. The vent should be high on the hull side and the opening facing downward *and* aft.

There are solid stainless steel fittings available as replacements for cheap plastic or zinc.

With the advent of direct fuel injection engines, even small amounts of water contamination become very damaging. Most boats are sold with cannister type, spin-on fuel filters. Not only are these things made of aluminum and steel and highly subject to corrosion, they do a poor job of filtering out water and neither can you determine when they need replacement. For these reasons we recommend the use of superior quality filters such as Racor, which have visual sight bowls that collect water in such a way that the condition of the fuel, and the filter, can be seen. While such filters cost several hundred dollars, they are more than worth their cost as you will discover the hard way if you ever have to face the cost of overhauling an injection system.

Bilge Pumps

The vast majority of outboard boats that I see are sold with inadequate bilge pumping capacity. Lower priced boat builders will usually use the smallest, cheapest pump, apparently just to be able to say the boat has a bilge pump. Never mind that the pump is hardly adequate to do the job.

There are two modes of thinking about bilge pumps. One can view the pump as merely the device that removes the water from the bilge that occasionally builds up there. The more experienced boater sees bilge pumps a little differently. To him, a bilge pump is more like a life jacket or fire extinguisher, an item of safety equipment. Because so many small boats sink - at the dock and otherwise - surveyors also see pumps as items of emergency equipment that should not be skimped on.

Things can go wrong with boats that cause the hull to start filling with water, especially small boats which do not require much water to sink them. The experienced boater doesn't merely want adequate bilge pumping capacity, he prefers to have emergency capacity in order to deal with the unexpected. Good quality bilge pumps today are so inexpensive that it's foolish not to have an abundance of pumping power.

Regardless of the size of the boat, it should have a minimum of two. Because pumps are submersible, they have problems with wiring and automatic switches, things that require constant maintenance. It is foolish to expect one pump to always work when you need it. Murphy's law teaches us otherwise: when you need it most, it won't work.

Rule pumps are the most widely used and have proven to be very reliable, even if the wiring isn't. The Rule 1500 pump is a good minimum size. I do not recommend any of the smaller pumps such as the Rule 1000 or 750 because the impellers and drive motors are too small and weak. These pumps can clog and jam up easily with the debris that

Fig. 8-22. This handsome looking hatch is beautifully finished and fitted with a bolted piano hinge. The only problem is that the hatch pull (center) goes right through the core.

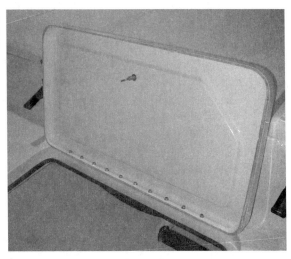

always ends up in bilges. The 1500 has a much more powerful motor and has proved itself over a period of almost thirty years this pump has been produced.

A good installation uses two Rule 1500 pumps set in the same location, one rigged as a primary pump, the other as a back up. The back up is determined by the positioning of the float switch in such a way as that it does not activate the back up pump until water reaches a certain level.

Wire connections are what renders pumps most often inoperable because water gets at the connections and corrodes them at an accelerated rate because the wires are energized with current. Far and away the best method for creating reliable connections is the use of a product called Liquid Electrical Tape for this stuff will seal the connection, whereas shrink wrap and other so-called water proof connectors don't really keep the water out.

And finally, the pump isn't going to work unless the float switch is installed properly and is free of any obstructions that prevent the float from rising and falling. Loose hoses and wires, sludge and debris in bilges are what most often interferes. Switches should always be installed with the flapper facing aft so that water rushing aft when getting up on plane doesn't tear it apart.

Bait Wells

These are a common source of grief because the plumbing and pumping systems are often poorly designed. I could easily devote a long chapter to why these systems often don't work right. The best I can tell you here is to test it before you pay your money and take delivery.

For any well that is below water line, take note of whether the well will pump dry and stay dry, or does it fill back up with sea water? If so, the system is not designed right. Centrifugal pumps will allow water to flow through them, so it may empty the well which then fills right back up again, if you don't have the right pump in the right place. For underwater intakes, you must have a positive displacement pump which prevents water from back flowing through it. Centrifugal pumps are okay for the discharge so long as it is above the water line.

There is one type of bait well pump that should be avoided; this is a plastic pump that threads directly onto a through hull fitting (See figure 18-23 facing page). The reason that this is dangerous is that due to slamming, the plastic pump can shear off, resulting in flooding of the hull. No type of pump or strainer should ever be threaded onto a through hull fitting. These should always be independently mounted and connected with a hose.

Sea Strainers

Any time you're bring water in from outside the hull, a strainer needs to be installed to prevent debris from damaging the pump. A good quality bronze strainer costs several hundred dollars; a cheap plastic one, a few tens of dollars. The difference is that plastic strainers are prone to breakage, and when this happens, they will almost always sink the boat.

Plastic Through Hull Fittings

The vast majority of boats come with plastic through hull fittings above the water line. The problems with these are (1) plastic is a very weak material and, (2) it degrades rapidly from sunlight. This causes them to crack and occasionally sink the boat. The price of bronze hull nipples has come down greatly in recent years so that these are available for around $10. I strongly recommend that you have any plastic fittings replaced with bronze.

Foot Coves

You know what a foot cove is, it's that notch at the base of your kitchen cabinets, the purpose of which is to allow you to stand closer without leaning over and getting a sore back (see figure 8-18). What we call a foot cove on a boat really means that the gunwale extends inward, beyond the side of the cockpit liner, which serves the same purpose. Doesn't it make sense that boats should have them too? But a lot of boats do not have foot coves, thereby making it awkward to stand close to the gunwale without having to lean a bit. Not only that, but some boats have cockpit liners that actually slope inboard, making it doubly difficult.

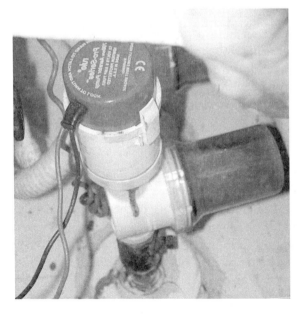

Fig. 18-23. A plastic pump threaded onto a plastic strainer threaded onto a bronze sea cock. All it takes is a light bump against these plastic parts to shear them off and start sinking the boat. These parts should never be installed in this manner.

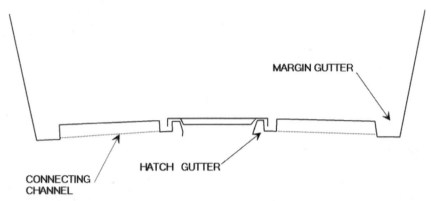

Fig. 8-24. One of the better deck drainage arrangements uses interconnected gutters

You will find that many boats have the foot cove in the aft cockpit but not the forward. The shape of the hull more or less forces this situation because the sides of the hull angle inward. Only by making the side decks much wider and cockpit narrower, is it possible to alleviate this problem in the bow area. This is an issue that fishermen should consider carefully. A boat without even a foot cove in the aft cockpit would not be acceptable to most experienced boatmen.

Deck Drainage

Years ago decks were almost always designed with a crown in them for the obvious reason of causing water to run off more rapidly. I've owned boats where the cockpit deck was flat and actually had low spots in it that would cause water to puddle. Not only was it aggravating, but this would leave big water stains as puddles of water slowly evaporated when the boat was not in use.

Another aggravating problem, as discussed in an earlier chapter, is when the boat trim and flotation is not right and water comes in through the scuppers, causing the deck to be wet all the time. There's nothing like having bottom slime growing on you deck! Well designed boats not only have crowns in decks, but also have a good guttering system to provide complete drainage. At the least there should be a drainage gutter at the margins of the aft cockpit, so that even if trim is not exactly right, or the boat is heavily loaded, back flow from the scuppers will usually be confined to the gutters.

And speaking of gutters, another important consideration is hatch gutters. There are two ways to design hatch openings: design for minimum cost, or designing it right for proper function. A well designed hatch, be it on a weather deck or cockpit deck, or even a seat locker, needs to have a provision for keeping water out. Simply having a cover sitting on a recessed lip not only does not keep water out, but can actually channel water into the opening. A well designed gutter catches this water and safely channels it away. Hatch gutters add significant cost to both design and manufacture, which is why we see so many boats that completely lack gutters.

There are a couple of places where guttering is critically important. First is any hatch that is far aft in the cockpit deck where water can either come in over the transom, or in through the scuppers. If water can flow over the deck and just go down through an unguttered hatch, then you have a risk of the boat sinking; that deck is not truly self-bailing.

Anchor lockers on fore decks also need gutters (Fig. 8-19), though many do not have them. Lacking the gutter, water goes into the rope locker, causing anchor rodes to remain constantly wet. This often ends up rotting out plywood bulkheads, causing severe mildew and rusting anchor chains. The same goes for seat lockers which are usually for storage purposes. Very often I find sodden heaps of equipment stored in these lockers that are ruined because the locker cover design does not keep water out.

Deck Hatches

Well-designed and constructed deck hatches are an important detail, particularly with center console boats that often have many of them. Poorly designed hatches often don't fit right. They may be warped with one side or corner sticking up that can cause a trip hazard. Also, we occasionally find boats which have a crowned (curved) deck, but the hatches are flat panels; this, too, can cause corners to stick up.

Nearly all hatches will have a core to keep them stiff and prevent them from sagging. Even so, at recent boat shows we found many boats with hatches that "give" when stepped on and therefore felt weak. The problem with this is that if a hatch bends when stood on, it is also likely to crack, allowing water into the core and eventual deterioration.

Fig. 8-25. A badly designed console. Note that shift levers are nearly vertically mounted, as is the wheel.

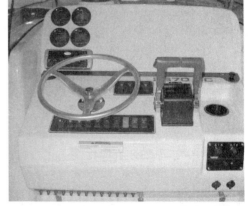

Fig. 8-26. This panel has almost everything right. Controls are near horizontally mounted, start switches at lower right and at least a small space where you can set something down. Note the large, cast aluminum wheel.

Another thing to look for is how the hardware is attached. Hinges should be recessed so you don't trip on them, and should be bolted, not screwed. These fasteners should not go through the core for obvious reasons. The same applies to the hatch pull handles.

On higher quality boats, hatches will usually have a gutter. Gutters always pose drainage problems. In the past, gutters were drained by a series of drain hoses that usually created a problem of getting plugged up with debris. In recent years designers have come up with the solution of molding in interconnected gutter-ways into the deck mold that drain off the hatch perimeter gutters to a gutter or water way that runs down the outer perimeter of the deck. Not only does this work to get water off the deck fast, but works well to keep water out of the hull, and below deck storage compartments dry.

To keep hatches from rattling and making excessive noise, the lip of the gutter should have a soft molding pressed onto the edge. Some are found to have glued-on moldings which you can expect will not stay stuck on once the sun hits it and heats up the glue.

Deck Hardware

It pretty much goes without saying that things like hinges and hatch pulls need to be recessed, otherwise when you drag your bare feet over these things, you end up getting injured. While most designers do this, there are still some that don't, and others that leave hinge barrels sticking up.

Attaching hardware to a fiberglass boat is never an easy proposition. Nothing has changed from the days of wooden boats where one had to prevent water from going through the screw or bolt holes into the wood. We don't have to worry about rotting wood, but we do have to worry about cores and something called crevice corrosion which causes otherwise "stainless" stainless steel to rust and make ugly stains. All hardware must be properly bedded with a bedding compound to prevent this. Any time you see big rust stains on and around stainless hardware, it's almost always due to improper or a lack of bedding.

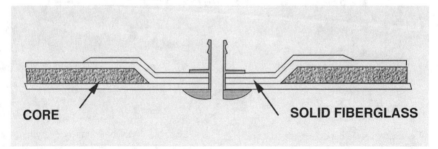

Fig. 8-27. Cross-section view of proper method of installing through hull in a cored hull. The same method can also be used for installing T-tops, towers and other hardware. In this way, no water can get into the core.

It's a fact of boating life that boats take a hard beating even with the most consientious use. Hardware, along with most everything else, needs to be the best of quality. Plastic just doesn't cut it; not only is plastic prone to breakage, but also to ultra violet degradation from the sun. Plastic through hull fittings on the side of the hull are not recommended for what should be very obvious reasons. When they break, these things can sink the boat.

One new invention that has proved to be less than great are pop-up cleats, which are invariably much too small to get decent size lines onto. Cleats on outboard boats tend to run small when it's hard to have a cleat that is too large.

Some builders have resorted to using anodized aluminum railings which, when the anodizing gets scratched, will start to corrode. Never mind that these things bend far too easily. When it comes to railings, what you want is stainless steel.

It's not often that we find plain steel hardware on boats until recently when numerous builders have taken to using pneumatic cylinders on hatches and doors that are steel. Not only do these things rust and fall to pieces in a short time, but make very ugly rust stains that are hard or impossible to remove. If you find these on a new boat that you want, make the sale contingent on replacing them with stainless steel cylinders that are readily available, albeit rather expensive.

Towers & T-Tops

Towers tend to make small boats, particularly outboards, a bit roly-poly. However, this is not always the case; the heavier the boat, the less affect the tower has. Another difficulty is that the boat's structure, usually the side decks, have to be reinforced to carry the extra load, particularly for cored decks. In most cases, the fiberglass work needed to strengthen the side decks is usually not extensive nor particularly costly.

T-Tops are usually fastened to both the center console and the cockpit deck which, because it is cored, needs special design considerations. It is not acceptable to be merely screwed to a cored deck. It should be through bolted with reinforcement built into the deck in place of the core. It is unlikely that you'll be able to see the underside, but you may be able to open a pie port and stick your arm in there and feel around for the method of attachment. Any time you see stress cracks around the tower or T-Top bases, that is cause for suspicion of deeper trouble.

Helm & Console Design

Here's a subject about which most people don't give any thought to, or if they do, the concern is about styling. While no one would deny the importance of styling, good ergonomic design is often over-looked. One can easily judge for oneself by standing at the helm and placing your hands on wheel and controls. Now, consider that you may be operating the boat in this position for hours. Is the wheel comfortably positioned so as not to cause you to hunch over, or unduly extend your arms? What are the prospects for sitting and steering?

While wheel positioning could be claimed to be a matter or personal preference, in a center console boat there is a good argument to be made for horizontal mounting. The reasoning here is that you can place your hands anywhere on the wheel to make tight, slower turns, especially while maneuvering, whereas with a vertical wheel you're limited to the top of the wheel only. This also explains why you often see knuckle-knocker knobs on high end boat wheels. These things facilitate very fast turning of the wheel useful in docking and fishing.

Next, observe the positioning of the engine controls. Very often you will find these set on a 45 degree angle, which causes a bit of a problem. With controls so positioned, to shift to reverse you have to push down; to shift to forward, you have to turn your wrist around, lift and then push forward. This is rather awkward, and certainly not the best positioning. A far better positioning is with the controls mounted on a horizontal surface where all you have to do is push and pull with a single, fluid movement of your arm. No lifting up and pushing down, just forward and reverse, like it should be.

Occasionally we also find that the controls are too close to the wheel, so that on turning the wheel sharply, your hands or arm hits the levers. There should be a comfortable clearance here so that doesn't happen. Nor is it a good idea to mount the various switches on the underside of the panel where one can't see them or read the switch labels.

One of the more aggravating things I find with so many boats, is the utter lack of any place on or around the console on which to set anything down. That may be a piddling complaint, but the fact is that I always seem to have something in my hand that needs to be set down, cell phone, piece of fishing gear, whatever, but short of setting it on the deck, there's no place.

Chapter 9
Used Motors

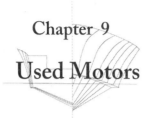

How Many Hours Will It Run?

This discussion concerns high horsepower outboards of 150 hp or greater. How many hours define the life of an outboard engine is probably one of the most common questions asked. My view is that people tend to place too much emphasis on engine hours. After all, an hour meter is just a clock that starts running when the key switch is turned on. They do not measure the amount of time the engine was sitting on the back of a boat in a wet, corrosive environment, nor what happens to that engine.

Meters can also be misleading in that it doesn't have to be that the engine is running; the meter will run if the key is inadvertently left on, so hour meters should not automatically be considered as accurate. Moreover, meters can be replaced. Both meters should read the same or within a few hours. At best, hour meters are an indicator of the amount of time an engine has been run, but it does not account for *how* it has been run or maintained.

Needless to say, the more a boat is used, the more hours one will get from it. A boat that is used very frequently could easily get two to three times the total number of operating hours over a boat that is seldom used. With good care, more use, i.e. higher operating hours, does not necessarily translate into much higher wear, and therefore a shorter future life. When thinking about used engines, think in terms of engine hours and years.

This question would be better framed in terms of what is a reasonable life expectancy of an engine. Obviously, that depends on a lot of factors, such as whether it's used in salt water or fresh, or whether the owner uses his engine(s) wisely, or whether he's the type who likes to run them wide open for long periods of time, or loves making jack-rabbit starts, and so on. It also depends on where the boat has been kept or stored. Was it afloat, in covered dry storage, or on a trailer outdoors? Obviously, engines kept in a sheltered, drier environments are less likely to suffer from atmospheric corrosion damage.

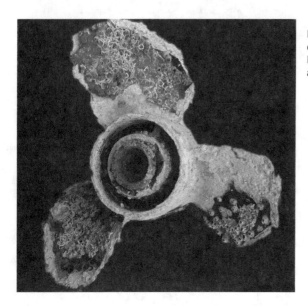

Fig.9-1. This is what a small amount of stray current can do to an outboard motor. Fortunately, its effects are easily identifiable as shown in this photo and on facing page.

Unfortunately, there's no way to answer many of these questions short of performing a thorough engine survey. Sometimes we can get a clue just from observing the general maintenance of the boat itself; if the owner doesn't keep up with general maintenance with the rest of the boat, he's not likely to keep up with the engines either.

Many outboard boats do not have hour meters, so I don't have a good feel for how many hours saltwater engines last. However, I do get a good feel for how many years they continue in service, and this varies greatly by engine manufacturer. It is not uncommon to find Yamaha engines still going strong after ten years or more. Only infrequently do I find other manufacturer products lasting this long. On average, my estimation is that outboard engine life (in saltwater, 12 month seasons) goes about eight years for engines that receive reasonably good care.

You should be aware that lack of use can be quite damaging to any marine engine. The oil that lubricates the internal engine parts and protects them from the very wet marine atmosphere both evaporates over time, and is pulled off them by gravity. Thus, an engine that is allowed to sit for long periods of time is going to suffer from some degree of internal corrosion, especially if kept outdoors. This type of corrosion damage to an engine is cumulative, so that corrosion damage builds up over time. The engine that is run more frequently and regularly will naturally last longer. So it is that an engine that has high hours is more likely to be in better shape than an older engine with very low hours. You can see here that the assumption is that the engine with higher hours attained those hours by means of more frequent use. That may not be the case, as it is possible for hours to be put on in large blocks of time, followed by intervals of long periods of disuse.

As a general rule of thumb, we figure seasonal climate boats get on average 100 hours annual use; in the south with either longer seasons, or all season operation, 150 to 200

Fig. 9-2. Corrosion pitting like this is an almost certain sign of stray current. This kind of pitting will continue even if the source of the current leak is eliminated unless the finish is properly restored.

hours is common. If you divide the total elapsed time on the meters by the age of the engine, this will give you a general idea of the extent of usage though obviously this won't be all-telling. It's entirely possible that the boat was used for an abnormally high number of hours in one year, and not at all in another.

So what are we to make of engine hours? First, if hours are normal for the age of the motor and geographic location, that is generally a good indicator. Secondly, if hours are either abnormally high or low, that is an indicator that a more thorough engine survey should be done.

Checking Out Engines

By their nature, checking out an outboard motor is not as easy as an inboard. I'd like to be able to tell you that it's a simple matter to perform a pre purchase checkout, but it isn't. The lack of a standard internal cooling, exhaust and oiling system means that when internal problems exist, they are harder to diagnose. There are only three things we can do to check out an engine: visual inspection, test operation and compression testing.

Because of the sensitivity of aluminum to corrosion and overheating, these are the two main trouble spots. First, remove the motor cover and check over the power head. If you see a lot of corrosion on both aluminum and steel parts, this probably means that salt spray had been getting inside the cowling. If you see it here, then it's inevitable that the carburetors have been sucking in salt too, so you may want to take a pass on that one, or at least have a compression test done. Check the inside of the carburetor or air intake throttle body; if there is rust and corrosion, it's likely that there is excessive internal wear. The exterior of the power heads should be generally clean and free of corrosion.

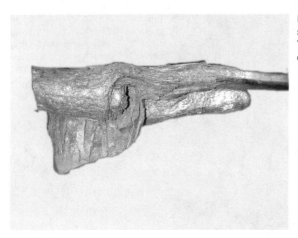

Fig. 9-3. Badly corroded tiller arm and rotator shaft bearing cap can result in steering failure. This can be expensive to repair due to being difficult to remove because of heavy corrosion.

Next, examine the gasket surfaces, such as around the cylinder heads, for signs of wicking, particularly in sea water, over time water will wick through or under gaskets. If you see white deposits or rust along the gasket edges, this is an indicator that there is water migrating through or under the gaskets. This could mean that water is migrating from the cooling jackets into the cylinder. In that case, it is imperative to have a compression test done. If the compression test turns out okay, it will be necessary to have all the gaskets replaced.

Note: if there are very heavy salt deposits along the gasket edges, along with considerable corrosion of metal and flaking of paint, it is very likely that the mating surface of the heads or water jacket covers is eroded and that new gaskets will not seal. In the case where very heavy wicking is obvious, it's best not to buy it.

Overheating often leaves no external signs, but if you see bubbling and blistering of the paint around the cylinder heads, this is certainly an indicator that the engine overheated. Hard cranking with a fully charged battery is another tip off that all is not well.

Failure of oil injection systems and problems related to incorrect oil mixture ratios are not easy to diagnose except by compression testing. While you might think otherwise, engines with low compression usually run smoother at idle speeds, but one sign may be excessive smoking at idle. An engine with good compression and proper oil mix should not billow clouds of smoke. If you are looking at an engine that does, beware.

An even better tip-off is when you have two engines and one smokes while the other doesn't. To test, start and idle each engine separately with the other shut off.

The loss of oiling with engines that depend on a fuel/oil mixture will usually affect the pistons and rings first, long before the bearings are damaged. If bearings become affected, once they receive even minor damage, they will not last long and catastrophic destruction will occur. If you take the boat out and successfully complete a test run, chances are there is no bearing damage. However, ring damage can occur without bearing damage, and this will show up on a compression test.

Above idle speeds the engines should not smoke at all, and if they do, you can be sure that there is a serious problem. Best to take a pass on engines that leave smoke trails while underway. The best way to check is to idle along at around 800 RPM and watch the bubbles coming up in the wake. Remember that outboards exhaust underwater! If you see bubbles rising to the surface with little puffs of smoke, there is a problem.

Check the seal around the base of the motor cover or cowl. It should fit tightly and lock firmly in place. If the gaskets are damaged, or the cover does not lock down without leaving gaps, rest assured that water is going to be getting in there and causing damage.

Check rotator and tilt bearings for wear. Outboards tilt up and down, as well as from side to side. Grab hold of the bottom of the lower unit and rock the engine in the vertical plane, looking for any sign of play in the tilt bearings. With the motor tilted up slightly, now rock the engine horizontally, checking for signs of play in the vertical rotor bearing. If it seems like there's too much play, there probably is.

With Mercury engines, pay special attention to the tiller arms and lower rotator bearing cap. These are cast iron and very prone to severe corrosion damage. Sometimes these things get so badly corroded that the major assembly has to be replaced.

Fig. 9-4. The large throttle body injection module on this Mercury engine at right easily identifies what type of fuel system it is. A direct injection engine is identifiable by the fuel rails on the cylinder heads.

Fuel Injection vs. Carburetor

The main difference between carbureted and fuel injection engines shows up in repair costs and fuel efficiency. Carbureted engines are problematical from the stand point of the fact that engines tilt, causing fuel to run out of them when they are tilted. This can cause an oily mess and hard starting.

On the other hand, fuel injected engines are very sensitive to water contamination and will be shut down by computers or sustain costly damage when water is run through them. Especially the Yamaha HPDI system which has a water sensor that will shut the engine down when water is present. Therefore, these systems need to be equipped with large, high quality filters such as Racor or Dahl.

With a carbureted engine water will work through the carburetor, only causing the engine to run rough so long as the quantity of water isn't excessive, and without causing serious system damage unless the water is present for a long time. Whereas water going through an injection pump and injectors is likely to cause costly damage.

Up until around 1985, all outboard engines required oil to be mixed with the fuel. Then came oil injection systems which injected oil at the base of the carburetors, eliminating the need for the owner to mix the oil and gas. These proved to be effective, but quite messy as oil ran out of carburetors when the engines were tilted.

Types of Fuel Injection

The first and so far most reliable type of injection is the throttle body type using several injectors that inject fuel into a throttle body as well as oil. Throttle body injection places the fuel and oil into the crankcase much as carburetors do. Thus, this did not change the fact that the engines were burning both fuel and oil. One way or another, the crankshaft and pistons have to be lubricated. Throttle body injection is very simple and reliable and is the type found on most cars. It is also inexpensive to repair.

This was soon superceded by direct fuel injection in which fuel is injected directly into the top of each and every cylinder. This does not mix oil and fuel together. Pure gasoline is directly injected into each cylinder. The crankcases remain lubricated by oil injection by reed valves, as are the piston rings and upper cylinders.

The FICHT system uses direct injection plus injection of oil into the crankcase. The Mercury OptiMax EFI and Yamaha HPDI systems are also direct injection. Both these systems bring a vaporized air/oil mixture into the crankcase and into the cylinder, thus the burning of oil is not completely eliminated, but is substantially reduced.

The issue as to which is best is debatable, especially considering the ill-fated OMC FICHT engines. In theory, direct fuel and oil injection is better than running a mix of

Fig. 9-5. The right and left side views of the Mercury OptiMax 225 direct fuel injection two cycle engine. The Injector rails are evident at left of left hand photo and center of right hand photo.

gas and oil through the crankcase. The critical point in all DFI systems is the computer-controlled timing. It relies upon high precision and numerous internal sensors. In theory, because whereas you once had a single system to rely upon, now there are two complex systems controlled by microprocessors. When it works well, it's better; when it fails, the result is not easy to repair and costly. Outboard motors have become incredibly sophisticated and complex, in fact so complex that they can no longer run without computers and can't be repaired without computers.

This also makes ownership of these engines a lot more expensive when something goes wrong. The manufacturers have done their best to stack the deck so that only their own dealers can do repairs, thus attempting to drive out all independent repair shops. Without the manufacturer's diagnostic computers and software, repairs on these engines can't be done. The objection to such sophistication and complication is not merely economic, but also a matter of reliability.

The Yamaha HPDI motors are a good case in point. You won't find many shade tree mechanics able to handle this mass and mess of wires, sensors, hoses and computerized components. These engines use numerous sensors to control the fuel, oiling and ignition systems. The question becomes one of how reliable are these systems and how long will the sensors last? That's important because when sensors go bad, the engine shuts down. Because these are new products, the answer is that we do not know. This is not a problem as long as the two-year limited warranty is in effect, after which you're on your own.

These computerized sensor systems also have another built-in disadvantage to the customer. The computer system records certain sensor system data for later reference. This includes things such as total engine hours, over heating, loss of oil and certain other data which can and is used to deny warranty claims.

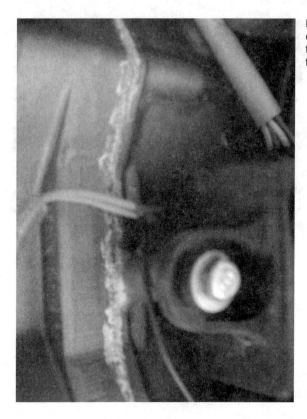

Fig. 9-6. Leaking cylinder head gasket are easy to spot. When they look like this, it's time to replace the gaskets and compression tests should be done.

Adding yet further confusion to the issue, particularly in respect to Mercury, is that the internal data processing units have been changed many times during recent years. While it is possible to have a dealer download the operational history of an EFI engine, different year and model engines do not all have the same data available. If you have access to a dealer, it is probably worthwhile to at least try.

Feedback on Direct Fuel Injection Systems as of October, 2001

Discussions on the Internet forums provide a means of monitoring product satisfaction to a degree that was never available before. We've been studying these forums for over three years now, ever since the introduction of the ill-fated FICHT system. In addition, we personally survey many repair shops of dealerships and marinas. While dealers have, to a man, refused to discuss these issues with us, simple observation of the numbers of engines we see in for repairs is yet another a very good indicator of what is going on. And, of course, our direct experience in our survey business.

OMC

OMC went out of business as of November, 2000. Based on our research, the fundamental problem with their FICHT system was resolved, probably around twelve months prior to their shutting down. Approximately 75% of warranty claims were resolved. While there are many FICHT engines out there that are doing fine, to purchase a boat with these engines will surely be a gamble. Non FICHT engines perform as reliably as they always have.

Mercury

This company had so many problems with its OptiMax engines that it stopped production in early 2001 after large numbers of warranty claims and complaints that the company was unable to resolve. These complaints continue up to the date of this writing. Our assessment: purchasing DFI engines 1999-2001 is a gamble. We continue to find large numbers of very unhappy owners. Unreliability and frequent breakdowns is the major complaint, followed by a seeming inability of the manufacturer to provide a permanent solution. Rapid fouling of spark plugs and the high cost to replace them also ranks high. Those models with throttle body type injection do not have these problems.

Yamaha

While we've been scouring the boating forums and marinas for feedback on how the HPDI system is doing, we've heard very few complaints, and those who did have problems report fast resolution. Moreover, the numbers of engines that we see in for repairs is substantially lower, another good indicator that they are doing well.

Honda Four Cycles

Until summer 2001, the Honda 130 four cycle was the largest available and after two years in service, there are no widespread reports of problems. Larger 200 and 225 HP engines were introduced in late summer 2001 and it is too early to draw any conclusions.

Carbureted Engines

The carbureted engine is cheaper, far easier to repair, but less fuel efficient and, of course, makes a lot of stinky smoke. On the other hand, they have proven reliability. As of spring 2001, there are no more carbureted engines in production due to EPA rules. There were widespread reports of remaining stocks of carbureted engines being bought up by commercial operators, which tells a lot about what knowledgeable people think of EFI engines. In our opinion, the next best choice is throttle body injection.

Inline and V6 outboards require three carburetors simply because fuel cannot be distributed evenly to all cylinders by one carb. Three carburetors, of course, become a bit more difficult to maintain, and because of their internal working parts, tend to have a limited life span, usually somewhere around 4 - 6 years. Corrosion, wear and aging gaskets eventually take their toll.

Carburetors, of course, can be rebuilt by any reasonably well trained mechanic, or just simply dropped off at your local carburetor shop. Not so with EFI; repair of these systems requires a higher degree of training, and that means higher labor costs. If you do have problems with EFI, expect your repair bills to be quite a bit higher. An engine with three carburetors can have a problem with one carburetor, and still run reasonably well off the other two. With an EFI engine, there is only one fuel system which, if it has a problem, the engine stops. This should be a consideration for buying a single engine boat. With a twin engine boat it's less of a consideration because you have a second engine to rely on.

The contrasting good news to all this is that with the coming of large four stroke engines, all of these recent problems with EFI engines may disappear as two cycle engines go the way of wooden buckets. I can only hope that it does, for the complexity and cost of the two cycle engines in my opinion has gone too far for the average boat owner to afford. Four strokes don't need all that complex unhappiness and rely on basic automotive engine technology which is vastly cheaper, more reliable, easily serviced and repaired. They will bring about a return of the independent repair shops, which the dealers surely will not appreciate.

Compression Tests

The compression test is one of the best diagnostic tools for outboards. Since there are no exhaust valves, low compression can only mean that there is either a blown gasket or bad piston rings, most often the later. And if it's got problems with the rings, then you can suspect crankshaft bearing problems also.

Fig. 9-7. Right: This lower unit was welded after apparently sustaining impact damage: It should have been replaced. Fig. 9-7. Below, left: Placing a pencil magnet into oil drain in lower gear case will determine how much wear metal there is. In this case, far too much.

Fig 9-8. Shaft seal oil leaks are usually easily identifiable as in the case shown above.

Fig. 9-9. The propeller shaft seal. A rubber o-ring, it is easily damaged by fishing line wrapped around the shaft.

The top cylinders are the last to get cooling water, so that if the water pump has been damaged it may not push cooling water all the way to the top of the engine. It doesn't take much imagination to see why the top cylinders are usually the first to show signs of low compression. If the bottom cylinders are good, but the top cylinders are off, you can anticipate overheating damage has occurred.

I don't recommend that you perform compression tests yourself unless you are a skilled mechanic. There is always the risk of breaking off or cross-threading sparkplugs in the soft aluminum heads, plus the dangers of igniting fuel vapors and causing an explosion posed by removing spark plug leads. Performing compression tests is best left to a trained specialist. Compression tests are not expensive and it is foolish not to have it done.

Motor Mounts

Yes, outboard engines have motor mounts, but you cannot see them because they're up under the power head. But you can test them by rocking the engine back and forth. Engine mounts can be damaged by abusive operation. The symptoms will appear as the engine power head rocking independently of the mounting bracket and rotator shaft. Tight mounts will not reveal any play to whatever pressure you can physically apply to the powerhead.

Damaged motor mounts can also be diagnosed on sea trials when excessive top end motor movement is observed. If the powerhead and motor cover seems to be shaking too much, most likely the mounts are damaged. Rough idling may also reveal the condition.

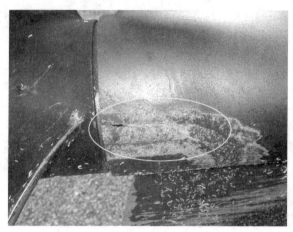

Fig. 9-10. A cracked drive housing, one on which a weld repair was attempted, making for a temporary repair at best.

Lower Unit

Check the lower unit over carefully. Purchasing an engine where the paint finish of the lower unit has been damaged is not a good idea, mainly because once the finish has been breached, the stage has been set for serious corrosion problems. First, look for signs of corrosion and pitting. If you see white corrosion deposits or pitted metal, you'll be buying into a problem that will only get worse without costly remedial measures. Properly recoating aluminum involves a bit more than just slapping paint on it.

The skeg, that fin under the gear housing, is fairly weak and can break off easily. If only a small part is broken off, that won't be much of a problem. If either the entire skeg, or even a small part of the cavitation plate is broken off, this will adversely affect performance, possibly seriously. The gear housing then needs to be replaced. Often the skeg has the paint worn off from being dragged through sand. This is considered normal and will not cause problems.

Check the sacrificial zincs. Are they completely wasted away? If so, this is an indication that the owner hasn't been very diligent about maintenance. If the zincs are eroded but also show bright, shiny metal, this is an indication of stray current (electrolysis). Beware! Costly problems may lie ahead.

Particularly avoid engines where barnacles have been allowed to grow. Barnacles attach themselves with the strongest glue known to mankind. While you can knock the body of the barnacles off, the circular heads or bases will remain. The only way they can be removed is by grinding them off, and when you do that, you damage the finish which then has to be restored.

Raise the motor with the power tilt and check up under the tilt/mount bracket. Check the tilt motor for corrosion; if it's all rusted — as many of them are — you may be

Fig. 9-11. A corroded cylinder head gasket seal between water jacket and combustion chamber. Typically a product of age, it usually occurs on the lowest cylinders in the bank and and will ultimately lead to catastrophic engine damage. This will usually be revealed by a compression test.

looking at a costly replacement. Examine photos in figures 9-1 and 9-2. This is what electrolysis and galvanic corrosion looks like in its various forms. Stray current — as from bad wiring or shorting electrical devices — can be very difficult to locate and correct. In addition, repairing this corrosion damage is time-consuming and costly. Any engine that displays these symptoms is an engine you probably should take a pass on.

With the engine in neutral, spin the propellers. Watch the gap between the propeller hub and the gear housing. The shaft and hub should rotate with no oscillation. If you see any sign of wobbling, chances are the propeller shaft is bent. Now rock the propeller back and forth rapidly. There should be no sign of play and it should not make any clinking or clanking noises.

Now check the lower part of the gear housing to see if there is any oil leaking out of the propeller shaft seal. Shaft seals can leak for two reasons. The first is from a bent shaft. The second cause is picking up fishing line which wraps around the shaft and gets drawn into the shaft seal. Normally, you cannot see this but it will show up either as an external oil leak, or an internal leak of water getting into the oil.

Cracked lower gear case housings can occur from hitting floating objects, or by wrapping objects such as rope around the propeller, which then forces itself between propeller and housing. If the bullet-shaped output shaft housing is cracked, the gear casing must be replaced.

Severe leading edge damage may mean that the housing has sustained an impact that resulted in distortion of the gear casing that could lead to future failure.

Check Lower Unit Oil

To check the lower unit gear oil, you need the correct size slotted screwdriver, a large one. The blade slot should be 1/16" wide; if it's narrower or the screwdriver blade is worn with rounded corners, you may well bugger the slot in the oil drain plug. If the owner is watching you do this, and you cause damage here, he may hold you responsible for it, so be sure you use a relatively new, properly sized screwdriver to open the oil drain plug. It's best to have a square shaft driver and use a pair of vice grips on the shaft to turn the driver.

Do not back the oil plug out all the way. If you pull the plug all the way out, you may not be able to get it back in quickly enough before a lot of oil runs out, so you must do this very carefully. Unscrew it very slowly just up to the point where some oil starts to leak out. Keep pressure on the plug so it doesn't drop out and that you can quickly screw it back in.

As you back the plug out and oil begins to drain, place a small magnet in the oil. Allow about a 1/2 ounce of oil or so to run out over the magnet, then thread the plug back in. First note the condition of the oil; is it clean or dirty? Most oils used today have a bluish color. If it is streaked with black or gray, this indicates high wear metals. Now check the magnet (see figure 9-7). If there are a lot of particles clinging to it, this will confirm excessive wear. If small chips show up, this indicates the beginning of bearing failure.

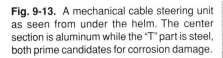
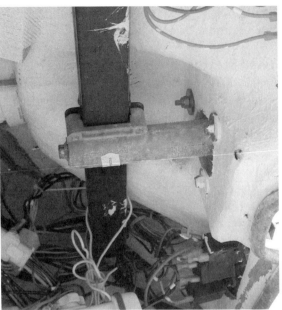

Fig. 9-13. A mechanical cable steering unit as seen from under the helm. The center section is aluminum while the "T" part is steel, both prime candidates for corrosion damage.

When excessive wear metals show up, this mandates a tear down of the lower unit to inspect how much damage exists and to initiate repairs.

Light gray or white streaks in the oil, or if it is generally milky-looking, indicates the presence of water. Water in the oil almost always means that the propeller shaft seal is worn or damaged, often from taking up fishing line around the shaft. Water contamination usually does not mean serious damage, but the unit will have to be dismantled and the seals replaced. At this time, water damage to bearings may be discovered, in which case those will also have to be replaced. This is usually not a deal-killer, but results in either the seller having to repair, or a price adjustment.

Controls

Hydraulic steering systems are usually fairly trouble free. Unfortunately, we can't say the same thing for shift and throttle controls, as many of the plastic jobs supplied with the engines tend to be of rather poor quality. Further, low quality controls have steel cable jackets which, if they get wet will rust and seize up. High quality cables are made of stainless steel.

Test controls ONLY with the engine running, and if they don't function smoothly, chances are that the controls are going to aggravate you for as long as you own the boat. And replacing them is not cheap. If they don't function smoothly, and result in incomplete shifting (the gears clank and fail to engage completely), you may be buying into a problem that's going to cost some money to fix. It may even mean lower gear damage, especially if you've checked the gear oil and found it to be dirty. Before you buy, ask the seller to have it fixed.

Test the steering system by rocking the wheel back and forth while looking back at the engines. You need two people to do this. There should be an immediate response to small wheel inputs with no slack or delays in engine movement. The feel at the wheel should be smooth with no sense of jerkiness. If there is excessive slack in the system, this will be visually and audibly obvious. It should operate smoothly and not make any noise.

Examine hydraulic steering lines and the steering cylinder for evidence of damage to plastic tubing and oil leaks. Locate the hydraulic fluid reservoir and make sure it is full. If it's very low, there's probably a leak somewhere. Look for kinks and any sign of chaffing or small cuts in hydraulic lines. Hydraulic oil evaporates quickly, so work the steering hard and then check for leaks. Be sure to look under the helm at the pump assembly which is under the wheel. This is most often where leaks occur.

Cable steering systems should be easy to turn. If not, then the cable may be corroded and need replacement. Check the steering cable end apparatus where it attaches to the engine; it should be relatively free of corrosion.

Check all the cables, wires and hoses at the point where they enter the engine cowling. Frequently they become pinched and damaged at this point. Be sure that there is enough slack in these items that the engines can turn fully without causing kinking.

Performance Testing

While it's just plain foolish to buy a boat sitting on a trailer in someone's driveway, the fact is that a lot of people buy boats without ever performance testing them. That's because it's a difficult and time-consuming process to launch and rehaul the boat, but this is something that must be done.

Performance testing is simple. Either the engines perform properly or they don't. The only real difficulty is with trying to assess what is wrong when engines don't run the way they should. As mentioned previously, most outboards will not run well at a certain speed range, usually somewhere in the range between 2,000 and 3,000 RPM. In this "dead zone" the engines will exhibit a tendency to either speed up or slow down. This situation is more prevalent with Mercury and OMC than Yamaha for most models that I have tested. This "dead zone" is also more prevalent on heavier than lighter boats, and is directly related to weight and the amount of torque an engine develops at certain speeds. The point where a boat is or has just gotten up on plane places the heaviest loads on an engine.

At all other speeds the engines should run smoothly and steadily. There should be no surging or alternating changes in the engine speed once you try to hold it at a particular speed. But be aware that throttle controls can be another culprit. If the throttle levers themselves fall back, then the throttle itself is the problem and will need correction. You don't want a boat where you have to hold the throttle levers all the time. A properly adjusted control will stay in whatever position it is set to.

If the tachometers are observed to be surging (the speed alternately rising and falling) this is an indication of electrical or fuel system problems. The same applies for any engine that misfires or surges dramatically. For twin engine boats, run the engines up to full speed (only if this can be done safely, and it's best to get the owner to do this). It's a good sign when both engines run up to within +/-100 RPM of each other. If you have a good ear, you should be able to determine if the engines are synchronizing at full speed. Synchronized engines will harmonize. If the boat is too fast to do this at full speed, back off to a more comfortable speed range. Adjust engine speed to the point where the engines are harmonically synchronized. Now check the tachometers. This will tell you how accurate these gauges are since, if the gauges are off by 300, but the engines are synchronized, then you know it's the gauges and not the engines. Now run back up to full speed and by the sound and the tachometers, you can determine if both engines are going up to full speed.

Engine manufacturers will only give you a maximum speed in terms of an RPM range such as 4400 to 4800. That's because maximum RPM is dependent on the boat, its load and type of propeller. In doing a performance test, the best you can do is determine if both engines are reaching the same speed, and that's basically good enough so long as top RPM is close within the specified range.

Rough idling and hard starting is a common problem with outboards, and its cause varies with the type of fuel system. All outboard engines will get fouled sparkplugs as a result of excessive idling. If the engines idle very rough, the thing to do before a test run is pull a plug or two and check; if fouled, clean them before taking a trial run. If the engine(s) still run rough, there's probably a carburetion or ignition problem. For fuel injected engines, the source of the problem is usually similar. Mercury Optimax engines are known to have widespread problems with chronic plug fouling, for which even the manufacturer has trouble with effecting a permanent fix.

Cavitation

The root of this word is *cavity,* as in hole in the water. A propeller can cause what looks like air bubbles but is actually a partial vacuum. The physics of this are complex, but all we really need to know is that cavitation is very harmful to engines and propellers.

Outboard motors, because their angles are easily adjustable, are very much prone to cavitation. As much as I'd like to give you a full description here, this is a subject about which a whole book could be written. Cavitation can be created by a propeller blade itself, without any outside factors, or induced by an outside factor such as a slip stream of bubbles going into the propeller.

Your ability to evaluate performance is going to depend on what you know, and what the owner knows. I often run across owners who haven't the slightest notion of how to trim their boats properly, and so they run around with their propellers cavitating and engines overspeeding. Stand on the shore of a busy body of water on a Sunday afternoon and you can just hear them out there.

Cavitation can be caused by the wrong trim angle of the motor, poor trim of the boat, or both. It can result from a stream of bubbles going into the propeller, damaged, undersized or improperly reconditioned propeller, among other things. Obviously, a propeller is going to turn faster in water that is full of air bubbles than water with no bubbles, which accounts for why these engine overspeeding problems occur. Most times cavitation occurs simply because the boat and motor aren't trimmed properly. However — and this is a BIG however — sometimes the design of the hull, or the mounting of the motors is at fault, resulting in a permanent and uncorrectable cavitation problem. By that I mean uncorrectable via the boat and motor controls.

Cavitation is distinguishable from engine surging relating to electrical or fuel system problems by the suddenness in which it occurs and the higher pitched sound. Surging occurs more slowly and does not involved sudden, high-pitched overspeeding, that whining sound that is so often heard with outboard boats. When cavitation occurs, the tachometers are usually going crazy!

If the cavitation is merely an engine trim problem, it can easily be eliminated by adjusting the engine trim. There are no set rules in how to do this because every boat is different. On single engine boats, achieving the proper trim is fairly easy. For twin engine boats it can be more difficult. The reason for this is that it's hard to get both engines at exactly the same trim, wherein only a few degrees difference (which is hard to detect just by looking at the engines) can throw everything way off. Getting them just right is an experience and skill thing, so if the owner hasn't mastered it, you are going to have a hard time determining whether you're facing a trim problem, or whether you've got a motor installation that induces cavitation.

If you are unable to eliminate cavitation by means of power trim adjustment, it's time to call a professional, for you may be looking at a situation that can be costly to correct. Believe me, it's no fun owning a boat that won't trim out properly and cavitates, particularly considering the damage this can cause to engines. If the owner manages to get it to trim out quickly at various speeds and under various conditions, then you can pretty much accept it as it is. You don't have to be an expert to figure this out; your ears will tell you whether the engines are running as they should or not. If it doesn't sound right to you, chances are it isn't. Look for smooth, steady performance as the key. Anything erratic is a sign that all is not well.

Cavitation is most commonly caused by motors not being mounted right, with the propeller not being set at the proper depth. The cavitation plate - the horizontal plate immediately above the propeller - should be set at a level equal to the bottom of the hull, or slightly lower. It happens more often on deep vee hulls with single engines that the cavitation plate is a bit too high.

It is a fairly rare occurrence, but cavitation, particularly on single engine boats, has been known to interfere with the water flow to the engine cooling system intake at the bottom of the lower unit. This can happen either in association with improper engine height, or something attached to the bottom of the hull, like a depth sounder transducer, which interferes with the water flow, directing a stream of air bubbles at the intake. This can even happen as a result of some peculiarity of the hull design which is almost impossible to diagnose. The easy way to check for this is to simply sight down the length of the hull and make sure that the engine water intake is well below the plane of the hull, and that there are no transducers or other objects attached to the hull bottom that would interfere with water flow. If not, you have cause to suspect a problem.

Boat Performance

Since boat and engine performance go hand in hand, I'll discuss boat performance a bit here. While it doesn't require a naval architect to properly design a small boat, the fact remains that there are far too many boats designed (or copied) by builders who haven't the slightest notion of what they are doing. I'm serious; I've talked to many of these builders and believe me, there are some who don't know anything about hydrodynamics, which is not even a very difficult subject.

Fortunately, the design parameters for outboard boat hulls is very forgiving even of serious design mistakes, so that only the worst of them cause serious problems. These usually involve (1) boat trim and, (2) motor mounting. We've discussed trim in a previous chapter, but just so we're perfectly clear on the subject of trim I will repeat it here. Hull trim relates to the placement of weights in the boat while it is sitting at rest. How it is trimmed in this condition affects how the boat will handle while underway. Motor trim involves only the vertical aspect angles of the motor itself, related to the boat, and always underway. Motor trim is adjustable by whatever controls are provided by the manufacturer.

Notice that as a boat gets up on plane, the trim angle of the boat changes rather substantially. This can cause the propeller to pull air down from the surface and cause momentary cavitation. In most cases, you can trim out (tilting the motor forward), which will change the propeller angle and usually stop this. Then, once you get up to speed, this trim angle is not right and you have to adjust again, because at higher speed the engines again begin to overspeed. This is an indication of a possible boat trim problem, for there should be an ideal setting at which the boat will get up on plane and run without having to trim.

You have probably noticed that a boat running at speed rises up out of the water. The faster it goes, the smaller the amount of hull that is in contact with the water, to the point where at about 30 mph or more only 25% of the hull bottom is actually touching the water. Unless the boat is properly trimmed, meaning balanced, it's not going to ride properly. Too much weight either forward or aft can seriously affect the performance and handling characteristics. With too much weight forward, the bow is going to 'submarine," meaning that the bow will dig in, a condition which can cause a serious loss of control. Too much weight aft and the bow rides too high, resulting in a loss of speed and greatly increased fuel consumption. Both conditions are highly undesirable.

Trim tabs will do nothing to solve the problems of squat during acceleration, a case in which the stern of the boat is too heavy and the bow rises too high. Trim tabs are intended to adjust boat trim (independent of motor trim) at higher planing speeds. The reason is simply that the boat has to be going fast for trim tabs to work, in the same way that an aircraft wing does not induce flight while taxing down the taxiway. If a boat squats heavily on acceleration, this is due to poor boat trim. Boats with bolt on brackets are most prone to this problem.

Ideally, you want to see the boat perform properly at one motor trim setting, and then use the tabs to make minor adjustment at higher speeds. If the owner is knowledge-able, he will already have the engines set at that angle, or make the adjustment as he gets underway. If he has trouble stopping cavitation and overspeeding, you have cause to be worried about poor boat or motor trim.

Porpoising is a condition in which the bow repetitively rises and falls without having anything to do with waves. The name adequately describes the motion involved. It is caused by improper trim of boat, motor or both. There are known instances where nothing anyone can do will stop it, and most often occurs with single engine boats. Be wary of a boat that does this.

Engine Speed, Performance and Propellers

Before you get any ideas about messing around with propellers, there are a few things you should know about outboard props. Outboard props are considerably different than props for all other engine types. This is because of the nature of these low torque engines which have specially designed props that are smaller in diameter, but higher in pitch. The blade area sizes are also smaller; thus these props involve a lot of slippage as compared, say, with an inboard propeller. Pitch is the angle of the propeller blade, and is measured by the amount of travel it creates with one complete revolution as though it were a screw. An 18" pitch prop advances 18 inches with one revolution.

These props are carefully sized by the engine manufacturer to ensure that the engine does not become overloaded. The engines are designed to run at a specified maximum RPM and it is extremely important that at wide open throttle, the engines will run within the specified range. Typically, this will be something like 5400 to 5800 RPM or 5200 to 5700 RPM. It is my recommendation that the top speed should ideally fall at the upper end of the RPM spread, rather than the lower end.

No load RPM, or running the engine at full throttle in neutral, will result in higher engine speeds; cavitation similarly reduces engine load and will also increase RPM.

The reason why this is important has to do with two things: stress and strain on the engine, plus completeness of fuel burn. Overloading an engine, either by means of pushing a boat that is too heavy, or by trying to turn a prop that is too big, can have a disastrous affect on engine life. These small aluminum block engines do not take well to very heavy loads. But not only is stress and strain damaging, but overloading also causes improper fuel burn which results in carbon build up which is also deadly to outboards. Overloading causes a higher fuel to air ratio that in turn results in incomplete combustion that causes the creation of carbon build up. The sure sign of overloading is failure to achieve recommended maximum RPM and carbon buildup as evidenced by frequently fouled spark plugs. Conversely, engines that do turn up within the recommended range, particularly to at least the mid point or higher, is a good sign that all is well.

Matching motors, boats and propellers is a complex issue, one for which there are no quick and easy answers. In fact, if a boat does have a performance problem and does not turn up to the recommended engine speed, don't make the mistake of thinking you can easily solve the problem by simply changing props, particularly with larger, heavier boats. If the engine does not turn up within the recommended range, there is a problem, though whether it's one of engine performance, boat weight or propellers is going to be very difficult and costly to discover.

Used Motors Without a Boat

Inevitably, someone is going to ask, "I'm buying a boat without a motor, so I'm looking around for a used motor.

The right question to ask is why would anyone sell a used motor independent of a boat? The obvious answer is because it is worn out. Equally obvious is the question of how to avoid buying someone's cast off. One reasonable answer is that perhaps the former owner upgraded to larger engines. I'd think twice about purchasing any used EFI engines, as it is very likely that you'd be buying into someone else's problems.

The only reasonable solution would be to have a qualified outboard mechanic evaluate the engine. The problem is how. How can you check out a 500 lb. engine sitting in someone's garage? Or maybe you are looking at one being offered by a dealer. One of those with a 30 day warranty. Thirty days go by awfully fast. If you go to all the trouble of buying it and having it installed, only to turn into a worthless chunk of aluminum, you got a big problem on your hands.

It's a much safer bet to consider a motor offered by a dealer with at least a 30 day warranty. A dealer is very unlikely to involve himself with an engine that he hasn't fully checked out himself.

The only thing you have going for you is that used motors sell pretty cheap. On the other hand, it's becomes very time consuming and costly to have to replace it soon. The best that can be said for buying used engines is that it is a gamble. There are rare occasions when someone decides to upgrade to larger engines, and most often this is done on a trade-in basis with dealers, but generally only on late model engines. Dealers are very unlikely to even consider trades on engines as old as five or six years for obvious reasons. But from a dealer you're going to pay a lot more.

If you are going to go this route, my suggestion would be to consider nothing older than three years, and only non EFI engines. The purchase of used motors from private individuals is a decidedly risky business.

What about reconditioned or so-called remanufactured engines? While there are a few outfits around offering reman engines, these apparently do not sell enough of them to have made any impact in the market, and therefore we've had no feedback on these.

Chapter 10

The New Outboard Motor Market

This chapter covers a general discussion of new outboard motors intended mainly for the novice or first-time boat buyer.

Most people ask questions such as, "What is the best engine for the price?" That is a question no one can really answer, for the only way to know what is best is by means of proof, and proof requires an historical record from which to judge. Therefore, when buying new products, all we really have to go on is a manufacturer's historical record of similar products.

The old saying that it is never a good idea to buy the first of any new type of product is a wise one for those who don't come by their money easily. And when it comes to engines, history proves this to be doubly wise, for new engine introductions historically have not had a good track record. The reason for this is fairly simple: new engines are extraordinarily costly to develop. We're talking near billions here. Not only that, once a new engine is ready to be brought to production, it requires a long period of testing, which manufacturers usually try to cut short. This is what accounts for the fact that so many first issue line of new engines usually do poorly. And when it comes to the changes in emissions standards applied to outboards, this has proved true in spades.

We can only hope that by the time this book goes to press, these problems will be worked out, but as of late 2001 they haven't.

Outboard motors come in size ranges from 1.5 HP up to 275 HP. In the under 150 HP range there are at least a dozen different manufacturers. These break down into two cycle and four cycle engines with a variety of different types of fuel systems. These engines otherwise all operate on the same basic principles and have very similar designs.

Fig. 10-1. Mercury OptiMax engine side and rear views. These direct injection engines are identifiable by the fuel rails above the cylinder heads.

Unlike in decades past, current offerings don't have a lot in the way of optional extras. These engines are sold as complete packages including controls, instruments, power tilt and alternators. The options choices usually consist of type of fuel system (which I'll discuss in greater detail) differing instrument packages, propellers, counter rotation and that's about it. With the larger engines, bigger alternators are sometimes available for boats with higher electrical demands.

My purpose here is to only cover the larger engines since these represent such a sizeable purchase. Above 150 hp, the number of different brands drop substantially up to the 200-250 HP size where there are only two major manufacturers, Mercury and Yamaha. However, in the big block four cycle market we can now add Honda with their very recent introductions of 220 & 225 HP engines .

The lower power size motors have a wide range of varying quality, design and bells and whistles wherein prices are very competitive. It's really not possible for anyone to be familiar with what amounts to hundreds of different models. Therefore the only reasonable basis by which to choose quality is going to be price, based on the theory that the lower the price, the more likely to be lower quality.

The four stroke technology of smaller engines has been perfected and proven so that the worst one has to face with these engines is manufacturing defects and not unproven designs or technology.

The American brands are OMC and Mercury[1] which, except for the EFI & DFI engines, are mainly proven older technology and which offer good value. Mariner and Force are both lower price motors by Brunswick Corporation that compete with the

---

[1] As of this writing, the Johnson and Evinrude brands have been purchased by Bomardier and continue to market engines under the original trade names. Owing to recentness of the acquisition, little is known about these products at this time.

rest of the field dominated by the Japanese companies such as Yamaha, Suzuki, Nissan, and Tohatsu. Suzuki engines, as near as I can tell, are identical to Yamaha and appear to be older Yamaha engines with different decals on the shrouds.

Choice and No Choice

In recent years many boat builders have adopted a tactic in which they offer their boats already rigged with a particular brand of motor, thereby leaving the buyer with no choice of engines. In many cases the purchase of a boat is a take-it-or-leave-it proposition because the dealer will not sell the boat without engines, or with another brand. It doesn't take much insight to see that boat buyers don't much appreciate having these choices taken away from them.

Some few builders offer the options, but make it difficult and more costly to chose those options. When going to a dealer, what we often find is that all the models they have in stock are prefitted with their preferred brand, and that to obtain the boat with our choice means a special order and a long wait. No dealer is going to want to take a prerigged boat and change motors because of a high amount of labor involved and all the mounting fastener holes that are left by installing different equipment. The dealers that offer choices in motors seem to be mostly higher priced, higher end boats.

The market seems to take on this generalization: Lower priced boats are usually fitted with Mercury engines, higher end boats, Yamaha. At the Ft. Lauderdale show in 2001, we did not see any boats with Evinrude or Johnson.

Engine Market Turmoil

At the time of this writing the outboard motor industry is in a state of serious turmoil due to EPA standards for emission requirements for 2002 and 2006. When I first started this book there were three major engine manufacturers; today there are only two. And with the advent of larger four cycle engines soon to hit the market, the market will become yet more confusing.

To fully understand what is happening in this industry requires a lengthy explanation which any buyer who wishes to be informed should know about. If you don't want to get into this level of detail, the best advice would be don't buy a DFI engine now. Or, if you do, be prepared for trouble. The exception to this are Yamaha HPDI engines that were introduced much later than OptiMax and FICHT, and appears to have been perfected before being unleashed on the boating public.

How Government Rules Design Products

Outboard motors are unlike automotive engines in that they do not have crankcases filled with lubricating oil. Until very recently, much like chain saws, outboard motors ran on a mixture of gas and oil. Instead of having an intake manifold, outboards have the carburetors mounted on what would be the bottom side of your car engine's oil pan. Sounds weird, but here's how it works.

There is a passage from the side of the cylinder wall which, when the piston is on its intake (and exhaust) stroke, sucks the vaporized oil/gas mixture through the crankcase and up into the opening cylinder. Instead of having Babbit slip bearings on the crankshaft journals, outboards have caged, open roller bearings so that the vaporized oil/gas both cools and lubricates them. The fuel flow into the combustion chambers is controlled by reed valves in the crankcase.

Two cycle engines therefore end up burning both oil and gas. But that is not what causes all the smoke and stink. Two cycle outboards do not have exhaust and intake valves as four cycle engines do. What causes most of the smoke and stink is the fact that the cylinders are exhausting and sucking in new fuel and air at the same time through what are called scavenging ports in the side of the cylinder. This results in as much as 30% of the fuel escaping out the exhaust side, and is what ultimately got the EPA on their case to do something about outboard emissions. This is also the reason why outboard engines are not fuel efficient and have been called gas hogs.

Imagine, for every 100 gallons of gas put in the tank, the old two cycle engine dumped 30 gallons overboard! With somewhere around 15 million outboards around, that amounted to hundreds of millions of gallons of gas dumped into the environment. Even the most uncaring polluters had a hard time arguing with the demand for changes. Engine manufacturers were given eight years until 2006 to reduce engine emissions by 75% in stages beginning in 1998. Hence the mad rush to meet the deadlines and the baffling array of design changes.

However, most manufacturers were not content to do it in stages, as this would be too costly. Instead, they seem to have attempted to come up with new designs that would meet the final, 2006 requirements. That makes sense, except that in retrospect it seems they didn't have enough time to get it right the first time, and there have been big problems.

Direct Fuel Injection

(DFI) is a two cycle engine system that injects the fuel individually into each cylinder at exactly the right time so that no fuel escapes through the exhaust ports. With direct fuel injection, the fuel is not run through the crankcase with the oil, and thus it cannot escape on the intake stroke. However, the cylinder still has to get a charge of fresh air, which it still does through the throttle body on the crankcase, and where it is mixed with lubricating oil.

The problem that comes with this new arrangement stems from the fact that the engines not only require new fuel systems, but also that fuel injection timing becomes so critical that a computer is needed to control it. Not only that, but many new systems and parts are required. And between the three major outboard manufacturers, it should probably come as no surprise that all three came up with different solutions, each claiming to be the best.

The genuine advantage of DFI systems is that the 20-35% of unburned fuel that went out the exhaust is substantially reduced. Better yet, DFI yields an altogether more efficient fuel burn so that fuel consumption rates are conservatively reduced 30-40% That's the good news.

The bad news is that these systems appear to have been brought on the market before they have been perfected. And also that these systems resulted in a substantial increase in engine complexity, thereby negating the original simplicity and reliability of the two cycle engine. These engines are now so complex that many dealer shops have yet to find enough adequately trained technicians. The computerization has meant that only dealers with manufacturer-supplied diagnostic computers and software can work on these engines, thereby putting many of the independent shops out of business. The days of the shade tree mechanic appear to be gone. But wait! There are more changes in the works and more on that in a moment.

Mercury DFI engines have quickly developed a reputation for severe spark plug fouling problems, something that we would have thought the electronic system would have eliminated. To make matters worse, replacement spark plugs for these engines are reported to cost as much as $25 each!

There is yet another type of fuel injection called EFI (electronic fuel injection) which is the same type as found on most cars. This is known as throttle body injection and uses a single injector to atomize fuel into a throttle body. (A V-6 engine will have three of them.) It is very simple, cheap and reliable, more so than a carburetor. This type does not, however, meet the final EPA 2006 standard, so its days are numbered.

Contrary to popular belief, OMC's Ficht system is not what brought that company down. What finally finished off OMC was incredibly bad management. By most accounts, the Ficht engineering remains very promising, but needs to be perfected. Whether it ever is or not remains to be seen.

In terms of reliability, the Mercury OptiMax system hasn't fared much better. Problems and complaints abound. So much so that in May 2001, Mercury announced that it stopped shipping its 200 and 225 HP OptiMax engines until they get the problems straightened out. Therefore, if you're looking for new engines of this size with proven reliability, you really have little choice but to look to Yamaha except for the few possible dealers remaining with older stock. If you're looking to buy used, it's probably a good idea to stay away from 1999-2001 engines.

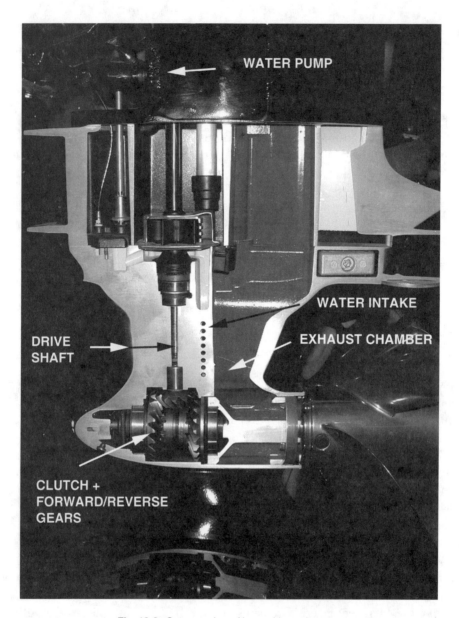

Fig. 10-2. Cutaway view of lower drive unit.

Yamaha uses a slightly different DFI system in that it injects fuel into the engine cylinders under very high pressure (700 psi), what they call HPDI (high pressure, direct injection). This helps in overcoming the critical timing problem, although it still relies on a computer and numerous sensors to read engine conditions and adjust fuel injection rates and timing. And although the Yamaha HPDI engines have been out for a much shorter time than Mercury OptiMax, there have been far fewer problems reported.

It should probably come as no surprise that dealers report that commercial engine users are going around buying up all the carbureted Yamaha engines they can get, as this is the last year they will be available.

The Rise of the Four Strokes

All of the engines in our cars are four stroke engines. The four stroke engine can also use all types of fuel devices and all use intake and exhaust valves and manifolds in the cylinder heads. Unlike two strokes, they do not have intake ports in the sides of the cylinders. The intake stroke sucks fuel and fresh air into the cylinder through intake valves and a manifold. The valves close, the piston rises, compresses the fuel/air mixture, the spark plug fires and the fuel ignites. The piston is forced down under the effect of the resulting explosion. As the piston goes down and back up again, the exhaust valve opens and the piston forces the exhaust by-products out into the exhaust manifold. Thus, the piston goes up and down two times, or in other words makes two complete revolutions, to complete a full cycle and is therefore called a four stroke engine.

Because the exhaust stroke is not a power stroke, there is a lot of friction and drag involved on the exhausting stroke because no power is generated. Whereas a two stroke fires once every up and down cycle, the two stroke develops more power cubic inch for cubic inch of engine displacement than a four stroke. But four strokes do not have the pollution problems that a two stroke does and will run even cleaner than a DFI two stroke. They are also more fuel efficient by up to 50%.

As of this writing, the largest four stroke is the Honda 130.[2] Virtually all of the outboard manufacturers have put the word out that they are developing 200 and 225 HP engines.

Four stroke engines have these advantages:

1. Four cycle engines closely resemble automotive engines, much as inboard engine boats do. They can use many of the same components as car engines. This presents a potentially tremendous boon to lowering both initial costs and repair costs.

2. There will be more trained mechanics available. This is a major problem because of the short season which renders the craft of being an outboard mechanic not very attractive due to less than full-time employment. This has a tremendous bearing on the caliber of mechanics currently available in many parts of the country.

[2] By the time this book goes to press, both Yamaha and Honda will likely have 200 and 225 HP four strokes on the market.

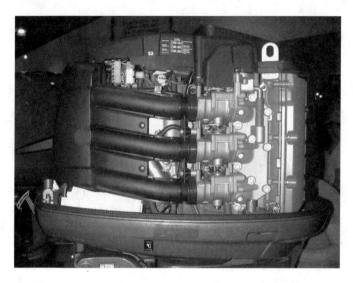

Fig. 10-3. Side view, Yamaha four stroke 225. Note how air induction ports are on outside of cylinder heads, making it very unlike a car engine.

3. Four strokes are less prone to catastrophic overheating, which translates to improved reliability.

4. Less prone to damaging carbon build up due to prolonged low speed idling. No need for expensive oil and fuel additives.

5. Vastly reduced noise levels. A four stroke engine makes roughly 1/5th the noise level as a two cycle engine.

6. Elimination or at least great reduction of the problem of prolonged low idle carbon build up. All things being equal, this should lead to greater reliability and longer engine life.

The following are some possible negatives:

1. More working parts leads to higher costs.

2. Possible sensitivity of exhaust valves to corrosion.

3. Belt driven cam shafts: If belt breaks, pistons will collide with exhaust valves, leading to catastrophic failure. Serpentine belts must be maintained in top condition.

4. Oil & filter changes required.

Fig. 10-4. Cutaway view of Yamaha 225 four stroke, rear view showing cams and valve train.

Is the four cycle engine perfected yet? From what I can glean so far, the answer is that they are very close to perfected, if not already so. There may be a few glitches, but certainly nothing like the FICHT and DFI fiascoes.

Are these engines just car engines mounted on a drive unit? Yes and no. The basic engine designs are car engines, but the Honda engines that I have examined are completely redesigned for their specific purpose. They're not, as some have claimed, just a quickie effort to turn a car engine into an outboard. Far from it. For one thing, a major problem with crankcase lubrication had to be solved because the engine stands on end. The second is weight, and a third, size. These facts also meant a major reengineering job of lubrication of the valve train. The engine blocks, while similar to the car engine, has significant differences.

The major problem that stood in the way of development of higher power four strokes is size and weight. Weight is very important from the standpoint that engines are mounted on the stern of the boat (and sometimes on brackets, several feet aft of the stern) and greatly affect trim. These engines can be significantly heavier because they have more parts, more metal and heavier metals, iron and steel versus aluminum.[3] Once these problems are solved, it is likely that four cycle engines will eventually overtake the outboard motor market.

---

[3] Weight of Yamaha 225 two stroke, 493 lbs. Target weight of Yamaha 225 four stroke, 583 lbs., 90 lbs. heavier per engine. With a total difference of 180 lbs. for a twin engine installation, this much additional weight will seriously affect trim in some cases.

Fig.10-5. The Honda 225 four strike. Note oil filter at right, fuel filter lower center. General servicing on this engine is pretty easy.

What are the down sides of four stroke engines? Some people will see more sluggish acceleration as a serious negative, especially those who like to jam the throttles forward for jack-rabbit starts. This is a terrible thing to do with an outboard motor in any case because of the terrible load placed on the entire system. For most people, this will not be a significant consideration. As with your car, and all other types of boat owners, you will have to do oil and filter changes.

Will Two Stroke Engines Become Extinct?

While the future is notoriously hard to predict, there are a number of factors to suggest that four strokes will catch on rapidly and bring about the demise of the production of two cycle engines. First and foremost is that the manufacturers may not be able to afford to offer both types simultaneously. To do so, effectively doubles their costs and halves the total market available to each type. For this reason alone, I would expect over the next five years, to at least see the beginning of the phase out of two cycles. Mercury will be the last to introduce a large four cycle engine, and a scenario could develop in which Mercury is the lone hold out for two cycles, though I doubt it.

Public acceptance of four strokes has been enthusiastic to say the least. While hot-rodder types may love the roar of their two cycle rods, most will come to appreciate the quietness of the four stroke. As for reliability two stroke versus four stroke, it is going to take at least a decade before we can answer that question decisively, though I fully expect the four stroke to prove more reliable.

How will that affect current two stroke owners? For most, very little because up until the introduction of DFI, most EFI and carbureted outboards were considered reasonably reliable, although somewhat cantankerous. DFI engine blocks are not the same as EFI and Carbureted engine blocks (which are the same). If the lines of DFI engines end up getting dropped, as in the case of Mercury this is very likely, then replacement parts for these engines could become a serious problem say eight to ten years from now.

Mercury -vs- Yamaha

While I'm as patriotic as anyone, and would love to promote Buy American First, the fact is that nearly all experts agree that Yamaha makes a superior product. Putting the two products side-by-side, the differences are starkly clear. The detailing and workmanship of the Yamaha products is obviously superior. On recent surveys, I found a multitude of faults with a pair of Mercury Optimax 225, 1999 vintage, then less than two years old:

- · Cylinder head water jacket gaskets were leaking.
- · One engine suffered a gear case failure.
- · It took two men fifteen minutes to remove two ill-fitting motor covers.   ·
- · Engine air intake through covers was drawing salt spray into engine on which steel parts were rusty and corroded.
- · Fiberglass cover was vibrating against engine block, creating fiberglass dust that was being drawn into engine air intake.

A similar survey of several pair of 1998 Yamaha 225's turned up no such problems, and despite being a year older, the power heads had no corrosion on them.

The engine control systems constitute another important consideration. Many of them are made of plastic, are poorly engineered and do not function smoothly, or are prone to wearing out rapidly. It is hard to appreciate just how annoying poorly functioning controls can be until you've had to live with them. The Yamaha, Honda and Suzuki controls are consistently among the best I have tested.

Granted, Yamaha engines can be 15-20% more expensive, but for those who demand quality and reliability the choice could not be more clear. And if you think Yamaha is good, wait until you see the new Honda four strokes; they're even better; they are almost as nicely detailed as race car engines.

Saltwater Designations

Yamaha, Mercury and previously OMC, offered what was euphemistically labeled "saltwater" engines, only with the 150 hp on up engines. This raises the question of whether engines not so labeled are only for fresh water. The manufacturer advertising is completely silent on the subject.

The only difference we can find in the Yamaha is the stainless steel propeller shaft, shifting gear and, for 2001, the cast iron steering or tiller arms that have always been such a rust problem. Plus, they use more water resistant connectors on the wiring. The basic aluminum alloy and the coating system are the same for the non saltwater designations.

For the Mercury engines, we do not see any significant differences and neither does their advertising spell out what they may be. On checking pricing differences between engines labeled saltwater and those not so labeled, price differences seem to be around $150-$200, so whatever the difference is, it can't be much.

Can Boats Get Too Big and Heavy for Outboards?

The answer here is definitely yes. A recent survey of a 29 footer weighing some 9,000 lbs. proved to be a rather slow and very sluggish boat, topping out a 30 knots and not being able to plane until at least 4000 RPM. At which point both 225HP engines had the fuel flow meters pegged at an enormous 24 gph. Any boat that takes 80% of full power just to get up on plane has something wrong with it, and in this case the boat was simply too big and heavy.

When considering boats this big and heavy, it is important to consider these issues and be sure to do a sea trial before signing on the dotted line.

How Fast Do You Want to Go?

Speed is a great thing, but with boats it always comes with a big cost penalty. The bigger and heavier the boat, the more power it takes to drive it. And if you want to go at speeds well above the norm, you can anticipate that the costs are going to be very high for larger boats.

For boats that weigh under 4,000 pounds, or boats under 22 feet, speed and selection of the right power is rarely a problem. That's because the average size outboard motor, say 150 hp, will push any of these boats at respectable speeds. Okay, so what does "respectable" mean? Well, 35 mph is a good minimum top speed for these boats. If you're the kind of person who thinks 50+ is a good speed, then you are beyond the realm of "ordinary" boats; you are a speed freak!

Outboards begin to run into trouble as boat sizes approach 28 feet and exceed 6,000 pounds and the reason why is the horsepower to weight ratio. Now we're talking about big block outboards in the 200 hp plus range. Keep in mind that all boat hulls are not created equal. Basic hull designs can be more or less efficient; Deeper vee hulls are less efficient than flatter bottomed hulls; one boat may have more windage than another. Outboard engines are lower torque, plus they are almost always rated at the top engine RPM, which is not where we're going to run them all the time, if we're smart, or do not have money to burn.

What we want to be careful of is to not pay too much attention to top speed, but more attention to what her *cruising speed* is or will be. Most well-balanced power to boat weight set ups have a sizable excess of power; that is, the boats will go considerably faster than desired. With outboards, this is not only not a bad thing, but usually a necessity because the main thing we're interested in is having a good cruising speed somewhere below 75% of full power. Thus, if we have a top speed of 45 mph at 5500 rpm, we would like to see a cruising rpm of 4000 rpm or less. And if that proves to be somewhere around 35 mph, that is definitely a respectable speed that should offer reasonably good fuel economy.

Moreover, it is most beneficial to have the broadest possible cruising/planing speed range. The wider the cruising speed range is, the greater is the opportunity to choose a more efficient speed. Let's say we have a boat that gives us the speeds mentioned above. It tops out at 45, but will plane all the way down to 2500 rpm at 16 mph and 18 gph. At our normal cruise of 4000 rpm and 35 mph, we're burning 28 gph and at 5500 rpm 48 gph. Here we have a very wide range of potential cruising speeds. Any boat/motor combination that sports a range like that is a well-balanced combination.

Now compare these numbers with another boat, bigger and heavier but same engines, that tops out at 40 mph, cruises at 32 mph at 4500, but will only do a minimum speed of 22 mph because, due to the weight of the boat, the engines will not hold that low speed. Numbers like this are the mark of an under powered, or inefficient boat because it takes too much of maximum power to bring her up to desirable speed. And when we get there, we're going to find that fuel consumptions are much higher across the board.

People often wonder why there aren't horsepower/speed tables that can be used to predict speeds with various power combinations. There are such tables, but because there are so many variables involved, in the hands of an amateur these tables won't prove to be very accurate. To get some accuracy, we have to account for many variables, such as fuel, fresh or salt water, windage, equipment and passengers. One final monkey in the gears can be propeller size.

Boat owners should not fool around with prop size, as these propellers are carefully mated to the engine power output. Unlike all other engine types, only outboard motors come with propellers on the engines, and with good reason. First, the lower units don't afford much increase in diameter. Secondly, due to the lower units being made of relatively weak aluminum, the gear casings can only withstand so much force. Changing to a larger diameter or higher pitch prop will *increase* the loads on these parts and likely lead to premature failures. Thirdly, the engines themselves need to run at certain speeds under certain loads. When an outboard engine becomes overloaded, it is highly prone to carboning up, a condition that can be disastrous to the engine. Ergo, engine manufacturers supply you with the propeller that they want you to use. And beware that if you change prop size beyond the recommended, you may end up voiding your warranty.

Taking the Dealer's Advice

Here's a case where it's usually wise to rely on the dealer to suggest which engines are best suited for a particular boat. The fact is that the dealer is likely to have the most experience with different power engines, and is likely to know which ones are best in terms of giving you adequate power. And the adequately powered boat is always going to go at least a bit faster than most people need or want.

If you have doubts about what a salesman is telling you, ask the service manager as he is likely to have more direct experience in these matters.

One caveat here: if you intend to add a tower, or carry heavier than normal loads, you should be sure to tell the dealer that. A typical example is a guy who loves scuba diving. He plans to frequently take out 4-5 friends for dive trips, plus he wants a small tower on the boat, unaware that tower, people and tanks add another 1,900 lbs. to his boat (people, 900 lbs.; tower, 400 lbs.; scuba equipment, 600 lbs.). His 6,000 lb. boat, with another 300 gallons of gas at 1830 lbs., now weighs 9,730 lbs. or nearly 60% heavier than a new, empty boat. Clearly, that boat is going to do nowhere near the same speed as the average boat with typical engines. Like it or not, that fellow is going to have to take a step up in engine power and face higher fuel bills.

Towers don't just add weight, they also add windage, as do T-tops. Typically, these can cut 3-4 knots from speed depending on wind conditions.

Cruising Speed as Horse Power Decision Benchmark

One way to approach engine power selection is to pick, not the top speed you want but a cruising speed, this being the speed at which you'll most often operate the boat.

One key to fuel economy and engine longevity is running an engine at lower RPMs. Two cycle outboards typically turn up to about 5500 RPM. A good cruising RPM is between 3500 and 4000, lower if you can manage that. Obviously, it's going to take a certain amount of horsepower to push a boat at those speeds.

One way to judge is to find the minimum efficient planing speed. That is the speed at which the hull gets up on step, levels out and will maintain that speed. One thing about outboards is that, due to their low torque, these engines often will not hold to lower speeds. You may notice that the RPMs will start to drop off and you keep having to add more power. The minimum efficient planing speed is also the lowest speed at which the engine will sustain a constant RPM. The lower the minimum efficient planing speed RPM is, the better the match between boat and motor. If that speed is 4000 RPM, that is not very good, for it takes 80% of full power just to maintain a rather slow speed. 3000 RPM is common for larger, heavier boats, while small, lighter boats should easily plane out at 2500 RPM.

Why is this important? First because it is an indicator of how well the horsepower is matched to the boat. Secondly, it gives you a wide range of cruising speed choices, which translates to a wider range of fuel consumption rates.

Typically, dealers try to sell you larger rather than smaller engines, so with a new boat, it is unlikely you'll be sold short. But you can use the recommended cruising speed as a bench mark to determine if you do have a good match. Then get that boat out on the water and test it out for yourself.

Builders are required by law to post the maximum horsepower that the boat is designed to carry. Many buyers simply go for the maximum rating, which is often a waste of power and money, for very high speeds are rarely usable except on protected waters. Check this first and determine if you really want or need to carry the max.

Warranties

Up to the time when they started using computers to record engine history, warranty service by Mercury and Yamaha was quite good. I'm referring here to the corporate policy of the companies themselves. Dealer service quality and customer satisfaction is another story.

Since the beginning of pleasure boating, the quality and service of boat dealers has always been a problem. You are making a big mistake if you think you can place the same level of confidence in a boat dealer as people normally do with car dealers. This is apples and oranges, night and day. This is not true of all dealers, of course, but is true of far too many of them. Many have good intentions but are unable to deliver, while others don't have good intentions at all.

Unfortunately, warranty service is often as dependent on a dealer's relationship with the manufacturer, as it is on the customer's relationship with the dealer. The unfortunate part is that we have no way of knowing the former except by the general reputation of the dealership itself.

Whomever you choose, in the north it's not wise to expect fast service in the spring when they are busiest.

Surviving, yet alone making a profit in the boat dealership business is a tough, tough thing. When you consider prices, you'll probably have a hard time understanding this. But consider that for most, it's a seasonal business that is vulnerable to recessions. Unlike the auto business, dealership loyalty between manufacturers and dealers is rather like the relationship between dogs and cats; neither has much respect for the other. That's why we see such an amazing game of musical chairs amongst the lines carried by dealers. Road side signs seem to change annually. Needless to say, the customer is the ultimate looser in this never-ending battle between dealers and manufacturers.

This is why I keep stressing how important it is to try to find a dealer that has a good reputation. Sometimes that is a tough prospect when you discover that the particular boat you want is only carried by someone whom you're heard bad things about. However, when it comes to engines, you are not obliged to return to the dealer from whom you bought the boat. Warranty work will be handled by any authorized dealer, and this fact may give you some better choices.

For more information on this subject, please see the chapter on Rigging.

What About Extended Warranties?

Understand this: Extended warranties are not warranties. By the laws of most states they are classified as mechanical breakdown insurance policies, regardless of whether issued by the manufacturer or an independent insurer.

I have personally studied the policies of both Yamaha and Mercury and can say that both are very good. There is very little that is not covered, and there are few fine print loop-holes.

Though rather expensive, you are definitely getting good value for your money. If you cannot afford to write big checks for expensive repairs, the purchase of an "extended warranty" is a good idea. My advice is to seek out manufacturer issued polices rather than after market policies, for at least you know the reputation of the issuing company. Most after market policies are from companies we've never heard of, and thus have no way of knowing who they are or what to expect from them.

One word of caution: Do not purchase extended warranties without reading the contract first. Get a copy and read it before you buy.

Shopping on the Internet

Is it possible to shop for new engines on the web as it is with so many other products? The answer to that is emphatically "no."[4] We have checked hundreds of dealer web sites and have yet to ever find any pricing on new engines. It would appear that dealer/manufacturer contracts prohibit this.

---

[4] As of November, 01 we did not find any large block engine prices published on the Internet. This, however, could change over time.

Chapter 11

Boat Rigging

Now that there are so many boat builders that are selling boats pre rigged at the factory, many of the problems we've had in the past with bad installations made by dealers has been greatly reduced, if not eliminated. Even so, I still recommend that you check over the installation carefully.

While this chapter applies primarily to new boats, it can also be used as a guide for evaluating engine installation on used boats.

Horsepower Ratings

By law, boat builders are required to affix to their boats a rating decal which indicates the maximum horsepower the boat is designed to handle. Exceeding this limit will probably void the warranty and may lead to hull or transom failure. (Fig. 11-1)

Steering Systems

It is important to have a good quality steering system simply because the system needs to be strong and durable enough to turn the heavy motors that steer the boat. The helm, or steering wheel, is also the thing you hang onto while the boat is bashing into the waves. With small runabouts, you will likely have no choice of steering systems and have to take whatever the boat is rigged with. Thus you may end up rejecting a boat based solely on the fact that you don't like the steering. One option would be to have the dealer install a better system at additional cost. Otherwise, you have to live with something you don't like. A steering system also needs to be highly corrosion resistant because it is always getting wet. They come in two basic types, mechanical and hydraulic.

Mechanical systems utilize a simple rack and pinion operating a push-pull cable inside a plastic coated, steel jacketed sleeve. The obvious weakness of these systems is that

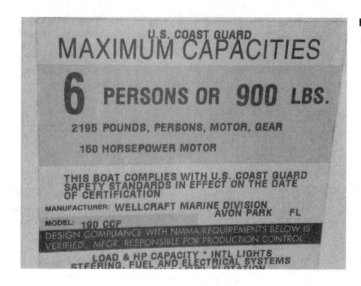

word "steel," which means that the cable can rust and seize up. I don't recommend these systems for saltwater use, but they're generally okay for smaller boats in fresh water. These systems are rarely found anymore. This type is most often found on small runabouts.

Hydraulic systems are by far the best type to have, although there are numerous manufacturers putting out a wide range of differing quality systems. Teleflex, for example makes systems ranging from very good to poor. Hynautic has an excellent reputation for making high quality systems that are basically the industry standard for larger boats. Sea Star, Wagner, Capillano are other makers of good quality systems. Hynautic is generally regarded as the best, and it's the one I'd recommend for outboards.

In some cases you will be able to choose your steering system, and it is recommended that you choose a top of the line system. You should get a brochure from the manufacturer you have selected. This info is usually available on the Internet, at boat shows or from parts dealers. Pay attention to the number of turns that the wheel will take "lock-to-lock." I recommend not more than three full turns, meaning 1-1/2 turns of the wheel in each direction.

You will probably be most comfortable with a wheel size of 14" to 16" diameter. However, wheel size is totally dependent on how it is mounted. Horizontal mounts, which is the way I prefer, definitely poses limitations on wheel size unless a boat has been specifically designed to carry a larger wheel, which some center console boats are.

Very small, "racy" looking wheels have become popular and are common on small runabouts. How comfortable it is for you is going to depend on your physical size and

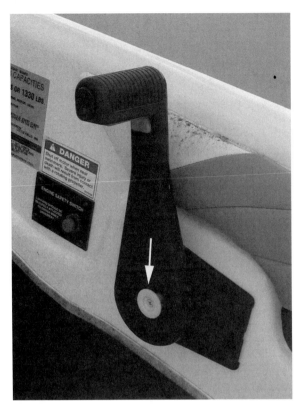

Fig.11-2. Plastic engine controls less than a year old, the neutral idle button has already broken and fallen off. This type of control is basically a piece of plastic junk that is almost guaranteed to malfunction. It's a perfect candidate for upgrading.

length of your arms, so check it out. As I noted in the Ergonomics chapter, stand at the helm and be sure it's set up comfortably. You should not have to hunch over to hold the wheel. If you do, operating the boat for any length of time is likely to give you a sore back.

Be wary of very small wheels; the smaller diameter affords you less leverage and therefore makes the steering harder, particularly on long trips. Avoid padded wheels and especially those foam covered wheels that absorb water; they will keep your hands wet and waterlogged. I would also suggest that you avoid those fancy race car wheels; they may look good but often aren't very practical.

Also pay attention to whether you are going to be steering with your feet, as many people, including myself, do on center console type boats on longer trips. You get rather tired standing up after an hour, so sitting back and steering with your feet is a very common method. Obviously, if you don't have the right kind of spoked wheel, you can't do this. It's hard to go wrong with the plain old spoked, stainless steel wheel. This is another reason why it's important to pay attention to the steering radius.

The deep, dished, aluminum alloy "Rybovich" style wheel made by Edson are becoming very popular, and are often seen with knuckle knocker knobs.

What about power steering? Power steering is not available for outboards, and don't need it. This comes only with stern drive boats which are naturally harder to turn. If you find an outboard system that is hard to turn, chances are something is wrong with it, and it needs adjustment or repair. The typical hydraulic system is very easy to turn.

Engine Controls

Engine control systems for outboard motors can be a real sore spot. Some of these plastic control boxes are just plain awful, with the shifting mechanisms so weak and flimsy that the things feel like they're going to break off in your hand. Some actually do. Or the mechanism is so sloppy that you have a hard time telling what shift position the engines are in. If you are really serious about boating, you'll demand nothing but the best, so I'd suggest that you compare the Yamaha system with all others.

Shifting systems in outboards have a natural weakness for the following reason: The control system extends from your hand on the lever, through the control box to the cable and thence to the powerhead of the engine. From there, a complex set of linkages travels down the inside of the motor shaft housing to the gearbox in the lower unit where the actual gear shifting takes place. The large number of turning points and the length of the system provides a lot of opportunity for things to go slack, along with the potential for high resistance, with the result that shifting may not be as smooth and easy as one would like. A boat with troublesome controls is not a happy state of affairs.

When it comes to used boats, cheap systems can wear out quickly, and the cost to repair or replace them is high. Pay attention to this if you're buying used. If the controls operate smoothly, they will probably be okay.

At this point, you should already have checked to ensure that the control positioning is ergonomically correct. You should not have to do hand contortions to operate them. Many control units are found placed on an angle, rather than a flat, horizontal surface. This causes the operator to have to contort his hand and lift the levers which, once they reach a certain point, he has to turn his hand around and start pushing them. This is sort of like having to reach through the steering wheel of you car to operate the turn signal lever, awkward at best. See Chapter 8, Design Details for more details on this.

In recent years boat builders have been resorting to offering their boats pre-rigged with no option of engine manufacturer. In which case, you have no choices. Lately there have been so many complaints about this that some builders have ended this practice. There is both good and bad in this. The good is that when the builder makes the installation, you have a much better chance that it has been done right. The bad is when the dealer is left to do it, you have a better chance of the dealer screwing up. Of course, reputable, experienced dealers are a lot more likely to get it right.

Most outboards are sold with a standard control system, occasionally an optional system, or the ability to upgrade to a higher quality system by a different manufacturer. This is one of the things you need to pay attention to before you buy. A lot of people have trouble with controls, and sometimes they never seem to get the systems working smoothly because the system itself is poor quality and has very poor tolerances. The end result is inaccurate shifting and gear chatter, the noise gears make when they are

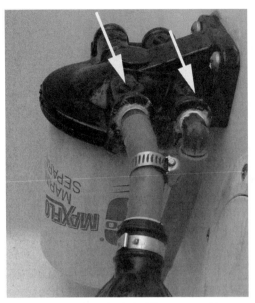

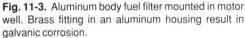

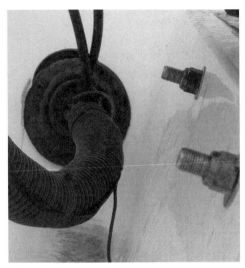

Fig. 11-4. Note the small washers under the motor mount bolts. These are much too small and are crushing the fiberglass. The cable pass through hole is near the bottom of this motor well.

Fig. 11-3. Aluminum body fuel filter mounted in motor well. Brass fitting in an aluminum housing result in galvanic corrosion.

not completely engaged, and hard, difficult operation. Needless to say, this can cause damage.

Outboard owners seem to get used to these sloppy systems, but if you've ever operated a larger boat with quality engine controls, if you're like me, you'll have a hard time accepting these junky systems. If there is a difficulty with changing to a higher quality system, it will be that the electric tilt/trim switches are built into some of the control units. For smaller motors, even the starting switch may be built into the controls, at which point you're pretty much stuck with what you get. As of this writing, Yamaha has by far the best control systems; the price-leader brands such as Force and Mariner, some of the worst I've seen. Even Johnson/Evinrude smaller engine controls (shown in Fig. 11-2.) leave a lot to be desired.

For larger motors, it is often possible to switch to a higher quality Morse, Hynautic or Teleflex control systems. With smaller boats, you're likely to be stuck with what they offer as there is usually no place to mount any other type of control system. As you can see in 11-2, this is a side mount system that leaves no option for mounting any other type. The former are good options for those contemplating the purchase of a high end CC boat, which will not have space limitations, and where dealers are usually more qualified to making these changes. Some engine manufacturers have separate rocker switch packages for the tilt/trim controls. In my view, it's worth the extra cost of doing this if you find those flimsy OEM controls intolerable. Look at some of the higher end outboard fishing boats and you'll even find some with dual, rather than single lever controls. Single lever controls will *never* work as smoothly as independent levers for

Fig. 11-5. Two different style fuel tank vent fittings: At left, recessed stainless steel. Right, stainless steel with plastic deflector. Both are good when installed properly.

throttle and shift because of the problem of a more complex mechanism that has more friction. Dual levers, though requiring more hand action, offer more precise control.

Personally, I wouldn't choose anything but dual lever controls because I enjoy the greater precision of control. The option of changing to dual controls will be completely dependent on whether there is sufficient space on the helm to install them.

Fuel Filters

With the advent of direct fuel injection, the problem of water contamination of fuel has become a critical issue. Water run through an injection system can cause not only engine failure, but costly fuel system damage.

The standard, spin-on cartridge fuel filters are no longer adequate, while these do a reasonable job of separating out small amounts of water from fuel, the capacity of these filters is very low and they can quickly fill up. Once that happens, the filter stops functioning and water passes through it. Not only that, you can't see what is happening inside the filter.

For these reasons, I recommend that high quality Racor or Dahl separators be purchased and installed. These filters have replaceable filter elements, but also have sight bowls where you can actually see the material that is being filtered out, including water. When the filter has too much water in it, you can see that and it has a provision for draining the water out. These filters need to be installed in a highly accessible and visible location so that they can be monitored frequently.

While these filters are fairly expensive, they are well worth the extra cost. Personally, I wouldn't have any kind of engine without them. If you do have them installed, be sure they are installed in a location where you can easily check them. It doesn't do much good to stick them in a dark hole somewhere.

Fuel Tank Vents

No detail on a boat is ever so minor as to not need attention. Shown in Figure 11-5 above are two tank vent fittings located on side of hull. Tanks must be vented overboard in such a way that no fuel escapes into the vessel. Naturally, this poses a problem with preventing water from getting into the tank via the vent.

Historically, vent fittings and location have been problematic. Vent fittings may be made of cast zinc or molded plastic, both of which are known to deteriorate rapidly and cause fuel supply problems. Secondly, the fittings must be located as high above the water line as possible, and certainly not in the forward section where the vent is likely to be subject to wave action. Thirdly, the vent opening should be angled aftward so that there is no tendency of wave action to push water back through the vent.

I recommend only stainless steel fittings, preferably either of the two types shown above. Be sure to check the vent fittings on both new and used boats. If they're plastic or zinc, are not installed in the right location, be sure to get it changed.

Engine Installation

After you have selected your boat and motor, the next step is rigging the boat. You may want to have the dealer provide you with a copy of BOTH the boat and motor manufacturer's installation instructions and diagrams. Read these documents and familiarize yourself with what is required. Why not just trust the dealer to do it right? Mainly because I've seen too many small dealers who hire unqualified, untrained riggers who don't know how to properly rig a boat. The only way you can ensure that it's done right is to familiarize yourself how it should be done. This is unlikely to be a problem for boats that are rigged by the builder, but you should check the points listed below.

You should not accept delivery until you are satisfied that it is done right, the reason being that any mistakes can be very difficult and costly to correct, and the dealer is likely to argue the issue if it's not done right. The dealer holds all the cards if you've already paid him the full price, so it's a good idea to hold back a few thousand dollars pending your final approval. Here are some tips on what to look for:

- Make sure the mounting bolts on the inside of the transom have large back up plates or at the least very large washers according to manufacturer's specifications. 2" squares of 1/4" aluminum plate are usually enough to prevent crushing of cored transoms. Small washers are almost guaranteed to cause problems. Minimum washer size is 1-1/2".

- Make sure the mounting bolts are properly bedded with 3M 5200 bedding compound. Silicone is not an adhesive and should not be used. If there is a plywood core in the transom, you want to make sure that it's not going to get wet after drilling the bolt holes. The best time to deal with this issue is *before* the engines get mounted.

- Check to make sure the distance between the motor cavitation plate and the bottom of the hull is at the prescribed height. This is one of the more common mounting mistakes.

- Make sure that the openings for the engine controls, whether in a motor well, platform or through the transom, are well above the point where the opening will allow water to enter the hull. For example, the openings should not be located within any recess or well in the deck such as a motor well. Those little rubber boots they put on there will not keep the water out. The preferred type are the spiral conduit tubes with appropriate connectors.

- Getting the cables in the right position can be troublesome. There should not be any tight turns or kinks in the cables or steering system lines, be they hydraulic or mechanical, but most especially mechanical. Pay attention to whether the boat builder designed this correctly. Did the builder provide a correctly designed, dedicated raceway for the controls? Or is the dealer just supposed to put them in any old way he can? Push-pull cables require a minimum of an 18" radius turn. Any less than that and the cable will bind.

- After the installation is complete, tilt the motors up completely. Is there adequate clearance for the steering cylinders, cables and wiring, or are they being crushed into the deck, damaging these components? If the motors won't tilt up fully without hitting the deck, then the boat wasn't designed right.

- Check the wiring. It should be installed neatly and be well secured. Think about what will happen to loose systems in a bouncing, slamming boat. There should not be any splices in the wiring between both ends that are exposed to weather.

- Where are the batteries installed? Will they stay dry or get wet? I recommend that if the dealer is going to use those cheap plastic battery boxes with the belt buckle straps, that you spend the extra money to get a better quality battery box with a cover that can more easily be removed. When selecting batteries, it's always better to go larger rather than smaller. Batteries labeled "auto/marine" are just car batteries, so don't pay more for them just because they say "marine".

- I do not recommend that the battery cables be attached with wing nuts on stainless steel studs. It's okay for the main DC system feed to be connected this way, but not the starter motor cables. They should be attached with properly swaged lead battery lugs that will not come loose when the boat is slamming. The proper type lug has the starter cable swaged into the lead lug, plus a stainless terminal post for the electrical system connection.

- No electrical equipment should be wired directly off the batteries, even if it does have an inline fuse. In one instance a dealer added nine in-line fuses, scattered all over the boat because the boat did not have an adequate electric panel from which to install additional equipment. Instead of installing a panel, the fuses were added wherever it happened to be convenient. This created a nightmare for the owner finding all those fuses. Many of them were installed in places where they got wet and shorted out. Before buying the boat, check the electrical system and see what provisions it has for optional equipment. You may need to add an additional fuse panel, and the best time to do this is now.

- Can the controls be placed in a comfortable location? If there's a choice where to locate them, make sure it's in the right place.

The best way to deal with most of these issues is BEFORE the rigging is done. Take the time to go over these points, not only with the salesman, but with the service manager as well. It's a lot easier to try to get them to do it right the first time, than it is to try to get an improper installation corrected. Most of these dealers operate on very slim profit margins, which provides the motivation for their resistance to correcting problems. You'll probably get even better results if you give them a list of your requirements in writing so they don't forget, and you have something to fall back on if it's not done right. Nothing like a little, "I gave it to you in writing," to make your point.

Tip: If you go to one of those giant dealerships, they are not going to do anything for you without asking you to sign and/or initial a heap of paper work. They are going to cover themselves from every direction. Why should this be a one-way street? All protections are for them, none for you. If you are giving them special instructions, get them to sign a copy of your written instructions. You'll get a pretty good idea of who and what you are dealing with when the guy says, "Sorry, but I'm not authorized to do that." Your response should be, "Then I'm not authorized to buy your boat."

Pre-delivery Test Run

Whether the dealer has a water front facility or not, you should try to get the salesman or service manager to take a test run with you. This is called a "shake down" run and is always done with larger boats, and there's no reason not to do it with smaller ones. The objective is to discover anything that isn't right, and to get the seller to see any problems with his own eyes, rather than you coming back later and complaining. Very often dealers will not fully check it out, causing you to have to return for corrections and adjustments. Far better to get these things out of the way at the outset before you become too heavily committed to using the boat. The following are the things that should be checked:

- Alternator is charging.

- Motor tilts fully up without hitting anything.

- No leaks in fuel system.

- Engines turn same number of degrees in both directions and steering tension meets your requirement.

- Engines start readily without excessive cranking.

- Engine controls shift smoothly without gears chattering when shifting. The gears should engage shortly after the shift lever is past the neutral position. If the lever has to be pushed a considerable distance before it engages, it is not adjusted right.

- There should be no slack or dead spots in the throttle advance. That's where the throttle moves but nothing happens. Engine idle should be 600-700 RPM and not stall when put in gear.

- All gauges are functioning properly.

- Boat gets up on plane quickly and trims out properly. Boat rides smooth without porpoising or tending to lay over on one side.

- The power trim works effectively. That trim tabs actually have an effect on trim.

- Engines will synchronize at the same RPM reading on tachometers at three speeds, slow, cruise and fast.

- Boat tracks reasonably straight with little effort to hold it on course. The boat should not veer off to one side when you let go of the wheel. If so, motor alignment may need adjustment.

- While underway at speed, make sure that there are no streams of water rising up and spraying the engines from the lower units or anything else. If so, the offending item will need to be adjusted to prevent this occasional problem.

- Check for things that are loose and rattle, like hatches and latches that won't stay closed, seat cushions that won't stay put, and so on.

- After running the boat for about a half hour and returning to the dock, check the bilges for evidence of water, oil or gas fumes.

Add-on Items

Any hardware that is added should be bolted and thoroughly bedded. It is not acceptable that major items be attached with screws, items such as convertible tops, T-tops, seating, railings and so on. There should be clear evidence of caulking oozing out the sides of any item attached to fiberglass. If you don't see any caulking, make them do it over again.

You should never make assumptions that the installer knows how to do it right. When ordering options, you should discuss installation with the service manager and if something is to be installed a certain way, have it spelled out on the work order.

The heavy items should also have back up plates on the under side. The size of the back up is dependent on how much stress the item will cause to the surface on which it is mounted. A T-top or anchor pulpit, for example, needs strong backing to keep the fasteners from pulling loose. Always consider the amount of leverage any item will transmit to the fasteners.

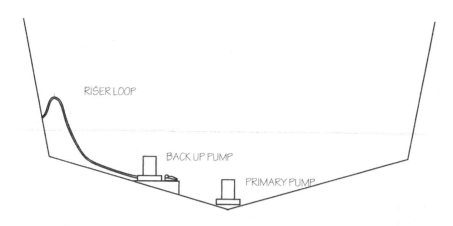

Fig. 11-6. A good installation scheme for a primary and back up bilge pump.

Another point: Pay attention to what these heavier items are being attached to. Recently we've seen quite a few T-tops and towers bolted and even screwed to cored decks. Unable to support the weight and load, the decks crushed under the tower and top feet. In many cases, the boats weren't designed to support these items, and serious damage was the result. Before automatically assuming that such items can be added with no problem, it's best to check with the builder or an expert such as a surveyor.

Selecting and Installing Electronics

The installation of electronics is normally pretty straight-forward, but there are a couple of points to be aware of. Flush mount instruments such as GPS and video recorders are preferable to bracket mounting. The reason is that with bracket mounts, the various electrical connections on the back side will be facing forward and are like to get wet with spray and become damaged. Flush mount instruments avoid this problem.

When flush mounts are installed, it is important that the face plates be bedded to the helm panel so that water doesn't leak in around them. Clear silicone is adequate for this job so as not to make a mess.

If there is inadequate provision for flush mount electronics and you have to go with bracketed installations, somehow these sensitive electrical connectors have to be protected against getting wet.

Bilge Pumps

The vast majority of boats that we see come from the builder with undersized and inadequate number of bilge pumps. Since bilge pumps are highly prone to failure for a variety of reasons, having one pump alone is never enough in any size boat.

We do no recommend that you rely on very small pumps, such as the Rule 500 or 800 pumps, the reason being that such small pumps are prone, by their very small size alone, to getting clogged up with debris. I recommend that you have at least a Rule 1500 pump. This can be in addition to one of the smaller pumps as a back up, but it is our contention that the larger pump is far more reliable.

For a 24 foot center console boat or larger, we'd recommend two Rule 1500 or larger pumps. A good way to install these is show in Figure 11-6. Having the second pump mounted at a higher level makes it serve as a back up only. And since the impeller is not constantly submerged in water, it will be less prone to getting fouled with debris that normally accumulates in the bilge.

One reason bilge pumps fail so frequently is due to corroded wire connections. Since these pumps are installed in a hostile environment, special treatment of the connectors is needed. Many of the various so called "water proof" connectors, including heat shrink type, have proved to be not so. We recommend the use of standard butt connectors and coating them with a product called Liquid Electrical Tape.

Float switches should be mounted with the flapper facing aft.

Dealing With Problems

It's the nature of the business that there have always been problems with dealerships and getting warranty work done properly. Once they've got your money, they're more interested in moving onto the next sale than in keeping you happy. Granted, that's not true of all dealers, but there are far too many for whom it is true. With the advent of ever larger and larger dealers however, these problems are reaching critical proportions. Far too many people are having to resort to hiring lawyers to try to resolve the problems. Even then, these efforts are often hampered because the boat owner didn't document anything.

My advice is that the moment anything seems to go wrong, you should treat it as if you will have to go to court, even if you have no intentions of doing so. The only real leverage you have is to document everything, first by taking photos of all the problems, then by reducing everything to writing. Keep notes of conversations, and back things up with letters from the very moment it appears that you are not getting full cooperation. While it may very well turn out that someone at the dealership is just having a bad day, if it turns out that they are trying to avoid making good, and you've done nothing to document the situation, then it's likely to cost you dearly.

All of this may seem like a lot of hassle at a time when all you really want is to be happy about buying a new boat. Unfortunately, it happens too often that what should be a happy occasion turns out to be less so. To protect yourself, it's best to conduct the purchase of a boat in a business-like manner: consider everyone guilty until proven innocent. This is your pleasure, but it's the dealer's business.

Rest assured that when you come back with a warranty issue, you are no longer quite the same valued customer you were before you handed over that big check. You now take on a different coloring because warranty claims or complaints are going to cost them profit. They will begin to conduct their business defensively, and so should you. Be polite but firm and businesslike.

In the event that problems turn up, do not delay in getting them corrected. Problems are often not successfully resolved because the boat owner failed to explain the nature of the problem fully. In addition to that, service managers are often harried individuals so that much of what you may tell them goes in one ear and out the other, and is never conveyed to the person assigned to do the work.

If you have to return the boat to the dealer with a list of things that need correction, you should take the time to make the list in writing and in detail with two copies. One for yourself and give the other to the service manager. He can then write down whatever he wants on his service order. It's highly inconvenient to have to go back a second, third and forth time because a problem wasn't resolved the first time. Handing the nature of the complaint to the service manager in writing can go a long way toward avoiding this. The larger the dealership, the more reason why you should do it this way.

In the event that the dealer seems unwilling to resolve a problem, or is clearly making only a halfhearted effort to correct it, such as in making shoddy repairs, it's time to seriously cover yourself. The very moment that you suspect that a dealer is attempting to skirt the issue, begin documenting everything that is done. Since your first notification was presented in writing, now follow up with a second description of why the problem was not successfully resolved. If it is possible take photographs of the condition, by all means do so.

You're much more likely to achieve a resolution to the problem when the dealer realizes that you are dotting the i's and crossing the t's. He's more likely to get the idea that you are covering yourself, building a record, and not taking the issue lightly. As you hand him the written description, you just might show him your photos as well. *See here, it's already on record, my friend.*

If he agrees to correct the problem, ask for a copy of the work order. If the work description is not clear on how it will be done, ask for clarification. Is the offending item going to be repaired or replaced? If repaired, then how? You should get an agreement on how the repairs are to be made. Just assuming that it will be done right could be a mistake.

One final point, if the problem is serious, or possibly difficult to understand, a good procedure is to get the service manager and the appropriate worker out to the boat to discuss the problem in their presence. There's nothing like discussing the problem in the presence of the problem to make sure that what needs to be done is understood by all.

Necessary Extra Equipment

GPS These navigation devices are more or less essential to any boat owner and they come in two basic types: fixed mount and portable, and two subtypes, position readout and plotters. They can either be relatively cheap or expensive, with the primary difference being the display plotter. The very small portable units with their very small displays are less than satisfactory for serious navigation. And because of the potential for getting stolen or dropped and damaged, I would recommend having a flush or bracket mount unit installed if there is room for it.

Note that GPS is not a substitute for learning how to read nautical charts and using them, as all but the largest chart plotters are inadequate to navigate by. If you don't understand why, then you need to brush up on the limitations of GPS.

VHF The marine VHF radio is not an option, but a necessity for even casual boating. It is definitely not recommended that anyone should try to depend on cell phones. VHF radios transmit on line-of-sight, which means that the lower the antenna height, the shorter the distance one can transmit. This is a serious limitation and consideration for small boaters who should be aware of the limitations of communication ability.

Depth Sounders It comes highly recommended that all boats should be equipped with at least a basic depthmeter unless you have good reason for not having one (like your lake is everywhere 100 feet deep). For basic navigation, a simple digital read out is best, and the larger the display the better. Instruments with very tiny read outs are hard to see in a bouncing boat.

Tops & Enclosures When it comes to convertible tops and enclosures, I have several points to make. As a general rule the types offered by the builder or dealer are usually not very good quality and usually not worth the price you pay for them. This stuff is expensive and won't last long. The best quality stuff costs only fractionally more than poor quality and is well worth the price. Additionally, you do not want to buy any top that has aluminum pipe frames, for this stuff bends too easily. Stainless steel is best.

In the south, and especially Florida and Texas, it is best to avoid black, red, and navy blue colors as these get extremely hot and can be very uncomfortable if the top is too close to your head.

Full Boat Covers These are particularly good for boats stored outside on trailers to reduce the effect of weathering. For boat covers to be durable and last a reasonable length of time, it needs to be custom fitted. Ready-made or mail order covers usually don't last long because the material is too thin and they do not have reinforcement at the points where it needs it, such as windshield corners, etc.

If you're going to get a full boat cover, it's best to have one custom made by a boat canvass shop.

Fire Extinguishers Though rarely needed, should the time come when you do need one, you'll rue the day when you made the decision to buy just one little cheapie. For 16 to 25 foot boats, I recommend two, 2.5 lb. size units with pressure gauges. Why two? Because I've heard numerous reports of people with just one that didn't work. They are prone to losing pressure is the reason why.

Life Jackets Not exactly optional, and called PFD's by the government bureaucrats, I emphatically do not recommend *floatation devices* but real, honest to goodness life jackets. Not the kind that hang around your neck, but the kind you wear around your torso. The reason for this is that this type will float your head higher out of the water than the other type, and will help retain body heat and retard the onset of hypothermia in the event you get dunked in cold water.

Personally, I prefer the zippered vest type worn by sailboat racers which can be worn with relative comfort when not in the water. These are specially good for little children whom you want to be wearing a life jacket any time they're out on the boat.

Anchors Small boaters naturally lean toward very small anchors as larger ones are harder to handle and stow away. But, the fact of life is that small anchors don't work well, so that larger is always better. Most casual boaters treat anchors like something they're forced to have aboard, but don't really want. An anchor is not only a general piece of equipment, but also a piece of safety equipment. Someday the boater may have to depend upon it to keep his disabled boat from going up on rocky shore.

My advice is to opt for larger rather than smaller. An anchor that isn't going to work well is less than useless. The Danforth or Danforth style is probably the best all-around choice. For example, for a 24 foot boat I would choose not less than an 18 lb. Danforth.

For anchor rodes, include at least a 6 foot galvanized chain lead and not less than 1/2" rope. Smaller rope is far more prone to tangling than larger, and harder to disentangle when it does. Rode length should be 3X average water depth or not less than 150 feet.

First Aid Kits Many, if not most, of the tiny first aid kits sold in marine stores aren't worth the sales tax you pay. The most important kind of first aid needed is for serious lacerations, which are easy to come by around boats. It is my personal opinion that you can make up your own at the local pharmacy that will be cheaper and far better. You want to be able to close up a badly bleeding wound. The most important items are gauze bandages, butterfly bandages, large and small, plus lots of tape and a tourniquet. A couple of lengths of surgical tubing is good have.

Spare Prop Operating an engine with a badly bent propeller can cause serious damage to the lower unit. Therefore, it's a good idea to carry a spare propeller. An inexpensive aluminum prop is good enough for use as a spare. A prop that gets damaged should be changed immediately, on-the-spot. Do not run the boat home before changing.

Chapter 12

Research, Pricing and Shopping

Research and Shopping for a boat can be very time consuming, so unless you have an idea of where and how to look, it's easy to end up wasting a lot of time. The following are some tips on how to refine and target your efforts.

Research Sources

The Internet

Thanks to the Internet, the task of researching a new or used boat purchase becomes much easier, although many people express their disappointment that there are not more objective sources of information. As I pointed out in the first chapter, because there are so many boat builders, it is simply not possible for there to be any comprehensive sources. There are a few publications, such as *Power Boat Reports*, and my own site, *www.yachtsurvey.com* that will review a relative handful of the most popular boats. For the vast majority, however, you will be able to find little or nothing.

I am constantly amazed at the number of emails I receive from people asking where they can get information on 15-20 year old boats. If you have a hard time finding info on late model boats, imagine how unlikely to find anything on boats one or two or three decades old! For the majority of old boats, the builders are no longer in business and there are no records anywhere about those builders and their boats. Many people express great chagrin that such information simply does not exist. You have to realize that small boat builders are just too small and insignificant for anyone to be interested in spending their chronicling the history of a small boat builder.

There is the possibility that you could run across limited information on the internet by simply typing in the model name, builder and/or size of the boat you are interested in. There are a number of web sites that have been put up by disgruntled boat owners who want to warn others about their experience with certain builders. Then, there are sites like *gripes.com* that provide forums for disgruntled consumers.

The number of sites or "clubs" dedicated to one manufacturer or model is constantly expanding. All of these are potential sources of good information. Try a search based on the manufacturer name plus the word "club" or "owner's club".

Discussion forums can also turn up good information, however, you have to be careful about from whom you take complaints literally. You'll need to be a good judge of character and try to discern whether the complainer is describing his problems fairly and accurately, or whether he is only one-half of the problem and a person with an ax to grind and is bent on revenge for slights real or partly imagined.

It can be very instructive for newcomers to boating to read discussion forums regularly. These can give you a good feel for what boat ownership is all about, although one should beware that forums involve all types of people and a lot of inaccurate and downright false information. To get the most out of discussion forums, it's best to read them regularly and get to know the participants. In a few weeks time you can get a pretty good idea of who are the knowledgeable ones.

When making Internet searches, I recommend using several different search engines as you will get different results. Try a couple of search engines such as Google, Alta Vista, Lycos, Excite, etc., using same key words. Technologies of search engines and their business practice are constantly changing. At this writing, Google seems most popular search engine, yielding more relevant results. If you search at directory service sites, such as Yahoo, the results will be further different. And if you don't get results at first, try typing in different variations of the boat name such as Aquasport 23, Aquasport 230 + Center Console. The more variations you try, the more sources you'll turn up.

Boating Magazines

Publications that depend on advertising will never publish negative information about boats, yet alone any of their advertisers, so you might as well save your money and avoid wasting your time looking in them. Moreover, publishing negative information is risky business as almost no one wants to take the chance of getting sued by an unhappy manufacturer. The most you'll find in the glossy magazines will be new and used boat ads.

Newsprint type magazines exist across the country, many of which are free, and include well-known national publications such as *Soundings* and *Boat Trader,* to lesser known local rags. These can contain ads for both used and new boats and are numerous in major boating centers, but may be hard to find in smaller boating areas. All of these are worth checking out and can be found at marinas, boat yards and marine stores.

Price Research

The Internet is particularly good for researching prices on used boats. Things can change, but as of this writing, I haven't found the Internet to be very good for finding prices on either new boats or motors. It is definitely best for used boat pricing. Unlike auto dealers who are forced to compete, boat dealers usually don't have a lot of local competition, so what advertising they do is normally intended to attempt to get you into their showroom so that you have to ask about prices in person. Of course, finding out who the dealers are, and then going around to see them can be very time consuming. I discuss how to make an appraisal further on in this chapter.

Boat Shows

Boat shows offer the opportunity to see a lot of boats all in one place, and do limited price shopping as well. Keep in mind that boat shows are normally attended by manufacturers, so that you are unlikely to find many competing dealers of the same brand. Boat shows are best for doing price comparisons *between* manufacturers. Even though boat shows have been turned into the equivalent of three ring circuses, and general public entertainment, thereby becoming extremely crowded, expensive and often inconvenient, it is usually still worth the hassle to go to these events if only because in no other way can you see so much in such a short period of time.

Depending on where you live, you may have more than one show to choose from. Shows will generally reflect the kind of boats people in the general area most often buy. For example, the Fort Lauderdale Boat Show isn't the best place to look for ski boats or lost cost runabouts. On the other hand, it is a very good place to find high end sport fishing boats, and where virtually every builder will be represented. Therefore, it pays to get some idea of the type of boats that will be best represented at a particular show. If you're planning to spend a considerable amount of money, you may contemplate travelling a considerable distance to attend a show. If so, be sure you know what type of boats will be most prominent.

Tip: Call the show management office a week or so before hand and ask for an advance copy of the show program which will have a listing of all exhibitors.

Show Types are Expanding

Many product manufacturers have recognized that boat shows have gotten too big. This has created an opening for new types of shows, or if not new types, at least smaller shows at times different from the main, big city events. These include used boat shows, specialty shows such as equipment only, outboards or sailboats only, and so on.

While the smaller shows certainly will not give you the best broad range of choices, they often make up for this in that the dealers are not swamped by huge crowds so you'll often come away with more information. Moreover, a quieter, more relaxed environment is more conducive to better decision making.

Among the most rapidly proliferating show types are used boat shows which is a tremendous boon to used boat buyers because these can be great time savers. The down side is that used boat shows tend to raise prices a bit. Show exhibition fees are costly so sellers tend to add these to the asking price. Moreover, with a large audience, sellers are motivated to ask higher prices. On the other hand, used boat shows tend to attract boats that are in better condition.

Buying At Shows

Judging by commentary on Internet discussion forums, the place to get the best deal on a boat is at a show. That is not always true, and the statement is based on the presumption that prices were researched prior to the show and were found to be higher.

My own researches indicate that new boat show prices *tend* to be lower, but that is going to depend on a number of factors. To understand this, let's take a look at it from the manufacturer's perspective. First, it is very costly to participate in a show, a cost which gets added on the price. If a dealer has a hot item in a hot market that is already selling well, why should he lower the price? There is no reason to, is there? On the other hand, if the market is less than hot, sales are okay but not great, he now has some incentive. In all probability, the dealer will start the show with something close to his usual price. Then, after a day or two goes by, if he finds that sales are not going well, he's likely to drop price. He may do this at mid point in the show, or only near the end.

Either way, it points out what times you should and should not consider buying at a boat show. Never buy on the opening day, and if you intend to buy, try do so on the last day, especially if the economy is fair to poor.

Shopping for Used Boats

The most common complaint I hear from used boat buyers is about the amount of time it can take travelling around looking to find the right boat. This can be very time consuming even in major boating centers, but in areas with fewer boats, driving around to look at boats for sale can involve considerable travel and time, so it pays to have a plan so that you don't waste your time going to look at boats that don't even come close to being what you want.

The first thing to do is to set your priorities and commit them to writing. As you travel around looking at boats, it will be very easy to become side-tracked and forget some of the specific criteria you're hoping to achieve. By making a list and referring to it frequently, this will help you to avoid overlooking important details. One way to avoid traveling to see boats that don't fit your need is by planning a list of important questions that you'll want to ask the seller over the phone.

One of the most important considerations is the condition of used boats. As you can imagine, most sellers, including brokers, will hedge quite a bit when you ask general questions about the condition of a boat. No one selling a used boat wants to admit that it isn't in very good condition, and so they'll come up with all sorts of ways to dodge a general query as to condition. If we can find a way to cut through the fog, we can save ourselves a lot of time.

Good interviewers are good because they know how to draw information out of reluctant subjects. They know that in asking blunt, general questions, they're likely to get evasive or misleading answers, so they devise questions that are less direct. They'll ask questions that are less general and more specific. For example, if you simply ask "what is the condition of the boat?" you leave it open for the seller to fudge an answer. "Oh, it's in really good shape," is the likely reply, one that really tells you nothing. Rather than asking this all-encompassing question, ask a series of more specific questions, such as whether there are any damages on the boat, the state of general wear and tear, what does the finish look like, the upholstery, how long the seller has owned it, how frequently he uses it, and for what purpose. What recent repairs and/or replacements have been made in recent years? When was the last time he compounded and waxed the boat? Any recent, major engine work and so on.

After you have looked at a few used boats, you'll get some experience and will become more adept at picking the right questions to ask. As you go around looking at boats, start a list of questions. Note all of the electrical equipment that the boat has, then go down the list, specifically asking about each one. This will put the seller on the spot, forcing him to either tell the truth or to lie. By employing this questioning technique, you'll either get direct answers, or evasive answers.

Evasive answers are nearly as good as very specific answers. A seller who frequently hedges or waffles does so for a reason, and that reason is always because he is reluctant to tell the truth. Thus, you are unlikely to be wrong by concluding that evasive answers constitute a negative reply.

Making Your Own Appraisal

What is the value of a boat, and how is it determined? It is often said that the value of anything is whatever someone is willing to pay for it. That is not entirely accurate since there are at times when unknowledgeable buyers will pay more than a knowledgeable buyer would. Therefore, anything that is for sale may be worth more to some people than others. This is really no help to us, so what we are really asking is what is the "fair market value" of the boat.

The fair market value of a boat can be defined as the price that more than one knowledgeable buyer would be willing to pay. The way to determine that would be to research recent sales records for what others have paid for a particular boat. Unfortunately, there is no agency that collects and makes such information available, so we have to resort to another method. That method is to look at current asking prices of either identical or comparable boats, or both, since such information can be collected and studied.

This is fairly easily done by collecting all available advertising media, including the Internet. For many years my own method of making appraisals was to sit down with publications such as *Boat Trader* and the various yachting magazines, scanning these for ads. Using an Exacto knife and a glue stick, I cut out the ads and glued them onto a piece of paper. Once I had a sufficient number of them, I make a list of all boats that similar engines and equipment, as well as making a guess about condition.

Let's say I find ten ads, each of which lists an asking price. Of these ten, the majority will fall within a certain price range grouping, while several others will fall into an extreme of highs and lows. These get tossed out as being unrepresentative and the remainder of the pricing is totalled and averaged out. We know, of course, that sellers ask more than they expect to get, but the question becomes one of how much. There are no hard and fast rules except that we know if one asks too much, their phone is unlikely to ring. We've already thrown out the high extremes, which are likely to represent those who are asking too much, and in taking our average, it's a pretty good bet that it will be fairly representative of the usual mark up of around 10%, perhaps up to 15%, over what a seller really expects to net.

Another thing to do is to evaluate each of the ads closely in order to determine how each boat relates to the others. This, in terms of extra equipment, engines and what-ever the seller has to say about the condition, which may or may not be true, but there's nothing we can do about that. Having done that, we make additional adjustments based on whatever differences we can glean from the ads.

It should go without saying that when an asking price is unusually low, there is a good reason for that. The reason will nearly always be that this particular boat is in lesser condition than others. Many buyers are immediately attracted to the one with the lowest price. My experience is that this is almost always a mistake. If you're going to travel far to follow up on the lowest priced ad, expect to be disappointed when search-ing out the lowest or lower priced boats.

Using this method will yield an appraisal that is as close as anyone can get. Naturally, the more boats one has in the sample, the more accurate it will be. Also, that this method works best for the more popular makes and models where obtaining a repre-sentative sample is most possible. But what do we do about makes and models that are more rare, and for which we may not be able to find any similar boats for sale?

In this case we have to turn the method of using comparables. Comparables are boats of similar type, size, quality and with the same engines, but not the same builder or model. Even if you're not very experienced in boating, if you assemble a grouping of comparably sized boats and simply average out the prices, even that will help to evaluate pricing better.

Appraisal Books

The question to ask about books is whether you think appraisal books reflect prices, or do books set the prices? This question is particularly valid in light of the fact that there are no central clearing houses for used boat sales. So, how do the book makers arrive at the pricing contained therein? In the used car market, there are large regional auctions where trade-ins taken by dealers are sent to be sold. This is how so-called "wholesale" prices are derived.

There are no such wholesale auctions for used boats yet there are books that list "wholesale" prices. Where do they get those prices? The answer is that they invent them. In nearly all cases, appraisal books derive their pricing from a declining balance depreciation method that is applied to tens of thousands of boats via mindless computers, and so the answer to our first question is that books set prices, prices do not make the book. The simple truth is that books are created for the benefit of brokers and dealers, not the boating public. As one who has been studying these books for years, I do not recommend that you use them, but apply the method I described above. Moreover, books cannot reflect current market conditions, but only past economic conditions, which may have changed.

For example, at the time this book was written, the economy was in recession and prices were falling. Books could not, and did not reflect that fact. In that case, would you really want to refer to a book and pay the indicated price?

Regional Variations

For larger, higher priced used boats, regional variations are likely to occur. This can result from factors ranging from popularity, to supply and demand. A lack of general suitability to a particular region can also play a part: inland type boats in coastal regions, sport fishing boats in inland regions and so on. If a boat is not well-suited to a particular region, it's not likely to command a top dollar price.

Yet another important factor that influences pricing is how well a brand has been established. Used boats with names that no one has ever heard of are a hard sell simply because such a boat is largely unknown, and smart people tend not to invest large sums of money in the unknown. Reputation is important, and lacking a strong reputation, a particular boat will not command as high a price as better known brands do. If you're going to be buying a relatively unknown brand, you'd best be paying less than the more popular comparable boats.

When To Buy

Outboard boat prices in particular are amenable to seasonal variations for several reasons, and for both new and used boats.

For new boats in regions where water gets cold and solid in winter, the obvious worst time to buy is late spring-early summer peak buying season; the best times are late summer through winter as these are the times sales fall off. Used boats will pretty much follow the same pattern but for different reasons. Winter is a terrible time to try to sell a boat, and anyone who is doing so may be a distressed situation, in which case you may be able to get a very good deal. Though there will probably be pretty slim pickings offered on the market, it certainly can't hurt to keep your eyes open for that outside shot a good deal.

The one big problem with buying in the dead of winter when the water is frozen is that you can't test the boat, a situation that makes buying very risky, particularly if you can't afford to make a mistake. When considering buying in winter, you need to balance whatever you may save on price versus the possible unexpected costs.

An exception to the rule is buying in regions where the water doesn't freeze in winter, such as the deep south. However, there will be much less in the way of seasonal fluctuations for this very reason. Boats sell all year long in Florida with no seasonal price variation. Texas and other Gulf coast states will be pretty much the same for used boats. In these states, slightly better deals may still be had on new boats in the winter months as sales fall off dramatically.

Salt Water versus Fresh

Yes, there are differences in pricing between fresh water boats and salt water boats. These are particularly justified for outboard motors where engine longevity is much greater in fresh water, while maintenance costs much lower. The variation typically runs 5-15% and where the condition of the boat is usually worth the extra money.

Long Distance Shopping

Shopping ads for boats located out of state, or otherwise far from home can be fraught with problems. The worst of these is misrepresentation of condition by the seller, a situation that in my experience is fairly common. Be careful about relying on photos, either on the Internet or photos sent by the seller. Photos can be highly misleading. Think about it; is the seller going to take pictures that include negative aspects? Many of my survey clients from out of state run into this problem. First, it is unwise to make an offer sight-unseen, or even just based on photos.

It is usually better to attempt to pin the seller down, as discussed earlier, by getting him to give a verbal report on specifics. Make it clear to him that you're traveling a long distance and you are going to be very unhappy with him if it turns out he has exaggerated the condition. Come right out and ask him to give you an accurate assessment. Chances are, if you handle it this way, you'll get the truth and not end up driving or flying hundreds of miles only to be disappointed.

Chapter 13

The Art of the Deal

New Boats

Once you have decided on the type of boat you want, the quality and general price range, it's time to start thinking about the dealer. There are, however, some things the first time buyer needs to know about boat dealers. In the first chapter, I discussed the nature of the boating industry so that you'd have a good understanding of why things are the way they are, so now we'll take a look at why the choice of a dealer is so very important.

Unlike just about any other major purchase that you can think of, boats are sold from an amazing array of differing facilities. From Honest John's roadside stand to showrooms as lavish as any car dealer you've ever seen. In between there are boatyards, marinas, storefronts, waterfronts and even those that look like vast junk yards set out in the middle of a corn field.

Boats are sold everywhere and anywhere, from ritzy multimillion dollar showrooms to converted gas stations and storefronts, and it is this fact of life that makes the task of buying one a bit more difficult. If there is any consolation, it is that you're far less likely to encounter the absurd trickery and overall odor of manipulation and dishonesty that permeates the auto industry. Generally speaking, boat dealers are more honest and less sophisticated in their sales tactics, except in those places that obviously mimic auto dealers. You can generally expect that buying a boat is going to be a more pleasant experience as long as you use common sense and are a reasonably good judge of character.

There are some very good dealers and some not so good ones, with others somewhere in between. In the commentary that follows, and in consideration of the historical track record of boat dealerships, I take the position of guilty until proven innocent, which does not mean that you should paint them all with the same brush, but to be alert to the possibility of running into one that lacks full integrity, expertise in service, or both. As Ronald Reagan put it, trust but verify.

My experience is that those dealers who have invested considerable sums in waterfront facilities tend to be more professional, carry higher quality products and have better trained service personnel. This is not absolute, nor does it mean that you should not consider smaller dealers or roadside dealers. In either case, I recommend that you do what you can to check out their reputation. If you're totally new to boating, you probably don't know anyone to talk to and basically don't know how to find out. In that case, I'd recommend staying with the larger waterfront dealers. Moreover, the independently owned or family run businesses are usually superior to the large dealer chains that are found in major boating centers.

On the other hand, established waterfront dealers are understandably higher priced. They've got all that overhead to pay for. Ultimately, it comes down to a matter of getting what you pay for. It's axiomatic that if you want the lowest possible price, you'll have to accept the fact that you'll probably get the lowest level of service.

Is it Really a New Boat?

It seems incredible that a dealer would sell a boat that has been used as a new boat. The fact is that I have seen a fairly large number of cases in which very late model used boats have been sold as new. It is hard to know how and why this happens. In some instances, it turns out to be a demo which, in most cases is perfectly legal with proper disclosure.

Unfortunately, there have been far too many instances in which boats that have had problems were taken back, repaired, and then resold. This situation may involve the dealer, the builder or both. In any case, this is illegal, and you should be on the look out for this possibility. It is actually pretty easy to identify such boats if you're alert to the possibility and are looking for it.

Be alert to so-called year-end leftovers with unusually low prices. Or boats with hull numbers that are two years off the current model year. The thing that most often gives them away are filled screw holes where equipment has been removed. It is almost impossible to fill a screw hole in such a way that it is not detectable if you look very closely. Pay particular attention to the transom mount of the motor(s) and if there is any evidence of motor changes.

A new boat should not have any signs of screw holes, filled or otherwise, there should be no evidence of equipment that has been removed, moved or otherwise changed, nor any indication of wear and tear. And while a dealer may offer a perfectly logical explanation for the existence of such things, you have to ask yourself, why would a dealer go the trouble of changing anything on a new inventory boat?

If you are suspicious about a particular boat, ask the dealer to show you his invoice or shipping papers. If he is telling the truth, he should have no qualms about showing them to you.

How About Demonstrators?

These are usually not a problem as long as you have every indication that the dealer will stand behind it. The biggest issue, of course, is warranty, and since you have two of them, boat and motor, pay close attention. What you particularly need to know is when the warranty period starts. Does it begin the day you take delivery, or did it begin the day the dealer started using it as a demo? That is something you need to find out about and get it in writing. *Do not just take the dealer's word for it.* Have it so stated on the purchase agreement.

If it begins the day you take delivery, then you are essentially getting a new boat with a few hours on it, perhaps a little scuffed up. But with the great advantage of a lower price. If the deal is based on the *remainder* of the warranty, then you are getting a used boat, and the price differential should be substantial. I can think of no better advice than to take the time to call the warranty department of both boat and motor manufacturer and ask them about their policy for demos. That's the only way you can be sure and it's normally a quick and easy call to make.

Seasonal Leftovers

These offer the chance of substantial price reductions at the expense of selection and very likely some wear and tear. Most new boats sit outside exposed to sun and rain and are going to be a bit worse for wear as time goes on, so that price reduction is not solely based on the passing of the model year. I have seen a lot of new boats sitting out for long periods of time that have considerable damage, including water damage to electrical stuff and the interior or upholstery.

Approach these boats as if they were used. For all you know, even the engine could have rusted internally from disuse. Check the inside of the hull to make sure that it hasn't filled up with rain water, and test the operation of everything. Do NOT assume that this is a new boat because unless they've kept it inside, it's not. Otherwise, it could be a very good deal.

The significance of model year is generally not as important for boats as for cars which always change every year. Many people are surprised to discover that it is perfectly legal for a manufacturer to change the hull number on a boat in his possession that did not get sold to a dealer in the year of build. But while a builder can do this, a dealer cannot. Because boat models often do not change every year, depreciation and pricing is not as critically linked to model year as it is with autos.

What About Builder Direct?

Most established builders won't sell direct because it will interfere with their dealer network. The ones that do sell direct are usually regional, if not local builders. They often do a lot of their selling at regional boat shows, and are the ones that never develop national markets. One cannot draw any conclusions about the quality of their products by the fact that they sell direct. Some are good, some aren't. Intrepid Boats, one of the very best high end builders, for example, only sells direct from its own sales offices.

Most develop avid local followings because people for some reason like dealing direct with the builder. They tend to be service oriented and usually well equipped, though you may have to travel a long distance to get your boat there for service. You can expect the quality of work they do to be commensurate with the quality of their boats.

Do they have lower prices? Generally, yes. Figure that they will halve the dealer's profit and costs and pass the difference onto you, while keeping the other half, or thereabouts. In South Florida there are many small builders that operate this way, builders that you've never heard of and probably never will.

What Are Dealer Markups?

This is the question everyone asks, but for which there are no pat answers. It all depends on the contract between builder and dealer. Some dealers are allowed to set the price at whatever they wish, particularly when a particular boat is a hot item and in short supply. That, fortunately, is a rather rare occurrence. As a general rule, dealer margins typically run 15% to 20%, lower for higher priced boats, higher for lower priced boats. Keep in mind that a dealer's inventory is financed, and he's paying interest; those costs either get passed on or the dealer goes broke.

If you're attracted to one of those places with the multi million dollar showrooms, you many want to bear in mind that somebody has to pay for all that elegance, and that someone is going to be you.

What to Expect From Salesmen

I've known a lot of dealers and boat salesmen over the years and it's not hard to separate the pros, or at least semi-pros from the sharks. Only a relative handful of commissioned salesmen manage to make a satisfactory living selling new boats. The likelihood that the salesman has a thorough knowledge of his product line is about the same as with car dealers. Most are just order takers.

Good boat salesmen don't act like salesmen. Generally they behave like ordinary human beings and don't come on to you like a long-lost friend, all covered in oily, insincere friendliness. That insincerity is going to tag along for the rest of the deal, right up to the paper signing, after which he will hardly know you. It's best to give this type a wide berth. Or, if you know how to cut through the muck, do so immediately and put your discussions on a no-nonsense basis, if you can.

My experience is that you will find the better ones in the established dealerships, particularly those that have very good businesses but not too much overhead. It's a simple fact of life that *you* have to pay for that overhead, as well as the salesman's commission. If a dealer wants to keep a knowledgeable salesman around, he has to ensure that he, the salesman, can make a living at it. And to do that he has to pay the salesman, not the overhead. It's as simple as deciding whether you want a fancy show-room or someone who knows what they are talking about.

The best dealers are usually in largish, but somewhat ramshackle facilities upon which they don't lavish too much money. They'll spend some bucks on service rather than just trying to wow you with appearances. Marina dealerships may be an exception to the rule in that marinas naturally attract more customers and therefore have a higher volume to pay for those facilities. Major rack and stack facilities are an example. The service and integrity is usually at least acceptable and major complaints are relatively rare.

Longevity is always a good sign, be it storefront or waterfront. That ramshackle joint up the road apiece, you know, the one with boats scattered all over creation, half looking like a junk yard or that a bomb went off in a boat yard. And then there's old Joe Crabtree, the proprietor, who looks as mean as a pit bull and is as coarse as a corn cob. Some of these outfits do remarkably well. Not trained in the Dale Carnegie School and perhaps lacking in good manners, if they have a big following, it's probably because they do good work at reasonable prices and are trusted.

Check out their service departments. Do they really have one, or are they fixing boats in the driveway or back lot? Good work can't be accomplished without a decent facility and good equipment. This stuff costs money and a lot of fly-by-nighters can't afford it. What kind of people are doing the work? Do they look like day laborers hired off the street? Are they there long enough to get work uniforms? Some of these folks passed off as skilled labor leave a lot be desired. It won't hurt to stand around and watch them a bit. Is the salesman in a hurry to get you out of there? A good service department is proud of its work and won't hesitate to let you see. Others tell you have to leave because of "insurance regulations."

Boat Loans

Most dealers will have financing packages available for new boats. Many people like the convenience of being able to apply for a loan at the place they buy the boat. Those deals will almost always be at higher interest rates than what you could obtain by shopping around. In part, that is because the dealer is doing most of the paperwork, and partly because the dealer earns a "loan origination fee," the cost of which you will be paying.

Obviously, then, you'll be better off walking in with your own financing prearranged. The three best places to find loans are banks, credit unions and specialty lenders. For boats under $50,000, banks and credit unions are the best bet. For boats over that amount, there are many specialist boat lenders such as First Commercial, Ganis and Essex, among others. The later are essentially loan originators who do not hold the paper themselves. That doesn't much matter because many banks will also take your loan and sell it to others.

Negotiating With the Dealer

The smaller the dealer, the less happy he's going to be if you walk in with your own financing. That's because the dealer gets a kickback known as an origination fee, the same as auto dealers. You will notice an immediate change in the salesman's attitude if you tell him this: his earnings just went down!

Many dealers will also arrange insurance for you and, of course, they make a commission on that too. It's probably better to throw him a bone by taking his insurance deal, but do your own financing if you can't get a competitive rate. At the time this was written, interest rates were at all-time lows, so who gets the loan may not much matter.

Test the dealer out first. He will ask you how you will pay for the boat early on. Say that you are not sure whether you're going to pay cash or finance.

The salesman's reaction to this is going to be very telling as to where he's coming from. Essentially what you're looking for is an indication that he's going to raise the price of the boat if he can't make more money from financing or add-ons. Chances are that he will fight to keep from giving you a price (just like the car dealer) until you tell him. Your job is to threaten to walk out unless he does. And don't be afraid to do it! You can always come back, but once you give in, that's it. Negotiating time is over because you just gave up your leverage.

If the salesman is willing to give you a no-strings price, chances are it's a high one, but at least he's not playing a numbers game with you. Take heart. At this point you have two choices: make him an offer, or show him a better deal that you've gotten elsewhere. If you make him an offer, he will probably come back cutting the difference by 25%, from which he'll probably not budge unless you've got some leverage. This then leaves you with the only option of walking out with a take-it-or leave it counter offer. In which case you can only hope that he will call you back tomorrow, which he probably will do.

Do you think for a moment he's going to let you go that easily? Oh no, he's much too close to a deal. We'll have to assume here, of course, that your original offer was within reason. That would be somewhere around 15-20% off asking, depending on price of the boat. The smaller the boat, the less wiggle room. For a $20,000 boat, that would mean an offer of $16,000. If he comes back with $18K, you are indeed close to a fair deal. Notice here that the amount of price spread in his counter offer will tell you a great deal about (a) how much he intends to sell the boat for, or (b) how much wiggle room he actually has.

The closer he comes to meeting you half-way, i.e. countering 50% of the difference, the more wiggle room he has. Thus, if he comes down more, you counter with proportionately less. If he counters with only 10%, this is a bad sign. If he counters with 30% of the difference, you re-counter with only 20%. Remember, at this point you are in control of the deal. Is it worth $500 to walk out and wait for another day? Sure it is.

Before launching into a protracted battle, consider whether the boat is already heavily discounted. If it is, the negotiating room is just not there and you are asking him to give it away with no profit. In that case, he'll probably have to let you walk.

Expensive options can provide a little extra lubrication, but you run the risk of driving the options price up. Optional stuff is usually priced very high and constitute a major part of a dealer's profit. If you negotiate boat price first, and then options, well, you can see what is going to happen. He'll try to make up for the boat discount with the options price. The only way to approach it is with the whole package, whatever it is. If either the dealer or you try to break it up into pieces, you'll loose whatever little control you had. It's like those children's toys where you push one peg down and another pops up. The higher price will just keep popping up again in some other area.

If you allow the salesman to break the deal up into pieces, say boat, motor, trailer and add-ons, you've lost control. If you've got one of those ex car salesman, you will discover that in a big hurry. He'll start juggling those numbers around so fast your head will swim. If he starts to play this game with you, you are in trouble. He should be working from one of those sales agreement forms. If you cannot get him to put all the prices down on paper, if for example, he wants to start with one item, move on to the next and the next, you are fighting a losing battle.

Do not negotiate any price until all prices are on paper. The objective is to negotiate only the total price so that you don't have pegs popping up all over the place again. If he will not do that, then you will just have to resign yourself to paying whatever he wants, or walking out. Make it very clear that you will not be manipulated.

Once all the prices are down on paper and you have worked the final deal, he can then rework his numbers anyway he sees fit SO LONG AS THE BOTTOM LINE REMAINS THE SAME. If for any reason he comes back with the final sales agreement that is higher than what you agreed, with whatever lame excuse he has to offer (be certain that there will be no end of them), then you are dealing with a dishonest person. "Oh, that additional amount is the dealer preparation charge." The shipping charge, the delivery charge, the whatever charge.

You had a deal and now he's reneging. This is a classic shyster. Take a walk and this time don't go back.

Changes and Alterations

In keeping with the maxim that there is no such thing as a perfect boat, in most cases buyers end up making compromises and settling for less than the ideal. However, unlike the auto industry where, if there is something about a car you don't like, there's nothing you can do to get the dealer to change it. With new boat sales, there is considerably more flexibility. Buyers can, and often do, get dealers to make changes, changes that are limited primarily by economics and the negotiating skills of the buyer.

When a self-survey of a new boat turns up faults that are neither extensive nor terribly serious, the buyer shouldn't hesitate to insist that corrections be made. Dealers will usually accede with sufficient jawboning and the demands are reasonable. A typical example would be something like hatch covers have steel pneumatic cylinders and buyer demands that they be changed to stainless steel. Keep in mind that if requested changes add up to an amount that would eliminate the dealer's profit, the dealer isn't going to deal.

Walking Away From a Deal

The thing that most prevents people from walking away from a deal they don't think is the best possible is the apparent loss of face that comes with being on the losing side of a negotiation if their last offer or demand isn't accepted.

Rather than risk losing a negotiation (which is like a game of poker), they simply don't attempt to negotiate further. In other words, let's say a buyer is reluctant to make a "final" offer, playing the bluff by being willing to walk out if it isn't accepted, mainly because he feels like a loser if he reverts to his previous position. The primary tool of haggling over price is the art of the bluff - the threat of walking away without buying, and then actually doing it. Salesmen are very good at this, while most buyers aren't. When you make any kind of offer or demand, you have to be mentally prepared to play the bluff - take it or leave it- and then actually walking out and playing the waiting game to see if the dealer will bend.

Just because you reach the point of your last offer - take it or leave it - does not mean that your previous position is irrevocable, so don't put yourself in this position by think-ing this way. Salesmen will often give a take-it-or-leave-it offer one day, only to call the customer the day after the customer turns it down, losing face by acceding the customer's last offer but gaining a sale. By all means make that "last chance" offer, but don't carve it in stone. If you really want that particular boat, returning to your last position is not a loss of face; it simply means that you have reached the limit of how far the deal could be pushed. Go ahead, stand on your last offer, walk out of the showroom without a deal, but be prepared the next day to say, "I slept on it last night and I think I can live with it." If the second to last offer really was acceptable, then you both win and there is no real loss of face.

Trade-ins

Doing a deal based on a trade-in is the worst possible deal you can make unless you figure your boat isn't worth much. First, you'll get nowhere near what your trade-in is worth, and you are giving the dealer the opportunity to juggle the numbers. In all likelihood he'll smell a very eager buyer and will raise the price of the new boat as well.

If there's any possibility that you can sell your current boat at a fair price, I recommend that you do so if your money means anything to you.

Used Boats

Dealing with a private used boat seller is usually quite a bit easier, although there are always a few tricksters around. You're not going to have the problem of a piecemeal deal since it should be clear as to exactly what the seller is selling. After looking the boat over, be sure to nail down exactly what is being sold with it.

It may have a bunch of his personal stuff in it. Pointedly ask whether there is anything that he intends not to sell with the boat. It's a good idea to go over the boat with him and ask about any item you're not sure about - electronics, fishing gear, loose stuff. Is he going to take the extra anchor with him? And so on.

When it comes to engines, if the seller makes any representations as to engine over-hauls or major repairs, be sure to ask to see the invoices. If the seller cannot produce them, then it's a fair judgement that the seller is not telling the truth. Only a fool wouldn't save invoices for such costly repairs.

In negotiating the deal, I would recommend that you follow the method commonly used for larger boat sales. This usually involves an initial inspection and test run, followed by an offer, acceptance, a 10% deposit and then a survey. The offer is made "subject to survey," which essentially means that if anything major is wrong with the boat, the offer can be withdrawn or renegotiated. If you are doing your own survey, then you can bypass the subject to survey part, but only after the test run has been made.

After the survey, a list of defects is drawn up, based upon which the offer is renegotiated in consideration of the cost to repair those defects. To the extent that we are dealing with a used boat, not a new one, the renegotiation is usually not made on a 1:1

or dollar for dollar repair cost basis. Most commonly, the seller splits the difference. After all, the buyer is not paying a new boat price, and the repair cost should reflect this. This is not to say that you shouldn't try for 1:1, but the fact is that big boat sellers tend to be pretty savvy, although you may do better.

If you're doing your own survey then I recommend that you not make an offer on the spot, but go home with a list of your defects, attempt to make an estimate of repair costs, and then come back to him the following day or whatever it takes. The important point here is to give yourself time to think about it.

It sounds easy enough but it's often not. If you're not using a surveyor, then you'll probably have a hard time estimating costs, so you can see why the surveyor provides a very valuable service.

Defects

When defects are involved in an used boat sale, as they almost always are, it is often the case that the seller will want to repair them himself with no adjustment in price. I trust that you can see the problem this poses. Experience proves that when sellers perform repairs after a survey, they will almost always perform those repairs as cheaply as possible, meaning that they often aren't done right.

The best position to take is that the boat was offered for sale in an "as is" condition, and that when serious faults are found, that is just cause for renegotiating the price. It is far better to do it this way, and to have the repairs made yourself, to your standards.

Contracts

Many people think that a contract has to be a fancy legal document with all sorts legal gobbledygook on it that no one but a lawyer understands. Not so. Courts will recognize any contract between two people as long as it is clearly worded and isn't outside the law. For example, if you try to cheat on sales taxes by phoneying up a sales agreement for $5,000 on a $30,000 boat, you'll find yourself in a bit of a bind if you have to take that document before a court.

Before you write a contract and hand over your deposit, ask to see the title. At this point you want to verify title information and make note of whether a spouse or co-owner is indicated. If so, you want to be sure to ask whether there will be any difficulty in getting the spouse's signature. Beware that boat sales may be involved in divorces, in which case you may not be able to get the spouse's signature. Pay special attention to the seller's reaction when you ask this question. If you don't like the answer, you may want to ask him flat out.

A contract can be hand-written, but both parties should have copies that should be signed by both parties. Below is an example of a simple sales contract.

* * * * * *

This document is a sales agreement between _____

Seller: <u>Name, address, phone number</u>
And:
Buyer: <u>Name, address, phone number</u>

Date of agreement_____.

The sum of $_____ has been paid by_____this day of_____to _____ as a deposit toward the purchase of _____ toward the total purchase price of_____. Buyer agrees that full and final payment and closing is to be made by _____.

_____
Buyer's signature

_____
Seller's signature

* * * * * *

When writing the sales agreement, be sure to include the make, model and year. That way you have in writing that seller is representing the boat as being a particular model year.

If there are any other special conditions, those should be spelled out too. Example: fish finder was at repair shop but is promised to be reinstalled in working condition by a particular date prior to taking delivery.

In the event that the boat has a mortgage, the closing will usually take place at the lender's office. If loans are involved on both sides of the sale, the two lenders will make the arrangements for the closing.

My recommendation is that a deposit should not exceed 5% of sale price. The only purpose of a deposit is as a gesture of good faith to hold the boat until the final payment is delivered. It is normal and customary to give the deposit to the seller, unless it happens to be an unusually large amount. In that case, an escrow agent is needed. Look to your banker or any licensed professional escrow agent.

Verify Ownership

In most states, boat titles are the same as for cars and transference is the same. Checking ownership and title interests is easy in some states and difficult in others. In some states, you can simply call the appropriate department with the registration number and they will give you the information over the phone. In other states, like California, they will not give out this info over the phone without the owner's permission. Documentation services that can be found in all major boating centers can obtain title and registration checks for a nominal fee.

Specifically check these points:

- Name of owner or owners
- Hull number is correct
- Hull number matches title and registration number
- Check that year on title matches year on hull number

Note whether a spouse is indicated on the title or registration. If so, you essentially have two owners and you need both to sign off on the title.

Insuring Your Boat

I know, reading an insurance policy is the most boring reading imaginable. On the other hand, if you buy insurance without reading a sample policy, you are literally buying a contract without knowing what the contract says. Most policies are written today so that just about anyone can understand them, and there is no excuse not to. This is particularly true for outboard boats where policy types are highly variable.

A good general rule of thumb is that you get what you pay for, so if you're just shopping for the lowest rate, odds are that you'll end up with the least amount of coverage. That doesn't mean the whole dollar amount of the policy, but the types of losses it covers and the method by which loss payments are calculated.

When it comes to outboard boats, there are two basic types of insurance available. These are known as ACV (actual cash value) and agreed valuation policies. An ACV policy is much the same as a car in terms of the amounts it will pay out. ACV means replacement cost minus depreciation. An agreed valuation policy will pay the stated value in the event of a total loss, plus new-for-old replacement cost for individual items.

For example, let's say for some reason the outboard motor fell off the boat and was lost in 500 feet of water. The ACV policy would pay replacement cost minus depreciation; the agreed valuation policy would pay the total cost to replace it. Naturally, you'd prefer to have the replacement cost policy but there is a catch. Few, if any insurers, offer replacement cost policies for boats valued at under $50,000, so the chances are that you'll end up with an ACV policy.

On outboard boat policies, boats and motors are insured separately; there will be a stated value for each. It is important to be sure to get these amounts right, particularly when purchasing an used boat where you are paying one price for both. When in doubt, it's a good idea to use a "book" value or get an appraisal from a surveyor (remember, book values tend to be high). If you underinsure and have a loss, you'll be out of luck.

When deciding on the amount of coverage you want on the boat, consider that if the market value of the boat is markedly different from what you paid for it, this could cause claim settlement problems, such as when insuring for substantially more than was paid. Normally a boat should be insured for the amount the buyer paid for it, unless there is a strong reason to do otherwise. The general rule of insurance law is that the amount of insurance should be equal to the boat's value. If the boat's value is demonstrably more than you paid, be sure you can prove that. Insurance underwriters usually refer to a price guide when considering issuing a policy, so if the amount of insurance requested is substantially different than what most books say, the underwriter is likely to question the amount questioned.

There are also major differences in the extent of coverage between policies that you need to pay attention to. One type of policy will not cover loss or damage *resulting from* wear and tear or gradual deterioration. Thus should some deteriorated part cause your boat to sink, the resulting damage would not be covered. Other policies will cover the resulting damage, but not pay the repair or replacement cost of the deteriorated part. Be sure to fully read the *exclusions* section of the policy.

Also read the *property covered* section to see what it covers in the way of equipment and how it pays.

Glossary

ABYC   The American Boat and Yacht Council, the primary US boating standards society. Publishes a voluntary set of engineering standards to which most of the industry adheres.

Abaft   A reference to anything aft of the mid point of the vessel; abaft the beams.

Abeam   Directly off the beam or along side.

Aft   The rear portion of the vessel, or referring to that direction; stern.

Amidships   Referring to the middle section of the boat, or that general direction.

Anodic   A metal in a galvanic cell that emits a positive electrical charge, and will therefore corrode. Zinc is anodic to aluminum, aluminum is anodic to copper.

Anode   The opposite electrical pole of a cathode. On a boat, refers to the sacrificial zinc *anodes* attached to the motor lower unit, the purpose of which is to prevent corrosion damage to the motor.

Bilge   The area of the hull below interior decks; the inside bottom of the hull.

Bimini Top   Originally a free-standing soft top, now corrupted to mean just about any kind of soft top.

Blister   A separation between the gel coat surface and the structural laminates beneath, usually filled with a fluid comprised of water and solvents in the plastic such as styrene.

Bond   The *grounding* as opposed to the ground wire in an alternating current system. A normally non current carrying conductor. Also: any wire or other metal conductor joining two pieces of metal together for the purpose of minimizing galvanic corrosion between the connected parts. This is normally a green wire or copper strap.

Bonding System The process of wiring all underwater metals together so as to equalize the electrical potential between different metals for the purpose of preventing galvanic corrosion.

Boot That part of the bottom antifouling paint that is carried above the normal water line.

Boot Stripe or Boot Top Incorrectly referred to as the waterline, a boot stripe is added above the waterline, usually as a means of distinguishing the scum line that accumulates, but also as a cosmetic adornment. The waterline defines the intersect between the top of the water and the hull.

Bow That part of the hull that meets the water, usually considered from the point where the hull begins to curve from the flat sections amid ships; the forward part of a boat. The *stem* is the leading edge of the bow.

Broaching The reaction that occurs from operating in high, following seas when the bow noses into the backside of a wave sufficiently to cause the vessel to change the direction and veer off course, usually resulting in a loss of control.

Bulkhead These can be likened to a load bearing wall in a house. Perpendicular to the centerline of the hull, a full bulkhead attaches to the sides and bottom and serve the purpose preventing the hull from twisting.

Bulwarks A ship oriented term that refers to any part of the hull side that extends up above the main deck.

Bracket A term describing any external structure used for mounting motors on the transom.

Cavitation The result of air being introduced into the propeller. In addition to causing engine overspeeding, cavitation is damaging to metals such as propellers and should be avoided at all costs.

CFR Code of Federal Regulation. CFR 33 is the applicable section relating to boating standards administered by the Coast Guard.

Cavitation A condition in which air is introduced into the path of the propeller. Since air is compressible, while water is not, this causes the engine to overspeed by reducing the load on the engine, with a resulting loss in boat speed. Cavitation is damaging to propellers and engines and must be avoided.

Cavitation Plate The horizontal plate above the propeller on an outboard motor. The cavitation plate prevents air from being pulled down from above, into the propeller slip stream. Damaged cavitation plates must be repaired.

Chine   The angle formed by the hull side and bottom of the hull.

Closed Cell Corrosion   See crevice corrosion.

Chine Flat   A horizontal surface on the bottom between the hull side and the sloping bottom sections. Normally added to provide extra lift to very deep vee hulls.

Chock   A piece of metal hardware attached to a boat that is designed to hold a dock or anchor line in a certain place, or create a fairlead at a particular angle.

Cleat   A metal device designed to attach lines to.

Coaming   Usually a raised, curved surface such as found around the perimeter of an open decked boat. A flying bridge structure is called the flying bridge *coaming*. A horizontal surface around the perimeter of a cockpit is called a cockpit *coaming*. The same for a horizontal framework around a hatch opening.

Composite   A term meaning the combination of two or more materials. Fiberglass reinforced plastic is a composite, but in marine terminology usually means a core material such as balsa or foam.

Core   Any type of dissimilar material sandwiched between two layers of fiberglass, whether solid wood, foam, balsa, plywood or even aluminum.

Coremat   Trade name for a thin fibrous material used as a core in boat hulls, usually hull sides but not bottoms.

Corrosion   Any of numerous causes of a metal being destroyed or damaged by an electro-chemical process. A process by which any material combines with oxygen in a normally occurring process of oxidation such as the rusting of steel. In marine parlance, refers to the natural degradation of metals. Electrolysis is also a form of corrosion.

Crevice Corrosion A form of corrosion caused by water in contact with a metal where the oxygen supply is cut off, in which the water forms an acid. The acid then attacks the metal. Commonly a serious problem with aluminum hardware and fuel tanks at the mounting surface where water gets trapped in an area that gets little or no airflow; also called closed cell corrosion.

CSM — Acronym for Chopped Strand Mat, a fiberglass matting in which fiber direction is completely random and fibers are less than four inches long. May come in the form of a manufactured fabric or blown out of a chopper gun mixed with resin.

Deadrise — The angle of the hull bottom to the horizontal measured at the transom. While deadrise can be measured anywhere, the general use of the term means the angle at the transom.

Deck — Any horizontal surface of significant size that attaches to the hull, in small boats usually an exterior deck. Soles are distinguished from decks as being decks within the cabin area as in *cabin sole*.

Deep Vee — Generally considered as any hull in which the angle of the aft section is more than 20 degrees to the horizontal. A *modified vee* is one that is very deep forward but tapirs to a shallower angle at the stern.

Delamination — Since molded fiberglass is a laminated material, when the laminations separate for any reason the term *delaminated* is used to describe this condition. Also referred to as ply separation.

Displacement — The weight of a boat or ship determined by means of calculation of the amount of water the hull will displace. This is done by measuring the volume of the hull below the water line.

Dog — A heavy duty latch, usually on hatches.

Doubler — In boat construction, refers to any construction intended to make a structure stronger, such as a *doubler plate* under a mooring cleat or a sea cock in a hull; a reinforcement.

Dry Weight — The weight of a boat as measured on a scale, with all tanks empty. Usually will differ slightly from displacement.

Electrolysis — The process in which an electrical current applied to a metal immersed in water causes the metal to self destruct. The end result is the same as corrosion, but the root cause on a boat is a stray current acting to cause the destruction of the metal. The distinguishing feature of electrolysis results from an outside electrical source. See also *galvanism*.

Epoxy — A high quality plastic resin or paste that is highly water resistant. Only marine grades of epoxy resins and glues should be used on boats.

Ergonomics   The study of how manufactured products relate to the scale of the human body with a view toward improving ease of use or operation.

FRP   Acronym for Fiberglass Reinforced Plastic.

Freeboard   The height of the hull side above the floating water line at any point it is measured. *Effective freeboard* is the height above the water to any opening in the hull that would allow water to enter the vessel, such as a transom cut out or a deck scupper.

Forefoot   The curved section between the generally straight line of the bow and the line of the keel. Also refers to this general space on the interior.

Galvanism   An electrical current generated when any two materials are joined which have a different electrical potential. The common flashlight battery generates electricity by means of galvanic reaction between two metals. Carbon is a metal, which is the reason why carbon rubber hoses cause corrosion problems. Joining copper and aluminum, for example, will result in a galvanic reaction that will destroy the aluminum. The most common cause of corrosion damage to metals on a boat.

Gel Coat   A pigmented plastic resin that is first sprayed into the mold, having the dual purpose of creating a molded-in finish, as well as providing a means of releasing the part from the mold. Gel coats tend to be very porous and not very durable. The highest quality gel coats can be buffed back to a good shine, whereas poorer quality gel coats are likely to suffer permanent degradation.

Grid Linder   A fiberglass liner in which the full framing system is included; can be partial or full boat size.

GRP   Acronym for glass reinforced plastic, commonly used in Great Britain.

Gunwale   The side deck that attaches to the hull side in an open cockpit boat; may also be referred to as a side deck when intended to walked upon. The gunwale is a major structural component that provides the strength to the hull.

Half Tower   Not really a tower at all but a pipe frame top, sometimes called a Bimini.

Hatch   Any opening on a deck or horizontal surface; the nautical term for a door.

Hawse hole   A hole in hull or deck, normally surrounded with a metal flange, through which dock or anchor line passes.

Helm   Literally any device used to steer the boat such as the steering wheel. The helm station or general area is also simply referred to as *the helm*. It is not proper to call it the dashboard.

Hose Nipple   A special male nipple with ribbed or barbed construction designed to grip hoses tightly when clamped and prevent them from slipping off. Same as hose barb.

Isopthalic resin   A specific type of polyesther plastic that is blister resistant.

Keel   Typically the vertical strength member on the bottom of the hull, sometimes called the *backbone* in wood construction. Most small fiberglass boats don't have proper keels, but the angle formed by the two sides of the bottom are still properly referred to as the keel.

Laminate   In reference to fiberglass boats, a laminate is any part made of layers of fiberglass reinforced plastic, with any number of layers. A laminate that includes a core material, is often called a composite or sandwich construction.

Laid Line   The term for rope in which the fiber bundles are twisted together, as opposed to samson braid, in which the fibers are woven together. Conventional nylon rope is laid line. Samson braid is both more flexible and stinger.

Liner   Any of several types of molded fiberglass components such as a cockpit *liner* or full hull *liner*. Outboard boats typically have a full deck/cockpit liner. In the cabin it may be a molded head compartment or a complete cabin liner including the seating, galley, etc. Generally the same meaning as *shell*.

List   A boat that is not floating level on the transverse plane is said to be *listing*.

Lower Unit   The lower drive portion of an outboard motor which contains the drive gears, and which is removable and replaceable.

Marlin Tower   As distinguished from a tuna tower, a marlin tower is shorter than a tuna tower, usually about 2/3rds height.

Nobility   A term that indicates a metal's resistance to galvanic corrosion. More noble metals are cathodic, while least noble are anodic.

Non skid   A pattern or texture on a deck intended to make the surface less slippery.

Orthopthalic resin   A name that refers to the specific type of polyester resin, as opposed to isopthalic resin. Orthopthalic plastics are prone to blistering.

Pie Port   Any of numerous types of small, round plastic ports. Name was derived from manufacturer name.

Polyester   A plastic resin that is known for its least resistance to water absorption or hydrolysis, the dissolution of the plastic by water.

Porpoising   A condition in which the bow of the boat is constantly rising and falling in an perpetual and uncontrollable cycle.

Port   Any opening in a deck, hull or other structure for seeing through or to provide access.

Powerhead   The engine portion of the outboard motor as opposed to the chassis and lower drive unit.

Quarters   For purposes of location and direction, it is common to divide the boat into quadrants and refer to it such as *the aft port quarter.*

Roving   A woven fabric of glass fibers in which the weave is at 90^0 angles and the bundles of fibers are flat. Its appearance is that of a tightly woven plaid pattern.

Sandwich Construction   Same as composite or cored laminate. A material placed between two skins of reinforced plastic to add strength or reduce weight.

Scupper   A hole in the hull, usually the transom, for the purpose of draining water off the deck.

Sea Cock   A marine valve in the bottom of a hull used to close off the water supply to any component that uses sea water. All through the bottom openings are required to have such valves. The common gate valve is not a sea cock and should not be used in boats. Only bronze valves are recommended.

Sea Hose	Those hoses which are recommended for marine use and which have the qualities of petrochemical and biological resistance, as well as strength to resist suction collapse, pressure and kinking. Typically rayon reinforced butyl rubber. Polyvinyl and wire reinforced rubber are not recommended.
Sea Strainer	A special marine filter used to remove debris from water taken into the vessel from without, particularly for pumps.
Shear Line	The line formed by the joint of the hull and deck, usually delineated by the rub rail. The *shear* refers to this general area.
Shearing Force	The force applied perpendicular to the length of an object, as in shears cutting paper. Interlaminar shear is a shearing force along the long axis, as in the force that can cause delamination of fiberglass.
Skeg	A fin-like protuberance, usually intended to protect a propeller.
Sole	An interior deck.
Steering Ram	The hydraulic cylinder that turns an outboard motor as a means of steering.
Stern	This term is often used interchangeably with the word transom, though stern more appropriately refers to the after area of the vessel. A canoe, for example, does not have a transom, though it does have a stern.
Stiffener	A small frame used to strengthen a fiberglass panel, whether on a bottom, hull side or other surface.
Strake	Formerly referred to boats with overlapping planking, now refers to the ribs that are often found on the bottom of a hull thought to create lift. Their purpose is often the subject of debate.
Stringer	The structural frames of the hull which run fore and aft, normally the entire length of the hull. In small boats usually consists of fiberglass laminated over plywood.
Tabbing	Strips of resin saturated fiberglass fabric, typically used to join bulkheads and frames to a hull. Also referred to as bonding.
Taping	Same as tabbing. Strips of resin soaked fiberglass used to join parts together are referred to as taping.

Toe Rail	A raised portion of the fore deck around the perimeter, usually an inch or so high. It serves the purpose of adding strength and to keep things from falling overboard.
Top Hat	Hollow stringers or frames formed in the shape of a top hat. May be foam filled but the foam is used as a laminating form and is of no structural importance.
Transducer	The device attached to the bottom of the hull that sends and receives the electrical signal from the depth sounder.
Trim	The manner or angle in which a hull rests in the water, either while at rest or underway.
Vinylester	A high quality plastic resin know for its water resistance and resistance to blistering.
Warped Plane	A hull form that is essentially a distorted vee.
Weather Deck	Any exterior deck that is exposed to weather.
Zinc	Refers to the metal anodes attached to outboard motor lower units to help retard galvanic corrosion.

INDEX